NORTH OF
HOLLYWOOD

NORTH OF HOLLYWOOD

*To Joan
With thanks and
warmest best wishes!
Rick Lenz*

RICK LENZ

CHROMODROID
PRESS

North Hollywood, CA

© 2012 by Rick Lenz

Chromodroid Press
13029-A Victory Blvd., Suite 365
North Hollywood, CA 91606-2925

CHROMODROID
PRESS

All rights reserved. No part of this book may be reproduced or transmitted in any form or by any means, electronic or mechanical, including photocopying, recording, or by any information storage and retrieval system, except in the case of brief quotations embodied in critical articles and reviews, without prior written permission of the publisher.

Although the author and publisher have made every effort to ensure the accuracy and completeness of information contained in this book, we assume no responsibility for errors, inaccuracies, omissions, or any inconsistency herein.

ISBN Hardcover: 978-0-9848442-0-3
ISBN Trade Paperback: 978-0-9848442-1-0
ISBN E-book: 978-0-9848442-2-7
ISBN Audio Book: 978-0-9848442-3-4

Printed in the United States of America

Publisher's Cataloging-In-Publication

Lenz, Rick.

    North of Hollywood / Rick Lenz. -- 1st ed. -- North Hollywood, Calif. : Chromodroid Press, c2012.

    p. ; cm.

    ISBN: 978-0-9848442-1-0

    1. Lenz, Rick. 2. Actors--United States--Biography. 3. Motion picture actors and actresses--United States--Biography. 4. Dramatists--United States--Biography. I. Title.

PN2287.L4329 L46 2012   2011961053
791.43/0280924   1202

Book Consultant: Ellen Reid
Editing: Pamela Guerrieri
Cover Design: George Foster
Interior Design: Ghislain Viau

*This book is dedicated to Linda
& Scott, Charlie, and Abigail
& to Debby
& in loving memory of Grace Kurth*

ACKNOWLEDGMENTS

I am deeply grateful to my lifelong friend Michael Norell for his limitless patience and wisdom.

Also to Bret Easton Ellis, who has taught me as much of the ABCs of writing as I've been able to absorb.

And to my dear friends Betsy Hailey, Don Eitner, Tom Blake, John Gallagher, Anne Collum, Susan Gleason, and Michele Winkler who read the manuscript along the way and gave me invaluable feedback.

Also to Dian Parkinson and Carol Summers, whose love and support have been unfailing.

And to Pamela Guerrieri of Proofed to Perfection and Kevin Cook, who edited and re-edited—both tireless and encyclopedically smart.

Also the brilliant Ellen Reid, who made it all happen.

And to Ann Stuart.

Finally, more than anybody, to Linda, for everything.

Everything makes sense a bit at a time. But when you try to think of it all at once, it comes out wrong.

—Terry Pratchett

FOREWORD

North of Hollywood is more than a look inside show biz with the usual celebrity encounters and amusing anecdotes. It is also an inside look at a man who chooses—without really believing in the possibility of success—to seek a career in Hollywood.

In his forties, after startling good fortune as an actor/playwright (he's had plays performed in New York and on PBS; played leading roles in films and on stage; starred in television series), Rick Lenz finds it all falling apart. One evening in North Hollywood, standing alone, naked—not only metaphorically—on the stage of a tiny Equity Waiver theatre, it hits him that his career has dropped out of frame and into helpless freefall. In some warped corner of his mind, it is what he has expected all along. It is vindication of the sure knowledge he's always had that he *will* eventually fail. If fear of success wasn't such a weary cliché, it would be funny—in fact, as he tells it, it often is.

He has worked with or had life-altering experiences with Al Pacino, Jill Clayburgh, Bette Midler, Goldie Hawn, Alan Alda, Richard Dreyfuss, James Caan, Lily Tomlin, Jacqueline Bisset, Jonathan Demme, Curtis Hanson, and many others.

As a young actor, he played major roles with some of the biggest names in Hollywood history: John Wayne, Maureen O'Hara, Ingrid Bergman, Shelley Winters, Peter Sellers, Jackie Gleason, Elizabeth Taylor, James Stewart, Van Johnson, Eve Arden, both Gabor sisters (at once), Teresa Wright, Angela Lansbury, Rod Taylor, Raymond Burr, Peter Lawford, Richard Boone, and Lauren Bacall.

Under the heading of "sometimes hilarious encounters with," he meets Lucille Ball, Frank Sinatra, Ella Fitzgerald, Bob Dylan, George C. Scott, Peter Falk, Jason Robards, Sam Shepard, Steven Spielberg, Mel Brooks, Billy Wilder, Otto Preminger, William Wyler, and Claude Rains (grandfather of Lenz's daughter, Abigail).

But the most compelling story is personal. Deeper than show biz are the childhood memories of his drug addict-cum-nurse mother and his doctor father (Dad once lost his drug license because of the huge number of narcotics he prescribed to his family).

Finally, this is a story of the astonishing courage and compassion of an actor's wife—in a sense, the book's protagonist. She copes with her husband's personal and professional fiascos, and also helps him find the resources to support his sister in her battle with cancer and his daughter in her life-and-death struggle with addiction.

North of Hollywood is not merely a memoir told with wonderful humor; it's a psychological cliffhanger that unfolds as it is being lived. Will the crises that give signs of merging into catastrophe permit a happy ending, or will our flawed and histrionic hero end up alone in a fleabag hotel room like the one he stayed in when he first moved to New York?

Lenz tries to hang onto the real-life life he's been blessed to find. But he can't do it alone any more than his daughter can beat drugs without the help of ... *something* greater than herself. He reads the diary of his friend, Ann, Michael Curtiz's late mistress, and imagines analogies to

Foreword

Casablanca. Will he remain under the house arrest of his show business compulsions, the incarcerating world of Hollywood, and most of all his own ghosts, or will he fly off to freedom with his wife Linda?

—MICHAEL NORELL, "WGA" award winner
and twice Christopher Award Winner

CHAPTER ONE

I was raised in Jackson, Michigan—population 50,000—a city that lies at the third corner of a triangle with Lansing and Ann Arbor, about forty miles from each. Those towns are home to Michigan State University and the University of Michigan. Jackson is home to the longest-walled prison in the world and The Cascades, the world's second largest man-made waterfall. It also lays convincing claim to being the birthplace of the Republican Party—it was host to the first official party convention on July 6, 1854. A large pile of rocks on Washington Street marks the spawning ground of the GOP. There is also a plaque in case the rocks don't ipso facto identify themselves as birth-of-the-Republican-Party boulders.

When it was time for me to spread my wings, I headed to New York because that's where my theatre professors at U of M told me *real* actors go. They didn't mention anything about real bill collectors, and very little time passed before it dawned on me that "real acting" and show business have a commonality factor that ranges from less-than-you'd-hope-for to zilch. Before I learned that, I once asked an old character actor, didn't he just love being an actor and not having to worry about little hollow people's little petty rules?

He told me I had a paper ass.

Show business as a career, for those of us whom it chooses—we never choose it; no one lacks that much common sense—is the most enticing siren the gods ever conjured, at least to those with the weakness. The only pathway to her lies between Scylla and Charybdis. Any wayfarer with even minuscule common sense would take whatever evasive action was necessary to avoid that route.

My first acting experience was with a summer stock company, a job I got partly because I fit the costumes. Also, I'd been in a few plays in high school, the result of washing out of football when it became clear I was more than averagely breakable.

I inhaled my first season of stock. It was like the county fair, a magic bottle of emotions and smells, a perfumed medley of canvas and sawdust; hot dogs, popcorn, fresh paint, and old lumber varnished temporarily new. Every day, a genie slipped out of the bottle—this was his only trick and nobody could have asked for better—and blew the pungent winds that signaled the summer rains. The reedy grasses around Clark Lake swirled like an ocean in a typhoon, and I felt a frenzy that made me want to run out across the field, down to the water, and hurl myself into it—except I had a show that night. It was all adolescent longings, and they lingered with me like Erin Bibbin's first kiss hung on the entire walk home after my first and final date with her.

I can still smell that summer. It comes to me in waves when I think of that spot on the lake where the Clark Lake Players lasted for an eternity of twenty-five years. When I think of the water lapping against the

Chapter One

dock that extended out alongside the old clapboard theatre building that had previously been a roller rink, and before that a prohibition era dancehall, I think of my wife's question: "Did you ever feel so good you didn't know what to do with it?"

The Clark Lake Playhouse was above a bar with a jukebox in it. You could hear the constant thrumming of rock and roll even during your loudest scene. I can still hear snatches of dialogue:

"Where were you on the night of August 23rd?"

"On watch, sir." (Me as a seventeen-year-old Navy Ensign.)

"And what were your duties on watch?"

"Well, sir ... to *watch*."

And then from downstairs: "Wake up, little Susie! Wake up!"

You could still hear the buzz of motorboats out on the lake, sometimes even after dark. None of these distractions mattered. It was all too lovely to be even slightly diminished by a trivial encircling din. The romance in the air was so intoxicating that nothing else mattered. The adult camaraderie, the playacting, the beer, and most urgently, the girls. Everywhere you looked there were girls. They paralyzed almost every other perception. It was acceptable to show off shamelessly for them. It was *sweet* to flirt with them. And they flirted back. It was even more fabulous than *that*. It wasn't only a mysterious whirlwind of infatuations, not just art for art's sake, not just pretending to be a grownup. It was bigger than all the exhilarating parts of itself. It was magic for magic's sake.

In theatre school at the University of Michigan, following my summer stock stint, I trotted out for my first-year acting class some of the scenes from Broadway comedies I'd done. I found out still later that *real actors* call all acting "the work." The response to my first anxious classroom performance—I'd wowed 'em in stock—was pretty much the same as it might have been if I'd taken the stage and done what

3

my dog does in the park and for which I plan ahead by bringing along a pocketful of plastic grocery bags.

About a half-hour after sunset on a February evening, I was driving home from Ann Arbor, where I was an undistinguished graduate student, to my first wife Sarah and our two baby boys in Jackson. My plan in those days was to teach theatre in college. Nothing else seemed possible. While I was briefly studying pre-med I'd watched my father, an eye-ear-nose-and-throat doctor, pack a bloody nose. I slid down the wall, unconscious. After my dad finished with the bloody nose, he stitched together the gash in my head and told me, "Young medical students faint all the time."

I was looking in a mirror at my stitches for the first time when he said that. I threw up in the sink. He shrugged and his eyebrows, which always spoke the truth even if the rest of him was lying, told me that some part of him had understood all along that doctoring and I would make a sorry match.

Outside my car, a warmer day and then a cold rain had turned the countryside into a vast snow pudding. Now, it was freezing over again and the car was contesting my right to control it. I had the feeling I was not where I was meant to be. I noticed by moonlight the discarded cab of an old road grader that had been abandoned on a defunct utility road, and it struck me that the road grader was as pointless as I believed my life was going to be if I stayed.

A mile farther toward Jackson I saw the slush-covered, rusted-out shell of an old Pontiac. I imagined the man who'd been driving it stopping one day, or maybe one winter night, and getting out. It could have been a night like the one that was shaping up now. The Pontiac had just frozen up and quit. He said *to hell with it*, and hitched a ride straight to

Chapter One

New York City. I pictured him living in a penthouse overlooking Central Park, telling his new friends how he had once been imprisoned in an Andrew Wyeth winterscape until one day he found he'd had it with the bitter cold and scraping ice off his windshield with the base of a tire jack, and he finally got smart enough to make his way out of that frigid hell and come to this civilized place, to live the way elegant people should.

And all the well-bred guests warm their hands by the fire and their insides with Hendrick's martinis. They laugh with captivating suavity and one of them says, "By Gad, sir, you are a character. A *Pontiac*. By *Gad*, sir." (Apparently Sydney Greenstreet is on the guest list.) And everybody smirks and chortles until they're contented as puppies wedged in and warming themselves in all the comforts of mom.

Then it hits me, in my case anyway, that's not a soothing thought—that being tucked in with mom is a lot like being outside in a freezing cold Pontiac.

"By Gad, sir," says Sydney. "You *are* a character."

It dawns on me: This is an improv.

"Which character *are* you by the way?"

Improv is torture when you fear there is only one perfect answer for each question. At any rate, I don't know the answer to this one.

"By *Gad*, sir." Sydney is frowning now, has a distinctly menacing look. "You seem to be in the wrong movie."

This story is about celebrity and non-celebrity and, from a very personal point of view, everything in between. It is about the stumbling progress of my life, and about Hollywood, and how I feel about both. Sometimes I feel cheerful, sometimes dark. I try to apply light therapy as I go—light is my preference—but there is no way I can make the dark parts go away (yet) at my personal whim.

One more thing: There will be no descriptions of anyone's tits—for example, Jacqueline Bisset's—which by the way I have seen, nor will I say anything directly bad about Lauren Bacall. Were I to describe Jackie Bisset's breasts or anything physically about her, it would be insufficient and redundant anyway. If you've never seen them, I suggest renting the *The Deep* and taking a look for yourself. As for Lauren Bacall, she's a complicated lady and it would be stupid and in poor taste for me to give you an appraisal of her personality based on my limited experiences with her. It wouldn't be fairly representative.

Besides, I really do hate being unkind.

In *Cactus Flower*, my first Hollywood movie, I played opposite Goldie Hawn, who became pretty much my best friend for a while. It was the first big part in a movie for both of us. Walter Matthau and Ingrid Bergman were in it, too. Walter told me he'd had a crush on Ingrid for years, and since he was the muscle in getting the film made, being very hot at the time, he insisted she play the role.

Ingrid talked to me at length about *Casablanca* because I was married at the time to Claude Rains' daughter (whom I'd played opposite in Buffalo in a stage production of *You Can't Take It With You*). I told Ingrid that Claude never saw *Casablanca* because he didn't like watching himself on film—had a phobia about it. She was surprised, but then acknowledged that she, too, was usually uncomfortable watching herself (I think it's an unnatural experience for anyone). She still spoke with wonder about the success of *Casablanca*. She had almost no relationship with Humphrey Bogart away from the set—their involvement was exclusively professional. She also expressed awe that the film worked as well as it did. She said that as they were shooting it, she had no idea where the story was going, that nobody really did. She was completely

Chapter One

baffled as to whom she was supposed to care about most, Victor Laszlo (Paul Henreid's character) or Rick Blaine (Bogie's).

I had very little firsthand knowledge about movie stars, but I speculated that Ingrid was different from the rest. She was in her very early fifties. I was twenty-nine. It didn't matter; she was *incredibly* sexy. Like Walter Matthau, I developed a crush on her. It was hard to be around her and not fall under her spell. She was elegant in a kind, centered way with something friendly to say to everyone. But also, one of her secrets, both on screen and in person, seemed to be the ability to make men fall in love with her—with the possible exception of Humphrey Bogart. I think she knew she had that gift, and I wondered if she wasn't turning it on just a tiny bit for me (I got the idea she wasn't particularly attracted to Matthau). She was especially kind to me, I thought.

One day, Gene Saks, the director, called cut on a shot in which she and I were dancing. He said, "Rick, your hand is covering Ingrid's face."

I had ruined Ingrid Bergman's profile! I was going to be sent to would-be movie-actor-failure hell. But she smiled sympathetically at me and petted the back of my head; she knew these things happened. Now I was positive she was *very* fond of me.

Seeing me at the premiere in New York several months later, she said, "Hi, Nick."

A year or two before this, I'd done the Broadway version of *Cactus Flower* with Lauren Bacall, who terrified me because she reminded me of my mother and who later told John Wayne—when I was in *The Shootist* with them—that she'd "discovered me." Wayne glowered at her and said, "Aw, shut up, Betty." (Her real name is Betty Perske.) He was "a little ill"—so they said at the time—and I guess not in the mood for Hollywood nonsense. I got along fine with him, although protocol called for me not to volunteer much chitchat. He asked me what my politics were—I think because I had long hair, a pretty good giveaway in those days. I told him I wasn't political. He studied me for a couple of seconds, then smiled and shrugged.

Goldie and I remained friends for a few years, but we drifted apart. Her career went better than mine. So I started to ask her for parts in her movies. After that, it didn't take long for her to stop returning my calls. She and I have the same birthday, different years. I'm older by six. Occasionally, we exchange cards.

One time, my late friend John Ritter did a staged reading of one of my plays, opposite Sharon Gless. I invited Goldie and she wrote me a note, saying she was sorry she couldn't come, that she was out of town. That was as close as we ever came to seeing each other since the unforgettable day that she and Julie Christie and I played tennis on Boris Karloff's court.

I'm lost. I don't know what movie I'm in. It could be *Star Wars*. It's as if I'm in a George Lucas spacecraft, careening around in a kaleidoscopic wash of ceaselessly merging space and time, illogically-sequenced, tumbling moments of my life. I hang still for an instant, then *whoosh*, I'm shot into the next moment, each time increasingly sure nobody I encounter knows my name—or anything about me, which in the business I've chosen to spend my life, is catastrophic. Sometimes these moments are happening to me right now. Sometimes they're merely memory. I never know until I get there.

I pray all of this is no more than a nightmare, that I'll wake up before I crash, but it doesn't happen. The harsh reality hits me that I've become one of those Hollywood people catalogued in the entertainment industry, because I'm over fifty and not famous, as old-to-dead.

Chapter One

I'm like a drowning man, watching his life in fast-forward—except there isn't the slightest sense of chronology.

I watch the Academy Awards with friends. *Brokeback Mountain* is nominated in several categories, and gay cowboy jokes are sprinkled through the opening of the ceremony. Jon Stewart, the host, introduces a montage—film clips that can be taken as sexually ambiguous, featuring cowboys of past Westerns taking off their coats, their chaps, opening their vests for the showdown; handling and caressing their guns. Then, near the end of the montage, they show a shocked and terrified frontier newspaperman as John Wayne in *The Shootist* inserts an immense Colt .45 into my mouth. (All I remember about that scene was trying to keep my teeth from getting broken.) My reaction to having a large, metaphorical penis stuck in my mouth in front of hundreds of millions of people on Academy Award night is that I'm *thrilled*. It's the largest audience I've ever played to.

About two weeks after that scene was filmed, I arrive in Carson City, Nevada, to do more work on the movie and find out that Wayne has been feeling worse than *a little ill*. He's been in the hospital with pneumonia for several days. "If shooting lasts much longer," the wardrobe guy confides, "he may not make it."

But I know better. I live in this culture. He's *John Wayne*.

My last scene with him is an exterior. It's the continuation of the gun-in-my-mouth scene.

He's shaky. When he hits me with his pistol hand on the back of my neck, he also hits me with the pistol. After we're wrapped for the day, I go to the hospital where they put two stitches in the back of my head.

Two weeks later, I'm on the Warner Brothers lot. I have one last scene with Harry Morgan. It's early in the morning, at least a couple of hours before I'll be shooting with Harry. I'm alone on an idle backlot street, sitting in a canvas chair with my name stenciled on it. I'm watching some extras at the end of the street, just sitting around, staring. One of them is in a telephone booth. Others are lined up, waiting to make *their* calls. They're spending these moments of (what seems to me) their virtually vacant today—trying to get themselves booked for a vacant tomorrow.

I hear a familiar voice, behind me.

"Did you know [director Don] Siegel used a double for me while I was sick?"

I swivel my head around and look up dumbly at John Wayne. I can't make myself say a word. People come to Wayne, not the other way around.

"A couple long shots in this thing are going to show some other guy being J.B. Books."

He's remembered the pistol slap and is telling me he wasn't himself that day.

"Anyway," he growls at me, "sorry about that." He briefly directs his gaze toward the back of my head. "I only ever did that once before."

He shows me a barely perceptible shoulder shrug, turns, and with his distinctive hitchy saunter, moves off toward his trailer.

I should have saved those stitches. I wonder what they'd bring on eBay?

Sometime after I've shot that exterior outside of the widow's house (the widow is Bacall's part) in Carson City I run into Ronnie Howard at a blackjack table in the Orchard Casino in Carson City. He's charming and affable and we chat about not much of anything. Then, out of nowhere, I'm surprised and gratified when he promises me that if he should ever have any success as a director, he will use me in all his films.

Chapter One

I still have a five-dollar chip from that casino. It's probably worth five dollars today.

Cognitive dissonance is the basis of most good acting. It means that you come to believe what you find yourself doing. You take a job working for a political party, and you come to believe in the cause. You are an actor playing love scenes, and you find yourself falling in love with the actress you're playing opposite. You are in an easy chair, in a warm pool of light. The rest of the house is in darkness. You're reading an especially scary mystery novel. You hear a noise from somewhere upstairs. You get up. You move slowly to the bottom of the stairway. You look up. Your anxiety builds. You hear the noise again. It sounds less like the squeaking you originally would have called it and more like moaning. You start up the stairs.

If you are any good, you should now be literally terrified.

If you hang around Hollywood long enough, cognitive dissonance becomes your genetic instruction. Your psyche gets bent into the shape of your eight-by-ten.

At first you say, "Not me."

I was given a sobriety test by the side of the road early one morning in Beverly Hills. When I was called on to say my ABCs, I got hung up around P or Q and failed. And I was sober. It was the pressure of the moment. It was real life that was the problem—my instinctive cognitive dissonance. It's a great acting tool. It can also work against you.

When I was ten years old, I used to play with a boy named Dixie Thorpe. He was nine. I have no idea where he got that name. I don't think his family was from the South. One day, Dixie's mother took us to Crispell Lake, one of the hundred or more swimmable lakes that pepper Jackson County, Michigan. Crispell was about a half-mile across, and the area around it hadn't been built up much. We were going to swim at the small county park.

Dixie changed into his bathing suit first and got down to the edge of the lake before I did. As I came out of the bathhouse, I saw a group of four or five boys in the water around the end of the swimming dock. Dixie and I didn't know these kids well. They went to a different grade school. They were a little older than us and the few times we'd run into them, they'd always harassed us with pre-adolescent taunting for no other reason than they *could*, and because each of them wanted to prove to his buddies that he was a tough guy.

Dixie had never been to this lake before and wasn't a strong swimmer, but I was. It was a pretty shallow lake, so no one seemed to be worried. I was almost down to the water when Dixie reached the end of the dock. I saw him look hesitantly down, apparently working up the courage to go in. The boys standing in the water jeered and yelled at him, "Dive in, pantywaist. What are you scared of?"

Dixie was a gutsy kid. He wasn't scared of anybody. I liked that about him. It made me feel gutsy, too; confident, just like Dixie.

As I reached the lake, he backed up a few steps. The boys, standing shoulder deep in the water, continued to goad him.

I felt something leaden in the pit of my stomach. I ran out onto the dock, yelling, "Dixie! *Don't!*"

But by then he was sprinting full tilt toward the water. He threw himself off, head first, launching himself into an awkward jackknife dive.

He seemed to hang in the air forever.

He hung on in the hospital for a week before he died. I never saw him again.

The boys had been standing on their knees.

Chapter One

Whatever punishment they got came from their parents. However much it was, it was surely not as much as they've had to live with their whole lives.

I should have seen what might happen to him before I did. I didn't feel guilty—not exactly. I suppose the right word is angry. I was older than Dixie. I'd been swimming at that park before. I knew how shallow the water was. I shouldn't have let it happen.

For a while, I tried to shut him out of my mind, to forget he'd ever existed. But it didn't work. In a sense, I've seen him grow up. At every crossroad of my life, I've imagined the benchmark moments that never happened to Dixie. In some small way it feels as if I've looked at the world through Dixie's eyes.

About twenty years ago, the anger started to fade. At the same time, I feel Dixie's presence more than ever. He doesn't speak to me, but he has quietly forgiven me.

Maybe guilt *is* the right word.

Anyway, whenever I do something that feels like it's the decent thing to do, or the kind thing, he sort of pats me on the back. It's hard to explain.

Darkness.

Every theatre goes dark sometime. There are always other stages, other shows.

Not for Dixie.

CHAPTER TWO

When I first arrived in Manhattan to try to become an actor, I stayed in a cheap hotel in the West 90s. It was the kind of place where two years later there would be a double hatchet murder in the lobby. I didn't go out much while I was living there. I was too afraid—although I did slip away from time to time to buy an armful of paperbacks: Charles Dickens, Jane Austen, Emily Dickinson, Oscar Wilde—authors I hoped would help fill up some of the holes in my Swiss cheese education and arm me for whatever lay ahead.

I slunk back to read them, alone in my room. I didn't want to be there. I didn't want to be in New York, but I had no choice. My wife, back in Jackson, wasn't crazy about the idea, but she seemed to understand I had to try this. So did my father. He'd advanced me enough money to get by for a while.

It was the first time I would become even dimly aware that others might pay dearly for my restless ambitions.

Back in the hotel, the night clerk says, "What do you do up there all day?"

"I'm writing," I say, even though all I'm writing are impressions of what I believe those great authors are conveying to me in the privacy of my garret.

"So you're not just another wannabe actor?"

"Well, not *only* that."

"How long have you been writing?"

"Since I was a teenager."

Usually by this time of day I've already drunk a pint of gin.

He studies me carefully. "What do you write?"

He's a man of average height and weight, with badly pocked skin. He's probably in his mid-thirties. He has oily brown hair, combed straight back from a high brow; white, even teeth and small ears with almost no lobes. I've never forgotten his face. He will be one of the murder victims two years from now.

"I write whatever I imagine," I say to the doomed night clerk.

"Well, what do you imagine?" he asks.

Stuck, I finally tell him: "There's nothing I can't imagine."

Upstairs, my first New York hotel room is a simple setting: unpretentious, paint peeling, a balding carpet, leaking radiator, a single creaky bed.

I look out the window, down at the street. On the corner of 93rd and Broadway people buy newspapers from a guy at a stand. A fat lady sits on what looks like a wagon. She has a lapful of some kind of material she's always sorting through. A little girl or boy—I can never tell—is crouched next to her. Fire trucks glide by with their sirens off. And nothing is going on in my head: just a vague awareness, just a murky perception, just an objective view of the world.

A cockroach runs along the windowsill and abruptly stops.

"Hello, roomie. Care for a nip?" I drop a fingerful of gin on him. He runs down to the floor and out of sight.

Chapter Two

He is in serious contention for being my best friend in New York.

When I finally get up the nerve to go out onto the streets, I study people. I never catch anyone's eye. You don't do that in New York. You look near them, never *at* them. The metropolitan horizon in Manhattan is so dense with people that it's always possible you're looking at somebody else when you look *near* the first person, and the first person, if he's become even peripherally aware of you, naturally assumes that's what's happening.

You can have satisfying people-watching experiences this way and at the same time look suitably anonymous and unthreatening. You can be scrutinizing everyone around you, *and* be altogether indistinguishable from every other blasé New Yorker. Also, a good thing: It doesn't take long to learn these skills; we're born with them. It's the same animal phenomenon that makes a dog look away when he's been watching you eat a hamburger and then you catch him at it and he casually gazes off, as if you've insulted him by even imagining he'd sink so low as to covet your burger.

I find myself wondering who I am as I walk the hectic streets of New York. Everyone else is unmistakably what he or she is, whereas I, manic observer, don't fit into the pattern. Not that there *is* a pattern, which is a nonsensical thing to say, I know, because there *must* be one—one of those rules. But whatever it is, it has zero relationship to me. After awhile, this realization starts wearing at me, and I develop even less confidence than the none-at-all I arrived with. This insight hits me at the same moment I become aware that it's time I crawl out of my hole and begin an actual search for acting work. If I went back home to try to do something else, I wouldn't be able to live with the ridicule I always imagine waiting in the shadows.

Then I learn the thing that jump-starts me. At the very beginning—and this only lasts a little while—they love "innocence." "Unsophisticated" *sells*, and they're not at all alarmed *at*—don't even seem to be aware *of*—"O, what a panic's in thy breastie!"

One day, a few years later, I'm at my agent's office. He's just negotiated a deal for me to do a television pilot. If it goes to series (it doesn't), I'll come as near as I ever could have dreamed to being rich. I feel attractive, wanted, and full of myself.

My agent's assistant, an ambitious young man who will later turn into one of the business's dominant shark-people, studies me—an eager scientist watching a thrilling new development in his petri dish. "You're like two different people," he tells me. "One is reserved and unassuming, and the other one's as shy as Milton Berle."

When I first arrive in New York, Uncle Stu, who's not really my uncle but a third cousin or something, takes me out to the theatre, to jazz clubs (Eddie Condon's, Birdland, the Village Vanguard) and up to his home in Scarsdale, where we play golf. He treats me as if I were a beloved son. He's a big, garrulous guy, generous and good-natured. He works in the snuff division of a tobacco company. Really.

Uncle Stu is a great memory. I'm sorry to have lost track of him for several decades. He still pops up in my mind unexpectedly. Maybe it's because I'm older, but lately it's as if someone has handed me several stacks of driver's licenses, and I'm riffling through them like decks of cards, not because I want to but because I'm trying to locate someone I've lost, thinking this misplaced whoever-it-is will solve all my problems, put to rest all my unnamable fears and longings.

If I can only hunt down that perfect *someone* who knows the answers.

Chapter Two

Then you'll be happy.

Or if I could just remember that crucial lesson I didn't fully appreciate the first time.

I recall something from childhood Sunday school. It's from the book of Genesis. Jacob wrestles with the angel. After the long night, a new day breaks and the angel says congratulations, you've prevailed. You're a higher consciousness.

Awesome.

Claude Rains was forty-eight when my second wife, Jessica, his only child, was born. He and I meet only once. Shortly after Jessica and I move in together, we drive from Manhattan up to Claude's farm near Sandwich, New Hampshire, for Thanksgiving weekend. Jessica spends most of her time in the kitchen with the cook while her father does hours of readings, grateful for any audience: Shakespeare, various classical poets, Shaw. (He had played Julius Caesar opposite Vivien Leigh in the movie *Caesar and Cleopatra*. With this job, he was the first actor ever to be paid a million dollars for a film. You could win a party bet with that one). I sit, wet-eyed, mesmerized, through his hours-long performance. The two of us—old man (seventy-six) and kid (twenty-six)—are emotional wrecks by the time Thanksgiving dinner is ready. Claude has no appetite at all. I'm able to snap back and eat like a starving actor.

The day after Thanksgiving, Claude plays tapes of his old radio and television guest performances: Edgar Bergen and Charlie McCarthy, Jack Benny, Bob Hope. He starts to nod off but then surprises me by doing his favorite parts along with himself—kind of a chamber choral reading: Mr. Rains accompanying Mr. Rains.

In conversation, there is a glaze in his eyes that I will later recognize in several other performers. It's as if he's expecting someone else to show up, behind me, right over my shoulder. When I ask Jessica about it as we drive back to New York, she says, "It's just him. He's always a little vague."

"I don't mean vague," I say, thinking about his desperate need to perform. "It was as if there was somebody else with us, or about to arrive. You know what I mean?"

Jessica shakes her head minutely and watches me steadily as if absorbed in a puzzle she never knew she'd been working on. Then she looks back at the lush hills of New Hampshire.

Claude will die a few months before Jessica and I are married.

I remember my favorite story about Claude. Jessica was with her father and his silly, fruity-voiced—according to Jessica—"lady friend," trying to get onto the Appian Way in Rome.

But Queen Elizabeth happened to be visiting at the time, and in fact was about to drive down the Appian Way with her entourage. When a guard stopped Claude's car and told them that because of the Queen's visit there would be a considerable delay—again according to Jessica—Lady Friend leaned over toward the guard, pointing at Claude, and trilled, "Joolio Chay-sarree! Joolio Chay-sarree!"

Who evidently, in her mind, outranked the barbarian Queen of Britannia.

(There are many such stories, as well as an illuminating account of Claude's amazing rags-to-riches life, in *Claude Rains: An Actor's Voice* written by David J. Skal and Jessica Rains.)

Jessica's and my eleven-year-old daughter and Claude's only grandchild, Abigail, wants to be an actress. My brain, like an iPod set to random shuffle, advances to the next scene and the central character of the pivotal crisis in my story.

Chapter Two

Abigail performs at a cabaret every Sunday afternoon. It's a variety show for kids and their dutiful parents. She sings and dances and does sketches. She's pretty good—as much as you can judge a thing like that about your own child.

For a while, I say some things, as subtly as I can, that might talk her out of any thoughts of a life in show business. By now, I'm not *quite* as fuzzy as I used to be about the pitfalls. She finally tells me she's having fun and that I should leave her alone.

I'm horrified to hear myself say, "I'm telling you this for your own good."

"People always say that when they're taking away something you like."

"It's not a secure kind of life," I tell her (I'm talking to an eleven-year-old about security).

"*You* do it."

"Yeah, but I started a long time ago and I didn't know any better."

"Well, I don't know any better *now*."

"That's why I'm *saying* this to you now." I'm becoming shrill. "*So you'll know better*."

"Well, I *don't* know better," she says. "All I know is that's the way you feel about it, but I'm not you."

So she goes into show business too.

Later on, it becomes a matter of life and death.

In some ways show business is about facing death. It's true in other professions too, particularly ones that include challenging presentational tasks. What all those comedians say about "dying out there" is no joke. Many of them—no more than average modern-day dysfunctionals, not at all sure who or what they are—have living, wheezing sensitivities to humiliation. And yet they go into that line of work—often, ironically, because they're good at it. It's another form of cognitive dissonance—in this case not an actor's tool, but a disease. Dissonance, Webster's tells me, means "out of harmony."

I'm embarrassed to say that for most of my life I've found myself drawn to lack of harmony. It's like someone who stops at car wrecks; you keep wishing you'd quit doing that, but then you hear the sound of smashing metal and you're standing outside your apartment door, listening to the redneck in the apartment across the hall screaming at his wife, telling her how pathetic she is. You don't know why you keep doing that, except you've just got to know how this comes out. And the worst part is not that you may be catching a cold out here in this drafty hall (this is when I'm first in Hollywood and the adjacent door is at the top of an outside stairway), it's the fact that you're standing here at all, listening to other people's pain, and even factoring in your adolescent grasp of truth—you know it's a lousy comment on your character.

Peter Sellers spent his life out of harmony. I'm sure in the beginning, he thought, "Not me." He longed for harmony as much as anyone. But he lived in constant fear that he was "dying out there" even when he was brilliant. He was a masterful actor, royalty among clowns, but in real life he was a shortsighted pawn, unable to see the whole board or anything beyond the square he was standing on. Not that it would have mattered. He *was* Dr. Strangelove: not one useable limb, not one tool to help him navigate the world—unless you counted his solitary vision of life or his impenetrable genius. When that was guiding him, he could find the improbable comic moment like a dog unerringly detecting a buried bone.

Chapter Two

But his genius was useless outside his work. It didn't help him even to be kind to himself or to know himself in any way. He couldn't pick himself out of a lineup. He said, "There used to be a me behind the mask, but I had it surgically removed."

With the exception of *Being There*, most of his work choices toward the end of his career were sad, or at least misfires. I acted in one of those. It was called *Where Does It Hurt?* According to my billing, I "starred" in it—although the truth is nobody but Peter Sellers ever starred in a Peter Sellers film. It made money and developed a sort of bad taste cult following, but you can no longer buy or rent it in the United States. It's politically incorrect, with something bigoted to say about every minority—which was, I think, meant to be part of the humor.

The Sellers character, a hospital administrator, is a letch, a money-grubber, and an equal opportunity racist, like Archie Bunker of the same era. The movie also takes shots at the medical profession. The rumor I've heard is that the American Medical Association applied pressure to make it disappear. I don't know if that's true, but I believe it.

One day I was waiting for the set-up on the location—a vacated floor of a hospital in Culver City, near MGM. The phone rang. I didn't turn around; I knew it wasn't for me.

Michael Caine answered the phone in his distinctive cockney twang.

I spun around.

Peter the impersonator was telling whoever had called that this was an extremely awkward moment. "I'm in the middle of a delicate operation," he said. "And now look what you've made me do! I've just severed this poor woman's aorta!"

He grinned, staring off into space, relishing the effect Michael Caine, the surgeon, was having on the nurse or hospital official who had accidentally dialed a number on the floor that had been leased to a film company and learned that he or she was an accessory to manslaughter.

Peter smiled a lot during the shooting. I had several scenes with him, but I never knew what his benign mask of a smile meant. He gave nothing away. He shared only his incredible talent and his distanced way of relating to people. He did look at you, but it was as if he had some goal he was forever trying to get to without really knowing what it was. It was just over my shoulder, this thing he was trying to reach.

He reminded me of Claude Rains, talking to me, also focused on something behind me—in Sandwich, New Hampshire. Like Claude, Peter *could* make eye contact—he listened to some of what I had to say—but I couldn't escape the feeling he was concentrating on getting to that thing behind me. At the same time, it felt as if it wouldn't really matter to him if he did. He just *had* to do it. It seemed a kind of bravery that he kept on trying so blindly to get to that whatever-it-was that might save him.

Not so recently as I'd like to think, I say to my children, "Why, kids, when I was your age, I was a has-been." As I say that, I remember Dustin Hoffman's response to George Gaynes, playing the old ham actor in *Tootsie*: "Were you *ever* famous?"

The ham actor looks sheepish.

I'm not quite that embarrassed; I've had my moments. I'm recognized sometimes. Occasionally, somebody still says, "Aren't you …?"

But that's pretty much it. It never gets more glamorous than that. Earlier in my career, I have a Q rating for a few years, which means somebody has bothered to test whether anybody knows me by name—mostly they don't. I tell myself I didn't set out to be a celebrity, but

Chapter Two

somewhere in the middle I develop a yen for it. I see what it usually does to people and you wouldn't wish that on a sleazy politician, but after I'm in the business a while, I begin my lifelong struggle with an irrational craving for it.

"*But wait a minute,*" says an alter ego, a boyish voice that reminds me of Dylan Thomas's *A Child's Christmas in Wales*. "*You weren't just a nobody*," he says. "*Tell us about the presents.*"

And I promptly do: I was once walking along 4th Street in the East Village with Al Pacino and Jill Clayburgh. (I was doing a play with Jill. She was living with Al at the time). Al, loping along in his characteristic gait, looked up at me and said in throaty tones I can hear now, "I think I'm going to do movies like you." He'd already won an Obie award and a Tony for his stage acting, and he'd been in one film, *The Panic in Needle Park*. I'd done two movies and was signed to do my third. I don't mean that I was as good as he was; I knew better than that even then. But I *was* playing more or less in his league. (Years later—I don't think he knows I'm aware of this—he put up the money, anonymously, for one of the productions of a one-man play I did about a college professor called *Last Class*.)

Around the same time, Katherine Hepburn, according to my agent, called the head of the William Morris Agency and told him he should try to sign me; that I was the best young actor she'd seen on Broadway in fifteen years. Another time, Joshua Logan saw me in a television pilot and said I had the best comedy timing he'd ever seen. (I knew that was a *bit* of an overstatement. I knew there were a *few* who were better—possibly Jack Benny and a handful of others.) Once I was in a supermarket with my son Charlie and a young man came up to me and said, "You're my favorite actor." And this was in a city overstuffed with actors.

Riiiight, Miss Desmond. You were *big.* "*It's the pictures that got small.*"

Anyway, those moments are of little comfort these days. I can no longer trust myself—confidence has become too infrequent a tenant in me—and all I can think to ask is: If those words of praise were true, then why aren't I a worldwide celebrity? Why don't people crowd up to me and say, "I loved you in *Grand Delusion* (or whatever my latest megahit is)" instead of, "Are you anybody?"

My greatest letdown in show business may have been when I went to the premiere of *Cactus Flower*, and realized I was distinctly *not* Robert Redford, the flavor of the year (1969). *Butch Cassidy and the Sundance Kid* was released about two months earlier.

I met Gene Hackman at the party afterward (he hadn't really hit yet—it was a year or two before *The French Connection*). He was on a publicity tour for another Columbia Pictures movie, *Marooned*. I tried to comfort myself that he wasn't Robert Redford either. But I had the sinking feeling that Gene Hackman was something even rarer than Redford that, once again, I was not.

I'm sitting in my best attempt at a lotus position in the little Zen garden I've scratched out of our backyard. I think of peaceful places from my youth; sanctuaries of the past, quiet, warm, or comfortably cool, usually country settings, but they vanish in a heartbeat.

I redouble my efforts, trying to reach a higher level of perception than my guarded sensibilities can usually manage on their own. I concentrate on the reasons I'm here, on my new overriding principles, and on the God various people keep insisting is inside me.

Then, I see myself, as if I'm watching a day's film rushes. I'm pleased to notice how peaceful and respectful I'm coming across, devoutly fingering my possibly Tibetan prayer beads, waiting as

Chapter Two

anxiously as I did to find out I wasn't Robert Redford to hear what I have to say to the Creator.

I whisper my line and wonder if it's too late to fire the writer.

"I don't think you really believe in me."

CHAPTER THREE

I was six when I decided I liked the name Rick instead of Dick as the nickname for Richard. Maybe I'd already anticipated how cruel kids could be to little Dicks. With a claw of fear in my belly I asked my mother Virginia, after we'd seen *Casablanca* together, if I could be called Rick like the Richard in the movie (this was in 1946). It turned out she preferred that too, so from then on I was Rick.

I played a lot of football as a kid even though I was too skinny for it. If I could somehow turn myself into the heroic type—playing football, basketball … *anything*, I'd have a lock on the beautiful girl and the golden future. I broke many of my important bones participating in a long list of athletic activities, such as skiing down the Cascades right next to the falls—an area of the hill where it shouldn't have taken much common sense to figure out what a suicidal idea that was. Poor C.A. Smith got so he cried every time I fell down and something went snap, because as my neighbor and friend, he had to take me home and face up to my extremely volatile mother, who never took the news good-naturedly. (C.A. was no wuss. He was the toughest kid in the neighborhood if you didn't count Katy O'Brien.)

I didn't have long to regret the end of my sports career; I quickly turned to acting. At the age of sixteen, I appeared at the Clark Lake Players as "Another Young Man" in *Sabrina Fair*.* I had no lines, but neither did the "First Young Man," and I watched him very carefully. I wanted to excel and be noticed.

As I kept on doing this, it crept up on me that kissing girls in rehearsals, then during the run of the play, was way more fun than getting your bones broken showing off for them from far across an athletic field.

I'm in my first moments of trying to decide on a career. I think of my over-stimulated, blissful, punishing mother. My baby sister Debby, my only sibling, has to deal with a painful social problem during middle school. She has a discoloration of her lower lip, called a hemangioma. Technically, it's a tumor. Actually, it's nothing more than a dilation of a group of blood vessels that very slightly darkens one half of her lower lip. It should be no big deal (later, it will fade away), but when you're a kid that age and must bring a self-confidence problem to school with you every day, it's a life-and-death issue. Worse, later on she has to wear a back brace when she's diagnosed with a mild scoliosis. The kids are cruel and make fun of her about both things. But she can do something about the brace; some days she sticks it in her locker during classes.

When she gets home, Virginia shouts at her, "You didn't wear it, did you? When you wear it, I can see the red marks! Look at you! You're grotesque ... a *cripple*!"

---

* The basis of *Sabrina* (with Humphrey Bogart) and the 1990s remake with Harrison Ford.

Chapter Three

Then Virginia gives Debby a fierce hug and cries and tells her she's sorry.

Around this time, I see the legendary husband and wife acting team of Alfred Lunt and Lynn Fontanne, both elderly by now, in *The Visit*. Fontanne soars like a conjurer over the footlights. She has returned to the small town where she was raised, then later seduced and disgraced by Alfred Lunt. Now, she smokes a cigar, has a sleek pet panther—and a coffin. She wants Alfred Lunt *in* it. She offers the impoverished town a fortune to kill him. The townspeople are piously horrified. But Alfred Lunt ends up dead anyway. It gives me chills.

Oddly, Virginia is the best audience I've ever had. In the right mood, my mother laughs at all my routines. So I do anything, take any risk, any pratfall, to get her to laugh. Once I've grasped that this is the key to survival in my family, I'm on stage every second. I *never* drop my guard. Like Lynn Fontanne, Virginia has icy intentions and the trick is to *keep* her laughing. That way, maybe she won't have me killed.

Based on this kind of logic, I begin to decide what to do for a living.

Sarah and I got married the summer I finished undergraduate school. I didn't really know her. She didn't know me. We were so unformed. Sarah was simply a lovely girl who made the mistake of her young life by marrying me. By the time this realization hit, our sons Scott and Charlie had been born. I don't know how it's possible to stumble along with only minimal good intentions—or more precisely, with a horror of causing pain because you've seen enough of that—and get so lucky as to end up hooked up with (or becoming a parent to) good people. And if your fortune holds, you can look back one day and feel grateful you didn't attract the killers you knew for sure you deserved; for example, you've sometimes felt you should have been in that hotel lobby when a certain psychopath came in that night to take his revenge.

Sarah and I lived in Detroit at first, where I tried to sell home improvements in the ghetto: the aluminum siding, the carports, the air-conditioning units. A middle-aged black man, standing in his front yard, grinned at me when I made my pitch. "What you doing here, boy? You not gonna sell none of that here." He was right. So I took Sarah, who was pregnant with our first son, Scott, back to Jackson.

I directed the Civic Theater in Jackson for the next two years. I was paid an okay salary for the time. Scott was born on the closing night of *Look Homeward, Angel.* Fourteen months later, Charlie made his entrance within hours of the final performance of Agatha Christie's *The Unexpected Guest.* Abigail was born seven years after Charlie. I don't associate her with any play, but like the boys, she is, if you don't count her recent troubles, "fair and wise and good," just as the nursery rhyme says Sunday's child is. (All three of them were born on Sunday.)

When Charlie is a month old, I leave my family and go to New York. After I land at La Guardia, a taxi takes me to the 34th Street YMCA. I tumble out of the cab onto the curb. I'd sprained my ankle several days earlier back in Michigan. The late morning light is draping itself around the skyscrapers, and midtown is neatly bordered by the usual yellowish-brown haze settling in for another day. Barely an hour in New York, I realize I've made a mistake. The cab driver is standing over me, telling me I should watch my step.

I apologize to him.

On my floor at the Y, I am, I'm told, the only one who's not gay. I make friends among my floor-mates. One night, I'm out with a couple of guys, and one of them, a marvelously sardonic character, tries to

Chapter Three

convince me that I ought to give it a go. "There are so many more things you can do," he says.

"Yeah, maybe, but I'm pretty sure I don't want to do any of them."

I go up to Times Square one night. I play skee-ball for a while and take in a newsreel. I see *Mondo Cane*, the lurid Italian "shockumentary" which has been running for a year. Then, I catch the last nightly showing of *Lawrence Of Arabia* at the Criterion Theatre. It starts with that mind-blowing score by Maurice Jarre. The titles play over a black screen. The lights come up on a bird's-eye shot of Peter O'Toole getting on his motorcycle. He takes off, then goes faster and faster through the English countryside until two men appear on bicycles, with big baskets on the front, and he has to take evasive action.

Then he careens off the road and dies.

I have two sons back in Jackson I don't even *know* yet. It's *shameful*—although I don't quite register this at the time. It's cognitively dissonant madness, but as Lawrence dies, I feel as if I'm being born.

I'm leaving my first New York hotel room one day (I'd moved out of the YMCA two months earlier). I press the elevator button and look through the crack down into the shaft and watch the ancient lift creaking its way up to get me. The pokerfaced janitor/elevator operator says nothing to me, so, wanting to be pleasant, or possibly not to be killed—or maybe, before Sarah and the boys arrive, to create more family in New York than my cockroach—I ask him how it's going.

"That old lady is plenty fat, too!" he says with astonishing passion. I can't think of one thing to say back to him.

He gets pokerfaced again.

Those are the only words I ever hear him say. It doesn't seem too surprising that he will turn out to be the hatchet murderer.

I walk over to Riverside Drive and down the steps to a small park, dominated by a prize-winningly shat-on statue of Joan of Arc, which is the subject of some annual Gallic ritual wherein, I think, they've pledged to clean her off in no uncertain oratory, and then they go back to their respective lives and whine at their wives who are home baking bread during the festivities: "Why did we leave Paree? New York is a peeg sty. I speet on eet. Ptooie!" And of course the bird droppings remain and accrue to the Maid of Orleans.

I continue through Riverside Park down toward the water, choosing my footing like a running back because it's spring and the dog shit of winter is blooming like dandelions on the green—it hasn't been legislated out of the parks yet, and downtown, Times Square has yet to be Disneyfied. (One day I'm watching a second-run movie on 42nd Street and behind me, in the lobby, a man is shot dead. They don't even stop the film.)

When I've gotten as near to the river as I can, I lean against the fence and gaze out at the Hudson. It smells good: of the sea, of freshness, of opportunity—which is quite poetical, I think, because in fact what I'm smelling is more shit.

I have roughly the common sense of a pigeon.

I got a five-year medal for Sunday school/church attendance when I was twelve. The minister said to us, "There is no health in you, miserable offenders. You will find the answer where? Inside yourselves. Let us pray."

God's actual spokesperson, as I'd been directed to understand it, as much as promised an answer to the what's-the-meaning-of-it-all question, then quick as a safecracker had me running through litanies that took up all my concentration trying to remember them. I'd think to myself: It's inside me. It's inside me. The answer is inside me. But by then, having to respond to him about how miserable I was, I'd forgotten the question. I wanted to shout: "Pardon me, Your Majestic Dazzlement, could I have one straight answer if you don't mind, and this time could it please be without any indecipherable parables?"

Evolved as I've lately come to hope I am, I might now add: "How about a little something to do with growing in compassion?"

Actors don't have compassion; they have "Look at me."

I'd like to answer *them* back with a little eloquence. I could tell them most living human beings have *some* form of *"Look at me"* haunting their souls. Perhaps they're trying to get God to acknowledge them, worried that after the Great Expulsion and we all put on our togas and doublets and Levi's and so on, to cover our nakedness, that God doesn't recognize us anymore, which makes us feel forlorn and cruelly abandoned.

I'd like to tell them about the end of *The Searchers*, when the racist John Wayne character lifts "tainted" Natalie Wood high over his head and saves her life and *his* soul and takes the crucial step away from hatred, toward humanity, and—with a little luck—back into God's good graces and out of all these garments of self-distrust, fear, and despair. It's unbeatable theatre. It's the human race improving. It's Joseph Campbell's "We must be willing to get rid of the life we've planned, so as to have the life that is waiting for us." It's almost religious—in the good sense. It's exhilarating!

But I don't say any of this because, to be honest, I'm terrified of these *voices* always lurking like a thicket of vampires in the back of my brain. I was born on Tuesday. "Tuesday's child is full of grace."

In my dreams.

A couple of years after my career begins its protracted tapering-off phase, I'm doing Equity Waiver theatre, which means you don't get paid. One of the plays I do is my one-man piece about a philosophy professor. He's gotten fired for inappropriate behavior at a faculty tea. Now, he delivers his final lecture, which he begins by preparing a large, dry martini. He tosses an olive into the air and catches it in the martini glass. He takes a soul-satisfying sip and begins his lecture.

The show is successful. I get some renewed attention for a while and a string of TV jobs. But my one-man show is lonely, unsettling work. People laugh, but it feels as if it's for the wrong reason, as if it's out of—I know it makes no sense—out of something like *scorn*. It's crazy. I like being in a cast with *people*. All there is with a one-character show is you and the stage manager. And when you get out on stage, all there is, is you and the audience. And every single move you make, every word you utter, has only one purpose—to try to make friends out of a bunch of strangers sitting out there in the … in the …

Darkness.

CHAPTER FOUR

On V-J Day (Victory in Japan) in 1945, with the war finally over, my parents celebrate by going out with their friends to the Fort McPherson Army Air Force base—where my father has been stationed, giving new soldiers eye examinations. I am five and stay home with a babysitter while Lincoln, Nebraska, and most of the rest of America goes apeshit. My babysitter isn't the celebrating kind, but it doesn't matter anyway; nothing could make her happy enough to make *me* happy.

I want to be with my mother and have my father in the background, keeping quiet as he does most of the time. I want to say just the right things to her, do the right dance or sing the right song with the right curlicue at the end and make her go *double* apeshit. But she isn't here. When she gets home, smelling of perfume and bourbon and cigarettes, she wakes me up and kisses me, which is fantastic, but I'm also jealous and angry with her for not including me in the celebration and in whatever has worn off her lipstick.

She kisses me again and goes out into our tiny living room, where she tells my father for the first time I can remember what a disappointment he is to her. He'd wanted to come home early, before she was ready to. It's clear he's always disappointed her in ways like that and from her tone of voice this night, she sees no hope for change.

I'm living in Beverly Hills. My second marriage is about to end. I'm trying to figure out what's gone wrong. I'm sitting in the bathroom, looking out the window down at Jacqueline Bisset, who is having an early morning nude swim in her backyard pool. I'm wondering what it would be like to be living just one house away—with her. I've had a few drinks through the night. It makes me see things more clearly—that would include Jackie's you-know-whats—unobstructed by preconceived notions.

I contemplate calling Sarah, and telling her I'm sorry I was such an asshole there at the end, but she's long into her second marriage—with, as far as I can gather from the boys, General George W. Patton's doppelgänger—and I decide calling her at six in the morning isn't intelligent. Also, I don't want Scott and Charlie to think badly of me. So far, I tell myself, I've been a good father—from a distance anyway, even if I wasn't so hot up close. Since I screwed up my first marriage, my sons' wellbeing feels like a bellwether of my own.

Instead, I locate the telephone number of an old girlfriend from college days, call her, and tell her I still have feelings for her.

It's eight a.m. in North Dakota. Lou Ann says, "What on earth do *you* want?"

"Aren't you surprised I got to be famous?"

"Beg your pardon?"

Didn't she hear me? I enunciated flawlessly. She says, "I didn't know you *were* famous. Nobody told me. Goodbye." She hangs up.

I remember sitting in Lindsay Wagner's trailer during the filming of an episode of *The Bionic Woman*, drinking aquavit. Why did she invite me there? Did she have something in mind? I'd known her for a while, but we weren't close. I would have *liked* to be, despite the fact that I was married. A year or two before that, we'd done an episode of *Marcus Welby, M.D.* together, playing a married couple. She got multiple sclerosis and I couldn't get it up anymore.

Right! Does anybody *remember* Lindsay Wagner in her twenties? She could have had leprosy; it wouldn't matter. I wonder if it's possible she asked me to her dressing room simply because she was lonely and wanted company. Maybe she was just being friendly.

Later, I'm not married and I'm doing a play with Vera Miles, most famous as Janet Leigh's sister in *Psycho*. We become very close for a while. She is ten years older than I am, and it feels more like *Oedipus Rex* than *Same Time, Next Year*, which is the play we're doing—like she's just gotten home from the party with my dad and come into the room to say goodnight to her little boy, except in *this* scenario, she doesn't go back out into the other room and berate my father; she stays with baby and daddy can get what's coming to him when baby says so.

I got hooked up—not in the same way I did with Vera—with other actresses older than me. When I was first in New York, I met Teresa Wright in Philip Burton's acting class (he was Richard's foster-father and he sounded just like Richard, or vice versa). Teresa had won an Academy Award for *Mrs. Miniver* and was a major star for many years. She kindly mothered me for a time.

Teresa played Gertrude to my Hamlet in class. We weren't very good; Burton subtly said so. Teresa had little Shakespeare experience. I had none outside of acting classes. Our scene was "not bad" and "valid," which might be okay for Gertrude. It sort of works—and the audience can imagine the rest—to play her as vague and superficial.

But it doesn't work for Hamlet. He has complex feelings about mom, mostly rage, and it's impossible to place any analysis of the acting of such feelings under the heading of "valid." I was best at playing three things in those days: really nice, really goofy, or really angry at mom.

You're supposed to recognize the difference between yourself and your character. I had unprofessional cognitive dissonance: adolescent and unpredictable. I remember a textbook from college: *Acting Is Believing*. I believed too much—but not always at the right time; sometimes I was too angry, sometimes too *nice*. People wonder why young actors behave so foolishly in their private lives; it's because actors often decide to *be* actors because they need serious help. Looked at from a certain angle, life as an actor seems as if it ought to serve that purpose. It doesn't.

I think Teresa Wright knew I was crazy and felt only kindness toward me. That was her best quality. Watch any Teresa Wright film. You invariably feel a compassionate woman, *underneath*, even when the character is not essentially sympathetic. I was incapable of yelling at her; she was too unlike Virginia.

Teresa died recently. I hadn't seen her for a long time. I still miss her.

I look at photographs I took a long time ago of my third and final wife, Linda. Her generosity shines through her hypnotic blue eyes, which she jokingly calls registered lethal weapons. I must have cheated to get so lucky, but I don't think I did; she just fell into my life, and all I've had to do to keep her is to be a little better than I used to be—which doesn't take much, and which she effortlessly inspires in me most of the time.

Although she's put up with a medical encyclopedia of insecure, self-involved shenanigans from me, she's been patient and constant.

Chapter Four

My friend Michael Norell said at the beginning there had to be something wrong with her. Now, when he recalls that, he says, "And I kept watching and watching, and you know what? There's isn't a goddam thing wrong with her."

More than once Linda has made me think of the maternal side of Teresa Wright. She also reminds me of Woody Allen's classic line in *Manhattan*: "You're God's answer to Job. ... 'I do a lot of terrible things, but I can also make one of *these*.'" She pulls me back from my loose-cannon impulses. I wish I'd had her with me when I had an actual career. She's never harsh on purpose, even though I take it that way occasionally. She's not wound as tightly as I am—well, maybe *sometimes*. She has anxieties like most people; she worries about her mother every day—not so it hampers her day-to-day living, but so I always know it's there, underneath, but in maddeningly sensible balance.

We can no longer have our cat in the house because of my "adult onset" asthma, so our current one, an orange male named Willy, has the most elaborate outdoor cat structure in the Western world—a kitty Taj Mahal made of wood, indoor carpeting, outdoor carpeting, a ramp, a scratching post, and an eating station—with a parasol over it all. It's nuts. On cool San Fernando Valley nights, Linda puts microwaved warming saucers under Willy's bedding. Paraphrasing Hamlet: "She wouldn't beteem the winds of winter visit Willy's tender body too roughly."

It's infectious. I've come, through Linda at first, and now for his own sake, to have affectionate feelings for Willy. I play with him through the window; it's as if there's no barrier between us, and I can see Linda even in our pussycat. I know it's creepy, too good to be true, but I can't find anything wrong with her—just little stuff, baffling stuff.

It's not only Willy. She performs a million kindnesses. When she's done drying the clothes, if it's a chilly evening and I'm watching television, her quirk is to spread them on top of me. She imagines it will be a warm and comforting surprise. Warm clothes tucked around my neck make a good metaphor for life with Linda. The little things, her small—you couldn't even call them faults—are almost nonexistent.

A year-and-a-half into living with her I go through several thin work months. I start telephoning a baseball trivia quiz company after I've had a few drinks late at night. Sometimes, I don't stop till dawn. After three months of nights like that, what I have to show for my time and money are about 120 unbelievably cheap baseball shirts that say Detroit Tigers on them. So, I send the company that sponsored the quiz a series of letters from a lawyer I pretend to be. I even have some letterheads printed for this lawyer, and I finally get all the telephone charges reimbursed—$1,128.00. I tell them my client is retarded.

Linda didn't know about the calls. She goes to bed and sleeps like a hibernating bear. It pisses me off—I've had insomnia my whole life—but I don't say anything. She doesn't find out about the baseball shirt fiasco until they begin arriving in the mail. After I tell her the whole story, it's her idea to tell the baseball quiz company I'm retarded.

It's not *all* warm clothes tucked around my neck with Linda. I get home from having my third back operation a few days earlier—I'm not sure exactly how many days because of the Vicodin they've given me for pain.

Linda doesn't think she has physical processes. It's another *little joke*. But I've done therapy. I know about these things. One night, I say, "That fish you cooked has made the kitchen smell like a fish slaughterhouse." She takes it as a comment on her cooking. It doesn't seem reasonable, but she does. She doesn't want to eat with me in our bedroom where, until I heal a little more, I'm still spending most of my time. She goes out and eats in the other part of the house.

I go mad. She comes back and after awhile says, "What are you so angry about?" I say, "Are you fucking kidding me?" I realize I'm crying. She tries to comfort me. I snorfle some more, but begin to come out of it and say, "Come on, you were really pissed off, huh?"

"No."

"No?!"

Now she looks like a bull about to charge.

"But you have rage, right?" I press.

"No!"

Her family doesn't believe in conflict. But what the hell does she think this is? If you don't believe something exists, you can't have it. She's slender, about five-foot-six. She's been drinking three glasses of wine a night, calls it moderate. When I tell her it isn't, she turns over and goes to sleep from the dose of alcohol she's already taken to medicate her rage.

Now I find myself really crying—out of my drug-induced psychosis (I hope, otherwise she's right; the madness is not temporary) and a heightened sense of frustration that my chosen one is not there to confront, because whatever it is in normal people at the root of their reason to deal with problems head-on doesn't exist in her.

Next day, there are all kinds of things to be done in the house that I can't do and she's out watering the fucking lawn for two straight hours. Jesus, I pick crazy women.

I'm breathing in burning steam. I study the rolls of fat on the misty human forms around me. They're trying to sweat away a heart attack—if they're at all like me—trying to make the cocktail hour less terrifying the morning after.

Outside the steam room, a head instructor is delivering a lecture to several students. This Adonis is buff and bronzed. He opens the door and six well-defined young bodies with heads direct themselves at the few older, foggy occupants.

"Excuse us, gents," the Adonis says.

Something about the way the Adonis says the word "gents" moves me out of the steam room, and I dress as fast as I can in front of the orange-and-blue pastel lockers. I hurry out of the club, passing a young man and woman, flirting with each other, both of them so exhaustively well toned it's impossible to look away.

I head to the Antelope Valley to meet a director who's out there with cast and crew, working on an independent film about some kids abused by a camp counselor. It's midday as I drive forty miles over the taupe-lavender mountains and out into the high desert north of LA. My ancient VW Rabbit makes its way heroically through the heat, up and down the hills.

When I arrive on set, the director seems surprised. "I'm really sorry," he says. "You're not quite what I had in mind." When I ask him what he had in mind, he shrugs and simply says, "Someone younger."

It is beyond my comprehension how he could say that to me. When I was young, I kept being surprised at how long I kept being young. Now that I'm not young anymore, I'm surprised how truly shocked I become when something like this happens. The habit of being young is that ingrained.

I head home. I'm not as disappointed as usual about the rejection. I was already feeling "a mite discouraged, sonny," before I went out there.

Chapter Four

On the way home, my brave little Rabbit inches back up the hills it flew down earlier. Struggling like Sisyphus up the longest, steepest incline, it gives up and dies. It has a cracked cylinder, or so I'm told later. I wouldn't know a cylinder unless it was clearly labeled. When it happens, I open the hood and inspect the engine. I bend over and take a closer look. I don't touch anything. It's easy to tell it's really hot. People pass me on the freeway as I perform my compulsory American male duty.

I look at the engine for at least half an hour before a cop stops and looks at it with me. Finally, he asks me if I want a tow. I say, "What are my other choices?"

He looks at me for a long time. "Well, you could live in your car the rest of your life. You could hire piano movers and have them haul it away. Or … you could just hit yourself on the head with a rock until you pass out."

I opt for the tow truck. He calls for it.

A new shuffle of my iPod kaleidoscope and it animates into fast moving, feathery white clouds that crown the radiance of a rare, clear San Fernando Valley morning. In the same millisecond, the world turns and I feel the Santa Ana winds slacken, knowing the smog will soon settle over North Hollywood again and that by noon, the overpowering heat will be accompanied by the usual still and poisonous air.

I force myself off the sofa and go over to my barber's house down the street, next to the house where my actress friend Ann Stuart used to live, so I can try to get in a swim before the heavy contaminants arrive. My barber and friend, Dale, who lets me use her pool, is at work. If she were at home, or if Ann Stuart was next door and still alive, I wouldn't go there. I hate to impose.

My asthma is not too bad so far today; I do laps for half an hour. It's an ordinary pool in a very pleasant small backyard in the San Fernando Valley, over the Santa Monica Mountains from Beverly Hills and Hollywood. Dale has several Buddhas and statues of little girls and bunnies along the walls, among the yellow-and-pink-flowered hibiscus bushes. Beyond the rear wall is one of the man-made tributaries of the Los Angeles River, as dry at the end of June as the rest of this once-picturesque *Bagdad Café* country. It's still picturesque, if you don't count the smog, the freeways, and the hopeless, crammed-together architecture.

Swimming in Dale's modest but caringly-wrought environment, watching my favorite side of the pool by alternating with each lap the way I turn my head as I Australian crawl through the splashing diamonds of sunlight, I realize that I'm almost enjoying the hibiscus blooms, that I'm almost enjoying all of it.

Then I look at Ann Stuart's house and think about her moment as Queen Nefertiti and her liaison with celebrity.

She was a lonely woman. Her professional acting name was Anitra Stevens. She was born Alice Ann Yoder. She had been mistress to Michael Curtiz, the director of *Casablanca* and pretty close to a hundred other major films. I have Ann's diary, which recounts the last four years of her life. It's a story that didn't have to be that way. She had money—not that that would have made the difference, but at least she could have *bought* help. She was tall, slim, and beautiful, or had been. In those last dispirited years she had the bearing of an imprisoned aristocrat. She was a princess whose beauty in the end had not worked for her the way she'd been promised.

Ann and I used to drink together and talk Hollywood. She told me her attitudes were based on what she had picked up many years earlier from Michael Curtiz. She made him sound improbably starchy;

a creative artist of his genius, I thought, couldn't have a personality that stilted. But I wanted to learn whatever I could about him (there's not much biographical material available), so I didn't argue.

Ann said Curtiz was typical of his age: a defender of old traditions who didn't approve of the *moral tone* that was beginning to sweep through Hollywood at the time of his death in 1962. This was consistent with the inclinations Ann had already had instilled in her under the unbending guidance of her mother, a first-generation American who had escaped an oppressive, strict-Calvinist European background. I wondered if she wasn't painting Curtiz in her own image.

She met him at a casting call for the first remake of *The Jazz Singer* (with Danny Thomas). He cast her in the tiny role of Yvonne. In his next film, *Trouble Along the Way*, she was Bobo, the saloon girl. The following year, simply in love with her by now, he cast her as Queen Nefertiti in *The Egyptian*. It wasn't really much of a part, but she *did* get to be the Queen of Egypt.

The year after *The Egyptian*, Curtiz bought her the house down the street, in North Hollywood.

She never worked again.

When Curtiz died, he left Ann most of his estate, which included all of the ongoing movie residual/royalty payments. Before she died she gave me several photographs of herself with Curtiz, and also two of her with Elvis Presley, taken by the still photographer on *King Creole*, which Curtiz had directed. In both photographs Ann looks as if she were made of porcelain, desperately afraid she might at any second make the tiniest wrong move and shatter the illusion.

During some thin times recently, I sold most of those photos to director/producer Steven Soderbergh. Among those pictures was one of Curtiz's mother. It's a portrait of what looks like a benevolent "mom," perhaps into her eighties. The picture is signed by Curtiz: "My Mother." It occurs to me that's slightly peculiar: an eight-by-ten of a mother, autographed by her child.

Maybe it's a narrow window into the effect of celebrity on its victim.

Aside from my interest in Michael Curtiz, I don't know why I'm so fascinated by Ann Stuart. I can't say I thought she was *nice*. Like most people whose lives are controlled by alcohol, her real focus was always on her next drink.

I guess the truth is I am horror-struck by the similarities between us.

Linda says, "Why have you picked her?"

I'm painting a picture as she asks me this. It's of a man painting a picture of a fantasy creature he wants to fly away on. "I don't know," I say. "She *defines* North Hollywood to me."

"You'll hurt my feelings."

"But you're not North Hollywood. I'm just saying in general, you know? Ann *screamed out* North Hollywood to me. I mean that as a show biz metaphor." I don't like the way she's looking at me. "Listen, I'm not actually focusing on Ann. I'm concentrating on Michael Curtiz. What does his relationship with this sad North Hollywood woman say about who he was and how he approached his work?"

I always hear Linda's silences; I mean *really* hear them, as if they add up to her own precision language, and it makes me doubt my own words, labels me a liar. And I *hate* that.

I once asked Ann how it felt to be Queen of Egypt.

She shrugged, her features crimping into a cynical smirk.

Still swimming in Dale's pool, I wonder what it would be like to be twenty-nine, clueless, and monarch of the civilized world.

Chapter Four

Then I remember that I was.

The morning I went in to meet Gene Saks, the director of the film version of *Cactus Flower*, he told me I would be reading that afternoon with Goldie Hawn.

I nodded and smiled, striking just the right note of cool.

"The only way you won't get this part," he said, smiling back at me, "is if you give a schmucky reading." He was assuring me he knew I wouldn't do that because I'd played the role several hundred times on Broadway.

As I read with Goldie that afternoon, I was pretty sure I was coming across, if not exactly schmucky, at *least* a little bit tense, and definitely not cool.

It had nothing to do with Goldie. She couldn't have been more charming.

It didn't matter. *I wanted that job!*

A couple of hours later, in a state of near paralysis from my mounting fear that *a little bit tense* had slipped over into *clearly schmucky*, I managed to dial my agent, Wally Hiller.

He told me my first rehearsal would be on the following Monday. I'd gotten the part.

The next three years were heaven. The whole world, especially Hollywood, treated me like royalty: the best dressing rooms, parties, limousines, multiple-star hotels, first-class plane rides. My God, people *listened* when I spoke.

Naturally, I assumed this was the way life would always be.

CHAPTER FIVE

I witness an argument between James Caan and Don Adams, whose television series, *Get Smart,* is in its last season. The argument is about "What acting is." Neither of them is drunk. Neither of them is a drinker. But together, they have enough testosterone to populate Indonesia. Adams finally settles the dispute by stalking into the next room and returning with the two Emmys he's won. He raises them triumphantly over his head and says, "*That's* acting!"

Thinking about celebrity and my own acting career, I hear Maxwell Smart's voice insipidly declaring, "I missed it by *that* much, 99." Everyone knew that Agent 99 (Barbara Feldon) was leagues smarter than Max, even though she went along with him, which she had to do in order for the show to work. Her common sense, her mystery, her power were infinitely greater than the poor dummy she partnered with. Nobody ever said much about it, but it connects in a way to the oldest story on earth: women having profound power at their cores and men scrambling around to thwart that power.

It's one of the great current show business fables, that women finally have power that can't be curbed. At times, they have *apparent* authority, but it's still, as always, under a routinely wary eye (Julia learns to disguise the high she gets from the opiate of influence until Caesar sees through it and sends her into exile). The soul is feminine and the feminine is the most intuitive, but the masculine wields the axe. Ask Sherry Lansing.*

Don Adams is at my house one evening. I offer him an hors d'oeuvre. He frowns at me and says, "What's your name?" I say, not entirely sure myself, "Rick Lenz. I'm a friend of your brother's." I *don't* say I've been at your house about a dozen times. We've spoken maybe fifty times before this moment (actually, I never speak, he does—more or less at me). For a time, Jessica and I go to Adams' house in Beverly Hills on Sundays. Lots of people are there: Peter Falk, Burt Lancaster—a glut of stars or would-be stars and killer comedians. We play tennis, swim, then watch a movie, usually followed by a couple of episodes of *Get Smart* or outtakes with Adams and other funny men (Lancaster and Falk have disappeared by now).

In my first Hollywood years, I don't learn a single thing from these and similar soirees about how I'm expected to behave. It makes me uneasy, and as I continue to be clueless about how to *be*—from these affairs, and at these affairs—how to work the system and other such fundamental-seeming show business skills, I begin to get depressed about it.

Then I have a tiny awakening. My accidental technique is at least giving me some longevity. Not knowing anything is not a stumbling block in Hollywood. When you don't know anything, everybody loves to have you around so they can tell you what *they* know. Also, you get a chance, once you learn to relax into it a little, to study the people who *can* work the system, and in a backdoor way you come to learn basic survival techniques.

---

* The first woman to head a Hollywood studio—20th Century Fox and later, Paramount.

Chapter Five

A couple of years later, before he becomes a star, Richard Dreyfuss does a staged reading of a play I've written. His energy is like one of the comedians at Don Adams' parties. It could blow you out of the room. He feels like a comic, touches a similar chord, only with a focus and commitment unlike any I've ever seen.

My killer agent, John Rival, asks me my opinion of him. Apparently Dreyfuss has come to him looking for new representation (it's after *American Graffiti*, but before *Jaws*). It doesn't happen. Killer Agent, who's happy to have me as a client—for the moment—does not recognize Killer Actor for what he is. Dreyfuss would have earned him a lot of money.

You'd think killers would recognize each other. But Dreyfuss, who has a passion for his work, which is about people, is different from the other killer, John Rival, and his passion, which is plainly about killing.

I look down at the marshmallow clouds below me—not sure where I've flown from and what I'm flying back to—and wonder how you make sure, if you have the compulsion to be a killer, you end up being the right kind, the kind you can live with.

Of course, if all you want to do is kill, such fine distinctions won't trouble you in the first place. I will learn, as I travel the path I've chosen, that killing is a pivotal part of the game. The late manager-producer, Bernie Brillstein, said, "You're nobody in Hollywood unless somebody wants you dead." The only good news in this is that, like sharks, the killers don't really care about *killing* you; in the end, they simply want to *eat* you. You can't take a thing like that personally.

Abigail, a Hollywood child, a high school dropout, and later a rock singer, gets on drugs, goes into rehab, then does it again. If it weren't such a vile cliché and she weren't my daughter, I'd laugh.

Quite a few years before the drugs, I catch her in a lie about where she'd been one afternoon after school.

So, I explain things to her, beginning—I tell myself—at the beginning. "Honey, you have to understand about your mother—" I keep going even though I hear one of my other voices scream: *Stop talking*! "Honey, you have to know about your mother that she doesn't like to face certain things."

She looks at me, puzzled. In those days, I have a reputation with my kids for having trouble getting to the point. And when I finally do, it can can come out harsher than I intended.

"Don't say it, Daddy."

"I have to say it once."

"*Please* don't."

"Honey, I've *never* told you this but I left your mother because she was unwilling to accept change. And life *is* change. Your mother wouldn't do it and she wouldn't allow me to either. She used to make me … *fib*, when we had company, about whether she'd cooked dinner from scratch when part or all of it had come out of a package."

She looks baffled. "But what did it matter?"

"That's what I told her."

"No, I mean, what did it matter to you if she wanted people to think that? So what? Why didn't you just let her have that?"

"Because it was symptomatic." I want to go back and find a word that's a little less cold, but it's too late. "Okay, listen, forget about your mother. This is about *you*. Think about your friends—those girls you were with this afternoon. Some of your friends think it's *hip* to lie." It seems as if she's looking at me with contempt, and I feel a blast of rage, remembering nobody says "hip" anymore.

"Okay, '*cool*!'" I say. "A lot of people tell themselves lying is *cool*! They insist on filtering everything through a prism of self-deception.

They're so concerned with how they're perceived by others that they end up living in a world of lies, and you can't do that without *everybody* knowing it—especially other liars; other liars sniff it out fastest. And it's them you end up living with because with them you can go along merrily lying to each other about how you're not lying to each other."

"I don't know what you're talking about."

"I'm talking about your damned friends; I'm talking about people who lie. I don't want *you* to be a liar. I'm saying how far do you think it is between lying about how the dessert got made and lying about everything?"

And now, remembering this, I'm alone, driving through Beverly Hills traffic at lawnmower speed, running through dialogue in my head, a machine gun conversation I *must* bring to an end; it's pointless and signifies nothing more than that I'm stuck in idiot traffic, chatting with and through—and a handful of other prepositions—the enemy in my head.

Abigail doesn't say anything, and again, I remember that she looked confused.

"I'm not telling you not to love your mother, if that's what you think. I just want you to know the difference between truth and lies. A liar's punishment is that he can't believe anyone else." *Schmuck!*

She gets up, scraping her chair across the floor. It makes an urgent shriek that sounds like a car screeching to avoid an accident. She looks at me, tears streaming down her face. "I don't know who you think this liar is that you're talking about," she says. "But it sounds to me like it's you."

"Don't act this way."

"*You're* the actor."

I see her quite a few years earlier, when she's seven years old, standing on the front porch of our old house in Beverly Hills. I'm picking her up for our father/daughter weekend and she's so open it almost draws my attention away from myself.

Now, she turns and leaves my house in North Hollywood and we don't talk to each other in any meaningful way until the night I bail her out of jail.

That's the night I *really* give her a lecture.

Linda gave me a book on meditation and I've been giving it a try. But to be honest, I don't have the feel for it. I'm more of a contemplator. Meditating, the book is saying, means you sit quietly and think of nothing. Then before long, the Universal Creative Force whispers breathtaking wisdom in your ear. What I get when *I* meditate is silence, which quickly turns into the need to scratch something or go to the bathroom. Once or twice I've found myself a tiny bit cross with the Universal Creator for choosing me as the only one He *never* whispers anything to. So I contemplate. I sit quietly and ponder important matters—like what's for dinner, or if by some chance I ever got to play *King Lear*, could I actually carry even a small-boned Cordelia, considering all the back operations I keep having?

Sometimes I think about Dixie Thorpe. I wonder if there's meditating and looking forward to dinner where he is.

The same year I'm in the film version of *Cactus Flower*, I do a picture with Jackie Gleason in Miami. It's a decent script based on a wonderful satirical novel by Peter de Vries, *Let Me Count the Ways*. The movie is called *How Do I Love Thee*? Go figure. In the story, I'm his son, a college professor. The very first day I'm on the job I have a scene with Jackie in a hospital, in which everyone thinks he's dying. I commiserate with my mother (Maureen O'Hara), then I'm to rush

Chapter Five

into my father's room, where I have to throw myself on him, give him a fierce hug, and beg him not to die.

Jackie is not the warmest man in the world. The ambience on the set is equally chilly (Jackie is the muscle in getting this one made, and the muscle always sets the tone). The only thing that *is* warm is the weather—and agelessly hot Maureen O'Hara. It's July. We're in a hotel, meant to pass for a hospital in Lourdes, France, where it's never this hot. It's ninety-five degrees, not counting the 170 percent humidity.

The assistant director introduces me to Jackie, just as Jackie says to the guy who's always waiting never more than five feet away to respond to any command he makes, "Butt me, pal."

The minion gives him a cigarette and lights it as Jackie gives me an indifferent glance and offers me his left hand like he's the Queen of Prussia. He says, "Whatdoyasay, pal?

I shake his limp moist hand, grin, and go, "Unnnh."

Fifteen minutes later, I heave myself onto his sweating chest and tell him with every bit of passion I've got, "I love you, Pop!"

This is my first lesson in shooting out of sequence and acting a deep, meaningful moment with somebody you don't know and in this case, somebody who's pretty much phoning it in.

Between shots, Maureen O'Hara comforts me.

"First time shooting piecemeal?"

I nod. (*Cactus Flower* was rehearsed for three weeks, then shot in sequence.)

She smiles sympathetically. "All you can do is grit your teeth and act your heart out. Don't worry. It's going to look fine. Just try to think how you'd feel if he were your own father."

A few years later, shortly after my career starts its lingering spinout, my dad loses his license to prescribe medications. He and Virginia have been doing prescription drugs heavily. I remember my mother, who suffers with a bad back—which I *have* to sympathize with—crying out at night, "Charles, I need a hypo." He finally gets his license reinstated and is able to come up with enough narcotics to kill all her pain.

I remember him telling me he'd talked to the pathologist who did Virginia's autopsy. The man said her organs were very soft, as if they were falling apart. And as my father tells me that, with this glazed, puzzled look on his face, I remember the sound of Virginia's midnight pleas. And every time, he gives her whatever she wants. I can see, I can *hear* the light snapping on outside my closed door and the scuffing of Dad's slippers down the hall. *My God*, he even *hums* as he goes off to get the drugs and the needle. And then he scuffs back and—no more pain for Mum, and an only once-or-twice-interrupted night's sleep for Dad. I'm surprised they don't—maybe they *do*—advertise in the medical journals: "Demerol kills the pain. SPECIAL for physicians' private use: kill two pains for the price of one, and before you know it, it's permanent."

But what if her pain *was* inexpressibly awful? I mean more than her lower back: middle-American housewife, post-World War II, no creative outlets aside from clubs and a kind of catchall community patriotism—not the good kind, but the hand-me-down, last-refuge-of-scoundrels kind.

What are you, her lawyer?

Debby is ten years younger than I am and never sees the upbeat side of Virginia's passions. She's never around when Mom is at her best—before the drugs have rendered her housebound. Debby is seven when I go away to college. She is the most spirited kid I've ever

Chapter Five

known, full of eager, mischievous energy. Despite Mom's cruelty, it's as if Debby has an electrostatic precipitator inside her, dissipating any cloud of unhappiness that might diminish her glow. The next time I see her, when I come home for Thanksgiving break, my freshman year, she's stressed and gun-shy. In my absence, Virginia has focused her indiscriminate rage on her like sun through a magnifying glass, and it's begun to shrivel my sister.

I got the benefit of Mom's benign years; she was still young and hopeful. By the time Debby was left alone with her (Dad spent long days at the office and the hospital—longer, I always thought, than necessary), Virginia had fully realized that marrying the doctor was not going to turn her disillusionments into rainbows, and not only that, he had become a major regret all on his own. But he wasn't home most of the time, so Debby caught the brunt of it—in such forms as out-of-the-blue elbows to the ribs—and it was a long, shitty road for her, getting over that.

She married Chuck, moved to Wyoming, and things got better. Then they got worse, because even though Chuck was a good, well-intentioned man, he had his own demons.

Wyoming still feels like home to Debby. She met Frank there and married him. Frank has family in Cheyenne, and they've gone back in recent years to vacation. Frank is not the rebellious type I remember Chuck being, but he, too, is kindhearted. Add to that: He is constant and reliable, a stand-up guy.

It's a good thing. He will need all of his strength.

Linda wakes me on a Sunday morning in April 1983 and says, "Your dad's on the phone." She looks at me with grief in her eyes. "Your mom died."

Dad, disoriented and doubtless drunk, manages to say my mother has choked to death in the middle of the night. He's too confused from alcohol and pharmaceuticals to tell me exactly how it happened—although I could make a pretty good guess. Linda drives me to Los Angeles International Airport, where I get on the next plane to Detroit. I drink four or five airplane gins on the way. I tell my seatmate what's happened, as much as I know. He seems to feel more pain than I do.

The minister of our church drives my hung over but still-intoxicated father and me the eighty miles back to Jackson. Soon after that, my sister shows up from Denver. She's the only one of us who's sober.

I am hung over for the funeral. My father and Debby and I sit together in the first row as the minister relates hollow, generic information about Virginia, who has spent her life on the other side of the world from the kind of excitement she'd longed for.

Debby sits impassively through the ceremony. I squeeze her hand as the minister speaks. She squeezes mine back but I don't know exactly what it means. It feels as if there's a battle going on deep within her. I happen to look up at the minister once and notice him frowning at us. Only much later do I realize that it's not a disapproving frown, but a compassionate one, and I remember that he drove 160 roundtrip miles with my father to pick me up at the airport.

We hang around for the next few days. Sometimes, when my sister is out, I go into my dad's room and find him in the marriage bed, weeping openly. I've never seen him cry in my life. I try to comfort him, but I give up. We're too awkward with each other.

He dies ten years later.

I think he loves me, but not nearly as much as he does my sister. I always have the feeling he's talking to me as he imagines a father

Chapter Five

should talk to a son, but he isn't an actor and can't play the role. I am, but can't play mine either except in the most superficial way. My father is never comfortable with human beings, even though he sees a stream of them every day in his ophthalmology practice (by this time he's dropped his ear-nose-throat specialty). Everybody likes him. People say, "Oh, you're Dr. Lenz's son, aren't you? We just love him. He's so gentle, so kind."

And he *is*—but not, in my experience, past a fifteen-minute appointment or ten minutes of family conversation. At his cut-off point, he goes away, anesthetizes himself and, as time goes on, my mother too—which, from my point of view, isn't all bad. Virginia is never lethal when she's doped up or asleep.

Although everything I say about my parents is true, corroborated in every detail by Debby, I can't shed the nagging sense that I'm too rough on them. It's crazy.

Another troubling notion having to do with my family: I wonder if I left for New York to be an actor a month after Charlie was born because of an earlier moment I'd had alone with Scott when he was a baby. His mother was at work, and Scott was being worse than fussy and wouldn't stop screaming. I imagined what it might be like if I were to grab him by the ankles, twirl him around, holding him at full extension, as in the hammer throw, and let him fly into the wall.

Good. Finally. You've ducked into the rabbit hole and come up with exactly what's there: blackness.

No! Jesus! I wouldn't have actually *done* it!

My next job—almost immediately after my mother dies—is on stage in *Equus*, playing the compassionate doctor awakening to the lifelessness of his life. The character has to dig to get to the intense, suppressed emotions within him. His bland avoidance of the guts of life is over when the play begins. If it were only about that, I could simply play my father before Virginia's death. But as it turns out, I'm playing the weeping new father I've just met, the one mourning the loss of the only human he's ever been close to, close enough to give her daily injections to kill *all* pain.

I'm not immodest when I say I get to the grief in my character. I can't hold my father when he's weeping. But my patient in *Equus*, the tormented young boy in my care, moves me every performance to tears I can barely choke down.

Between my second and third marriages, I'm very jittery, not yet my new wrestling-with-the-angel self. Michael Gordon (director of *Pillow Talk* and the movie version of *Cyrano de Bergerac*) casts me as the lead in a stage production of Eugène Ionesco's *Rhinoceros*, with Ionesco in residence. It's a great opportunity.

I learn the lines, work hard on the role, and then, the day before rehearsals are to begin, I call Gordon and tell him I can't do it. I don't remember what reason I give him. Whatever it is, it's not true. I've worked on stage a lot lately and tell my friends and myself that I'm becoming overexposed, implying that I'm steering a course of sensible career management. The real reason is that I'm afraid people are going to see through my thin veneer of actor's tricks and that I'll be exposed for the fraud I am.

Instead, I go to Kansas City and do *The Owl and the Pussycat*, a skillful enough but lightweight comedy, in dinner theatre. After the show each night, I drink myself into unconsciousness.

Chapter Five

The same Michael Gordon had directed the Gleason movie. One day I'm watching Jackie and Shelley Winters, who is playing his mistress, work on a scene together.

Jackie is a genius comedian and entrepreneur, but an up-and-down actor. (I see him on television recently in *Requiem for a Heavyweight* and am reminded that when he decided to take the trouble, he was brilliant.) This summer in Miami, he's on the wagon. He's getting married in a couple of months, so he attempts sobriety for a while and it's making him testy. Also, he believes this movie isn't going to do much for him other than give him a paycheck.

When Jackie is not phoning it in, his performance is full of blustery energy, but it's empty at the heart of it. On this day, Shelley stops in the middle of a take and says with her typical directness, "Jackie, are you even trying?"

You don't say a thing like that to Jackie Gleason. He turns crimson. If it were his television show, he'd have her fired on the spot. But this is a movie and he can't do that, so he retreats into his lifelong refuge: the bottle.

He never re-emerges. For the rest of the shoot, he's sober in the mornings, for the master shots. Then, in the afternoons, when Gordon moves in for the close-ups, he's slurring drunk—it's obvious in the dailies and in the movie itself when it has its fleeting run in theatres. Gordon can't control him. Russ Metty, the superb director of photography, quits the movie. (He had earlier photographed Orson Welles' *A Touch of Evil*—including the famous three-minute, twenty-second opening tracking shot, which inspired or at least influenced the jaw-dropping opening sequence in Robert Altman's *The Player* many years later.)

Everybody else on the crew stays with *How Do I Love Thee?* They all try their best. They need the paycheck. Besides, this could be something good.

But it doesn't matter because Jackie carries forever a wound in his heart. And every day, for the rest of the shoot, he drinks himself into the lonely abyss of insensibility.

CHAPTER SIX

I'm playing *Man of La Mancha* as a guest artist in Michigan. I'd never get to play it in a major production, so I grab the chance when it comes along. I love the role and the show. I've read *Don Quixote* twice and feel full of myself and scared to death. The cast is amateur, but they're mostly not bad. Being "professional" at *anything* doesn't necessarily mean you're any good, and being amateur doesn't mean you're not. Big news on the penetrating wisdom front.

The only small problem I have is that I'm not a trained vocalist (a few obligatory lessons in New York and some coffee house folk singing). I can do the higher ranges passably, but when I get to *The Impossible Dream*, I let myself and everyone else down—the cast, the audience, everybody whose opinion I've ever valued; even if they're not there to see it. Otherwise, I'm made for the role. It feels like I'm good at it. But when it comes time for *The Impossible Dream*, I wish they would play Richard Kiley's version of it over the sound system. Then I could lip-synch it and everybody would be transported by my power and passion. This is not advanced-level thinking, I understand, but it's all there is at the moment.

When I get back to Los Angeles, I'm waiting next to the Northwest Airlines luggage carousel. About a hundred feet away, I see—also waiting for his luggage—Richard Kiley, who invested blood, guts, and money in *Man of LaMancha* as it made its way toward its first New York production in Greenwich Village. Then he played Cervantes/Don Quixote on Broadway with all his heart and uncanny craft.

I get up a lot of nerve, go over to him and say, "I just got back from doing your role. Thanks *a lot*. You ruined my *Impossible Dream*."

He smiles and tells me I'm very kind. He's as gallant as Don Quixote.

In the first years away from my hometown, I work as a hotel night clerk, always with a wary eye out for janitors, always checking to make sure that's a mop they're carrying and not something sharp. I work at office jobs through a temporary agency, filing, answering telephones, some typing. I'm a substitute teacher for a few months.

One time, I teach at a grade school in the ghetto. The kids' regular teacher—black, of course—has been in the middle of reading *Huckleberry Finn* aloud. It seems awfully sophisticated for kids this young, but I'm just the substitute. I pick up where their teacher has left off, acutely aware that except for a couple of black acquaintances from college who fell under the heading of "wanting to have some black friends," I have next to zero experience with minorities.

Here's where I pick up the story:

> When they told me there was a state in this country where they'd let that nigger vote, I drawed out. I says I'll never vote agin. Them's the very words I said; they all heard me; and the country may rot for all me—I'll never vote agin as long as I live. And to see the cool way of that nigger—why, he wouldn't a give me the road if I hadn't shoved him out o' the way. I says to the people, why ain't this nigger put up at auction and sold?

Chapter Six

That's how far I get before I look frozenly up at my audience. They are third and fourth graders, equally boys and girls. I don't know if it's the fact that the Civil Rights Movement is only in its early stages and isn't really in these kids' consciousness yet, or if it's Mark Twain's writing and it's just a good story, or if it's—*empathy* with my discomfort? That doesn't make sense, that a class of third and fourth graders in a ghetto in 1965 would be that ... *evolved*?

Nevertheless, except for a bit of giggling, the kids are attentive and respectful as I read clumsily to them about "Nigger Jim."

There is no doubt that I'm not able to grasp the core of whatever their feelings are and that I still couldn't.

At any rate, I'm indebted to those kids for their—kindness probably isn't exactly the right word. Maybe it's instinctive grace.

I sing when I'm working around the house. Today, it's a few bars from Elton John: "What do I do when lightning strikes me?" Linda, walking by, says, "Run get help."

Several years before I met her, she dated a slick Hollywood guy for a while. They were in Las Vegas once. The Hollywood guy knew the crooner Vic Damone. They went to see Damone's show at one of the casinos. After his set, Damone came over to their table. The Hollywood guy introduced him to Linda. Damone looked at her, I imagine captivated by her registered lethal weapons, glanced briefly at the Hollywood guy and back, then said to her, "If you ever get tired of this clown, let me know."

Linda said, "Why? Do *you* want him?"

Once, shortly after I'd met her, we were shopping at Ralphs Grocery. Coming down an aisle from the other direction was Ted

Neeley, who'd played the title role in the movie version of *Jesus Christ, Superstar*. Linda dipped her head and crossed herself. Neeley smiled.

I'm at Jason Robards' house at the beach. He's drunk. George C. Scott is here and he's drunk too. The house is full of drunks, famous and otherwise. It's been called to Jason's attention that the flag is askew on the flagpole above the house. Still smashed, he shinnies up the pole and fixes it. Later he will get in a bad car accident and won't be drunk again for the rest of his life.

But for now, he is great fun to drink with—friendly, witty even. Of course I'm a bit drunk myself and am probably not a reliable judge.

When I'm in the Broadway production of *Cactus Flower* with Bacall, Jason's wife at the time, he comes around the theatre and hangs out.

One night I'm with him at the Theatre Bar—which burns down a few years later. He slips off his barstool and through a big grin, just before he hits the floor, says, "Catch a falling star?"

Another time, just after Lloyd (Bud) Bridges replaces expert farceur Barry Nelson in *Cactus Flower*, opposite Bacall, there's a problem. Lloyd gets a laugh Barry had purposely not gotten because it was a setup moment for one of *Bacall's* big laughs. Bacall isn't able to adjust and she delivers her surefire punch line right into Lloyd's laugh. She is furious.

There is a scene later in which her character is angry and she starts beating on Lloyd's chest. Only she is *really* beating on it because she is still—after several performances—irate about the earlier lost laugh. She is *wailing* on Lloyd's chest. She drives him down to the apron of the stage. To keep from falling into the front row, Lloyd grabs her arms. After only a few performances of this continuing scenario, Bacall has developed hand-shaped bruises on her upper arms.

Chapter Six

She goes home and apparently tells Jason how Lloyd has brutalized her.

A few evenings later, Robards comes to the theatre, before the show. He is drunk, has a couple of rough-looking Damon Runyon types with him. *They're* drunk. They're all in the hall outside Lloyd's dressing room, a few feet away from mine. I hear Lloyd say to one of the henchmen, "That's a beautiful tie." The distracted henchman says very drunkenly, "Awrrrh, thanks, Bud."

Now, I hear Jason say to Lloyd, "I hear you've been roughing up my wife."

Lloyd explains what happened.

Jason says, "Aw shit, Bud, you're right, Betty's a cunt."

During the time I'm in *Cactus Flower*, I occasionally take the bus to the theatre with Bette Midler. She's playing one of the daughters in *Fiddler on the Roof*. She's as charming and sunny then as she still is. Her ambition shines serenely beneath the surface. I see her the day I take over the role I've been understudying, the part I'll later do in the movie.

She grins at me and says, "Hello, star."

When I'm still understudying *Cactus Flower*, I'm also assistant stage manager. Among my duties is to knock on Lauren Bacall's dressing room door *once only* when it's time for her next entrance. I never call her Betty to her face, always "Miss Bacall."

After I've done the movie version with Ingrid Bergman (in the role Bacall created on stage), I run into Miss Bacall at Bloomingdale's in Manhattan one day. Once we've greeted each other, out of my hopeless self-consciousness and not being able to think of a single other thing to say to her, I ask if she's seen the film. She gives me a look that feels as if it could melt my skull, her voice drops into its most disdainful, pained register and she says, "Noooo."

It reminds me of the mournful call of a foghorn.

In Miss Bacall's defense—not that she needs my defense—in the previous story about Jason and Lloyd Bridges, Jason *was* drunk. I must also add that what she said to John Wayne about discovering me was true. She gave the original thumbs up for me to get the Broadway job in *Cactus Flower*. My biggest break in show business came from Lauren Bacall.

I'm doing *Arsenic and Old Lace* on stage near Chicago with Zsa Zsa and Eva Gabor as Abby and Martha, the Brewster sisters, sweet old ladies with the unusual hobby of poisoning lonely old men as an act of "kindness." They've never worked together before and if they even like each other, you can't tell it by acting with them. In fact, it seems to be the reverse: They are extremely competitive and appear to essentially despise each other.

In the script, one of the Gabor sisters has more lines than the other, Abby more than Martha or vice versa, I can't remember. The director, Harvey Medlinsky, spends *days* with the real-life sisters—spirited, ear-splittingly shrill sessions; they're balancing out not just the number of lines they each have, but the number of *words*, so they both have equal *validation,* I suppose—no, I'm wrong; it goes deeper than that; murky as a dozen husbands. Two sets of programs and posters are printed for the production at the Arlington Park Theatre, just south of Chicago; one puts Eva's name first, one set has Zsa Zsa with top billing.

John Carradine plays the role created by Boris Karloff on Broadway and played by Raymond Massey in the original 1944 movie version

(Karloff was unavailable). I play Mortimer Brewster (Cary Grant in the movie), and my girlfriend is Jane Merrow, who acted Alaise in Peter O'Toole and Katharine Hepburn's film version of *The Lion in Winter*. The great comic character actor Philip Leeds (*Rosemary's Baby*) expertly performs the Peter Lorre role.

Rehearsals are a wearying nightmare of celebrity aggression. One day the sisters scream at each other in Hungarian, then Eva faints and the stage manager calls 911. A handsome young paramedic revives Eva. Under other circumstances she would no doubt be flirting with him. She regains consciousness and is beginning to lift herself to one elbow as she hears him say into his radiophone, "White Caucasian female." There's a short pause, then everybody hears him say, "Middle-aged."

Not a smart thing to say about a Gabor sister, *ever*.

Eva swoons again.

I'm later told the reason she fainted the first time was that she'd found out that Zsa Zsa passed herself off as Eva, then charged a few thousand dollars worth of clothes to her in a Chicago department store.

One night I'm in the hotel bar with Jessica and Phil Leeds; five-year-old Abigail is with us. The show's costumer comes in, and is soon crying on our shoulders. In a fit of diva fury, Zsa Zsa has torn up all her character's hand-sewn costumes right in front of him. None of the rest of us has ever witnessed this kind of screwy behavior outside of movies about the theatre, the opera, or ballet—or movies about movies. We thought that was just Hollywood.

After the show has opened, I'm at a cocktail party one night, talking to Zsa Zsa. Three feet from us, his back to his wife, is Zsa Zsa's then-husband, a short, seemingly humorless man with a huge head, talking to a pretty young publicity agent. Zsa Zsa says to me, "He has a leetle teensy-weensy theeeng, darlink." She makes a small span between the tip of a forefinger and her thumb. I glance over her shoulder to see if her husband has heard (I can't tell). When I look back, I'm aware she's been watching my eyes. She wants to know if she's made him suffer.

She isn't the only one in the cast who can be mean. I don't mean Eva. I'd worked with Eva earlier in *Green Acres*, and she's entirely pleasant and professional—when she's not working with her sister—not to mention sexy. The show is held over and because Jane Merrow has a previous engagement, my wife takes over her role for the final week of the run. On her second night, I'm onstage doing a scene with a cop who's investigating one of Martha and Abby's acts of euthanasia. Jessica is due to make an entrance.

She doesn't show up.

Finally, running out of adlibs, I rush up one of the aisles of the in-the-round theatre, throw open the door, see my petrified wife and hiss under my breath, "What the fuck are you doing *standing* here?"

It could have happened to anybody. She was doing this without having rehearsed with the cast. She'd had two rehearsals, mostly with me. She was understandably terrified.

Later, I apologize. I am sad, angry, and ashamed, but I can't take it back. And I don't know how to make up for it.

The production has done good business and could have traveled the world. We are all asked to do that. We don't, because some of us want to do other things, but also because the sisters can't stand to be near each other one second longer.

What seems like an eternity earlier, not yet pals with people who mock their husbands' penises at cocktail parties, I get a job acting with J.C. Penney in a movie. Yes, *that* J.C. Penney. In a way, he's the biggest name I've ever worked with. It's an industrial film. The story is about

Chapter Six

generations of men who are having careers working as executives for the retail giant, J.C. Penney. I'm playing the youngest generation—in my very early twenties, the just-starting-out set. It goes up in age until, at the top is—well, the actual James Cash Penney.

It's like acting with Thomas Edison. It doesn't seem possible Penney is real, at least not in my lifetime. He's ninety-three, slim, vaguely friendly, not warm—but then, he's working with a bunch of actors with whom he has nothing in common, except our mutual humanity, to which he offers an amiable enough nod.

I never try to get a copy of the film for my actor's reel. The role is a little one-dimensional. The emotion I've chosen is "young executive"—hard to really involve the audience with that unless *they're* young executives, preferably working for J.C. Penney Inc., in which case, maybe they'll read into my callow, blank canvas of a face whatever set of J.C. Penney characteristics they'd like to see there.

Later, I'm in the New York casting office of Universal Studios. They will turn the camera on and ask me to, "Tell us a little bit about yourself—" so that the executives in Los Angeles can look at me and decide whether I have star quality or if I'm just another panicky wannabe. I cover my nerves with a friendly, wetly confident persona.

Nothing ever comes of the test. I know why. I'm neither friendly nor confident. At best I'm bland, at worst: not fully formed.

And I can't act my way out of that.

When I first start to write plays and short stories, I keep a file with the heading, *Rejections (incomplete)*. I tell myself it's funny. In acting, when they reject you, you never hear from them; when a piece of writing is rejected, they send you evidence. Sometimes they spell it out—exactly *how* you've failed. After the rejections have piled up for a while, it no longer seems so amusing and now that file is untitled, or else I throw the rejection letter out so I don't ever have to think about it again. Bastards.

I think of an evening when Abigail is about fourteen and Linda and I go see her sing in public for one of the first times. As we take our seats in the little auditorium in Burbank, we're handed a piece of paper listing the songs and singers. Near the bottom is my daughter's name.

It lists the song (I forget) and the singer: Abigail *Rains*.

It shouldn't bother me. Her mother and I are split. Why shouldn't it occur to her to leap up a rung or two by capitalizing on her grandfather's name, even if by this time it probably won't mean a thing, and she's in the wrong branch of the business for it to matter much anyway? She's only *fourteen*. Maybe she's still mad at me for leaving her mother. Lord knows her mother is still mad at me. Maybe it's rubbed off.

But, my God, that was eight years ago! Her mother wouldn't go along with the direction I *had* to grow in or die. Why the hell would Abigail not use her own name? I know my career is slipping a little, but I'm not dead. I'm still insultable.

Shortly after she's born, I get up to the obstetrics floor at Mount Sinai Hospital in New York, having lacquered my lungs with a fresh coat of cigarette sludge during a dawn-to-dusk marathon of pacing, and almost faint when I find out I have a baby girl. I already have two terrific boys, but I've always had a case on my little sister. I want to have a daughter. And there she is. She fills me with joy and gratitude since the day she's born and now she doesn't want to carry my label.

I study the look on my mother's face. My father is suturing my scalp. My last memory before that is running down the basement hall of Bloomfield Grade School, chased by the Nelson twins, their

Chapter Six

simultaneous cries of warning imbedded in my brain forever as I hit the partially opened door at the end of the hall. Next, and sequentially for a change, Virginia squeezes me so hard I wonder if my sutures are going to pop.

And *now*, in what feels like the same breath, I start directing the Civic Theatre in Jackson and ask her why I feel so happy doing it. She says, "I have no idea, but I feel the same. If there's a heaven, I hope God takes it easy with me and doesn't give me too much at once. I can hardly contain the joy I feel in *this* world." She smiles at me with such intensity I feel stifled to death by it for the thousandth time.

She says, "But you have to try to find a way not to have it be too blissful because the unavoidable flip side of it can kill you."

No shit.

CHAPTER SEVEN

Barry Nelson, former MGM contract player, aforesaid male lead in the stage version of *Cactus Flower*, and a shy, kind man, dies today in his car near New Hope, Pennsylvania. Years earlier, I do my second professional show at Bucks County Playhouse, in New Hope. Alan Alda (later, famous as Hawkeye in the TV series *M*A*S*H*) is the star of the play, *Sunday in New York*, and like Barry he is un-self-centered and open.

One evening Alan, Bibi Besch, April Shawhan, Dan Frazer, and I are walking along the canal next to the playhouse. We're on our way from dinner to an evening rehearsal. We say "hi" to two teenage girls, then stop for a few moments in the relaxed evening air along the canal in summertime New Hope and make casual conversation. One of the girls points at the sign over the old barn theatre that displays: ALAN ALDA IN SUNDAY IN NEW YORK and says, with the perennial teenage curl of the lip, "Who's Alan Alda? I never heard of him."

Alan spreads his arms and his usually genial smile turns into an expression of faint squeamishness, signifying he agrees it's crazy to put such a nobody's name on the marquee.

We walk on, and it seems that he really doesn't have illusions of self-importance. It's a rare and appealing trait in a young actor who's had a taste of success. Years later, I get to know Bret Easton Ellis, the novelist (he is *not* one of the *people*—the *voices*—who keep sticking their nose into my story). He's kind enough to critique my first attempt at a novel. It's a story about an actor. In one of the margins, he scribbles, "Actors! Eeew! Yuck!" So here I am again, another narrative about an actor. I doubt if I'll send it to Bret.

Back in New York City after we've closed the play, Alan invites the other five of us in the cast to do some improvisation. We meet at the New York offices of the old MCA split-off agency, Ashley-Steiner, in one of their conference rooms, and for several weeks play "theatre games." Alan acts as leader. He's experienced at it. He was one of the cast members of *That Was the Week That Was,* a forerunner to *Saturday Night Live,* hosted by David Frost, years before the Nixon interviews. I've never been in a happier workshop situation, thanks mostly to Alan's intelligence and unselfishness and his sunny nature. We do all sorts of exercises, intended to free up our intuitive creativity.

I remember this as the moment it starts to dawn on me that it's possible for life to be not a right-or-wrong examination, but a multiple choice test given with simple kindness. In an atmosphere like that—which I only barely begin to realize I *could* live in someday—there is no wrong answer.

In no time, we're playing the theatre games unselfconsciously, easily managing the most fundamental actor's task—not always so easy to pull off—being yourself.

That's odd. I thought you got into this line of work so you wouldn't have to do that.

Chapter Seven

I'd like to change places with my cat. He's hardly ever troubled about who he is, or celebrity, or much of anything else. Whenever he's hungry, he doesn't even think about it. He improvises—invents new tactical assaults on his food bowl, which we keep full except during ant season. Maybe sometimes—as I imagine this role—I find my mind snapping back to issues at hand, a moth that I've got to take a swipe at or a squirrel up in a tree that catches my eye and at the same time breaks the flow of whatever's going on in my absurdly self-confident head.

Oh sure, as a cat I have real concerns: like perhaps a car comes down the street in my direction and without realizing it, I've inched out from behind the tire of that parked Chevy in order to take in a little more of a ray of sunlight that's streaming through the Chinese elm in front of the house where the people who feed me live, and onto the pavement, and I'm relaxing in that beam of sunlight. And even though I'd recognize that this was a mistake if I had my everyday wits about me, I'm so happy in that peaceful spot, nothing else seems to matter. And maybe I'm taking a terrible chance doing that, but I don't think that way because I'm savoring witness to the birth of the sun, my insides all brand new and grateful for just being—grateful for *everything*—even things I might not normally find so wonderful. It's harmony beyond description. The point is, I don't let my concerns take away from the smile I always feel on my face despite the fact that life comes without guarantees.

Some cats are just cooler than others. Some people are just healthier than others. And then, every once in a while, you run into a cat that is *totally* cool, or maybe warm is the word. And you know you can trust him. And he sort of draws you in. And maybe without understanding why, you find yourself imitating him a little, seeing that the world is a better place with him in it, and maybe you'd like to have an effect like that.

Last night I see a story on TV about a photographer who is filming on the Golden Gate Bridge and sees a woman about to jump. He says, "I was hypnotized."

But then he abruptly stops filming and shouts, "Hey!" He runs and grabs onto her jacket and is able to pull her back up and over the railing, and instead of being *lost in his art*, he saves a life.

That's the cat I want to be.

So what happened? Did she come back again and jump anyway?

I don't know! That's not the point. The point is to try to be more than just another particle of the noise. The point is to speak up when it counts.

Like maybe when your friend is about to break his neck?

I'm very young, seeing Christopher Plummer as *Cyrano de Bergerac* in Stratford, Ontario. He plays the scene where he's fallen from the moon, and it could be Pablo Casals at the cello, Van Gogh at his easel, or Gene Kelly, singin' in the rain. In the death scene, the falling leaves are *choreographed*. The whole production is sublime. Plummer is sublime. It's like watching Magic Johnson in his prime, moving the ball up and down the court, looking to the right as he's passing to the left. Best of all, there is no death in this death scene—Cyrano smiles at Roxane, and tells her he wants only one thing: "my white plume." Curtain.

One of my old college textbooks, John Gassner's *A Treasury of the Theatre*, puts *Cyrano* under the heading of *Departures From Realism*. I like that. The world I'm seeing at this moment is transcendent and, to my amazement, at the same time lovingly watched over.

Chapter Seven

After a few years of doing theatre in and around New York, I go out to Hollywood to do a television pilot in which I play a country doctor. The pilot doesn't sell, but the producer puts me under contract to Filmways, and I become a recurring character on *Green Acres*—as Eddie Albert's law partner and redundant straight man to Eva Gabor's Hungarian malapropisms.

The producer likes me so much he takes me to dinner one evening and tells me his new pilot idea, spinning off Arnold the Pig, the real star of the show anyway. I will play Arnold's lawyer and Arnold will inherit a lot of money, and I will accompany him on worldwide tours.

I tell my agent that I'll walk out on my contract if such a project materializes, which it doesn't. Virginia hasn't raised—erratic as her child-drearing techniques are—any kids dippy enough to think it's a clever career move to be seen by millions as the international sidekick to a pig.

Back in New York and before this, I study Shakespeare with several first-rate acting teachers.

I'm not bad, they say. But it turns out I never act in a Shakespeare play. I'm better at light comedy. That's how I'm cast and that's how my career goes. The lesson I've learned by the time I'm permanently settled in Los Angeles is: Look as cool as possible, playing beautiful, light-comedy death scenes that never actually risk death; but on the other hand, don't be so dumb as to get caught acting with a pig—no matter how big a star he is.

One time, after Jessica and I have bought our house in Beverly Hills, I'm offered an okay Shakespearean role (Oliver) in *As You Like It*, at the outdoor Pilgrimage Theatre in Los Angeles. The cast includes Roscoe Lee Brown, Kristoffer Tabori, Penny Fuller, and a handful of other excellent actors.

I'm not in it because the American Shakespeare Theatre in Stratford, Connecticut, is going to do a play of mine in their new play series. Michael Kahn, the artistic director, will stage it. I can't miss a chance like that. The play is about a Shakespearean actor who falls apart because he isn't being hired anymore and moves into a squalid hotel, where he spends an hour and a half of the audience's life feeling theatrically forlorn. The actors are David Rounds and Caroline McWilliams. The show gets rave reviews, or rather the actors do, and it moves on to New York, where it has a limited run at the Lucille Lortel Theatre. Later, Kahn directs a taping of it for Connecticut PBS.

I see it in a motel room in Connecticut. Unfortunately, it doesn't gather enough interest to be distributed nationally to the other PBS stations. So I lick my minor wounds, not worrying much about it, because I've told myself things are going well for me back in California. I return to Beverly Hills, where I sit in my bathroom, staring down at Jacqueline Bisset and glancing from time to time at the script for an episode of *Love American Style* that shouldn't be this hard to learn.

I get a call from Jessica. Abigail is missing.

Missing! There are no words to describe my feelings, hearing that—knowing the company she's been keeping—hearing that she's … Jesus, *missing*. She's entered an expensive LA rehab facility, then, as soon as she's checked in, disappears. No one knows where she is—other than on the street somewhere. Her drug is crack cocaine. She was given her first taste of it by a famous rock singer, whose name I can't say, or bear to think of.

Abigail has had a four-year high (mostly natural) as the lead singer/songwriter of a band called Swamp Boogie Queen. The producer, Phil Ramone, has also produced Ray Charles, Sinatra, Streisand, Elton John, Bob Dylan, Bono, and many others. He has signed Abigail and "her boys" and for a while, it looks as if they're going to have a wonderful career.

Chapter Seven

It doesn't pan out. It's a good group, the songs are exceptional, Abigail has the passion of Janis Joplin and the voice of an angel, but the music business is as certain as whatever the opposite is of death and taxes, and the band breaks up. She has cared more about her singing than anything in her life. And now it's gone and she's been on crack for a year and in my mind, she's *alone* out there. Her "friends" occasionally die from what she's doing.

I spend the night watching television, channel surfing, and glancing every once in a while at my liquor cabinet. I go to the telephone and stare at it. I can't think of a single thing to do. I watch an infomercial that's selling songs from the '50s and '60s, mostly about how tragic it is to be a suburban teenager in love. I make and sip at a small martini, and remember a night when Jill Clayburgh and Al Pacino were at our house, and Al spent the entire evening playing with Abigail, ignoring everybody else there, including Jill. He was preparing for his role in *Scarecrow* with Gene Hackman and, in his Actors Studio single-mindedness, I guess, didn't feel like talking to adults.

He talked to Abigail, who was three.

Years later, when Abi is about twelve—I shouldn't have allowed this—I watch *Godfather II* with her. As the film nears the end, I realize she's been looking more and more crestfallen. She's remembered Al sweetly and can't believe he can be so mean.

Naturally, I figure her drug problem is Al Pacino's fault.

Remembering that Robert Mitchum told Abigail, "Your grandfather could knock 'em back pretty good," I fix myself just one more tiny martini, then find my copy of the superb *The Making of Casablanca* by noted film historian Aljean Harmetz. I wonder if Abi knows what her grandfather designed for his own gravestone. It seems to me, as I read it again, there was a sad wistfulness for life as his was coming to an end from liver disease:

CLAUDE RAINS
1889—1967
ALL THINGS ONCE
ARE THINGS FOREVER.
SOUL, ONCE LIVING,
LIVES FOREVER.

For what seems like a year, although I guess it's only a few days, I don't know where Abigail is, but oddly it feels as if I do. It's as if I can see what she's seeing, feel the blues she's feeling, lost, standing in the middle of a street full of strangers. She knows she's due someplace, but she doesn't know how to get there. She doesn't know where to go, so she sits down on the curb, rests her chin in her hands, and stares. She's huddled up inside her coat like the Little Match Girl, feeling a pain she can't put a name to.

We come home one night during this time and find the following message on our machine:

Dad? Linda? Are you there? You don't screen your calls, do you? No ... no, I know you don't. Daddy, I was hoping to talk to you. I don't know where to go. I mean I can go to a couple of "safe" places. But I wouldn't know what to do there. ... Television. I can't read right now. Fucking television! I'm sorry. I don't mean to talk to you like that. Not to you. But anyway, I was hoping you could give me some advice about ... About ... I know, I probably wouldn't act on it ... but ... but at least I could think about it and, you know, begin to make some really ... good decisions, do something constructive, get out of this hole and, I don't know—Live. That's all I want to do. I just want to live!

Chapter Seven

I tell Linda, "We should have *been* here!"

She holds me for a long time, then pats my face dry with the scarf she wore out tonight, takes off her coat, goes into the kitchen and makes a pot of coffee.

I feel aloneness, although I'm not alone. I don't know if it's about Abigail, or Linda and me, or if this one's simply my own. Ann Stuart chafes at my mind again, but I don't draw anything like a conclusion from it. The ache of isolation is a topic nobody can really make sense of, not therapists, not preachers, not blues singers, nobody.

After my marriage is over, I check into another hotel that features a lobby like the axe murder lobby. There's not much to do in the cheerless rooms of these places, so I end up getting pissed on either gin or vodka. I've always preferred my liquor clear—I want to be sure it isn't concealing something poisonous, something that might mess with my sense of time, which reminds me to wonder which marriage has just ended. It has to be the second one.

I turn on the television. They don't do news anymore, or if they do, my point of view has gotten so bent around that I can't tell the difference between the real news and the showbizzy kind. I see a press conference in which the police chief or the sheriff of the municipality in question in some sniper murders names all the people who've worked on the case. It screams out show business. He recites a long list of deserving peace officers and detectives.

But I keep expecting acceptance speeches. "I'd like to thank the commissioner, my sleuthing coach, my producer; and Mom, Dad, *this is for you!*"

"Richard!" I feel John Rival's voice go into pleading overdrive. "There's a lot of bad feedback coming in about your drinking. Sid [Sheinberg, the head of Universal Studios, with whom I'm now under contract] heard you're doing booze and pills." How the hell would Sid Sheinberg hear that? How would *anybody*? I don't call around and announce this stuff. There's a pause. "That can kill you." He breathes into the mouthpiece. "I'm concerned for you." More breathing. "Richard?"

For a moment, I wonder if he's got the wrong number. Then I remember my professional (not to mention otherwise) identity crisis: that I've been switching my stage name back and forth, between my given one and my *Casablanca*-prompted one. I'm billed as "Richard" in *The Shootist* and a few other things.

"They want to test you for that pilot. Can you do a test?"

"John, right now, I couldn't learn the names of the other agents in your office."

"Goddam it, Richard! *Richard*?"

Maybe he's *always* called me that, I can't remember.

"I care about you." Oh, bullshit. You care about money. "I'll messenger you the script. You want it messengered to your home?"

"I don't have a home, John, and messenger is not a verb."

"Where shall I send it?"

"Just a second. I'll switch you to the front desk. They'll give you the address, if somebody hasn't decapitated them."

As if he's just come up with the perfect, penetrating question, he says, "Rick? Is it simply that you're lazy? Is that the problem?"

"No, John, I'm not lazy at all. I'm terrified, which can sometimes be confused with lazy."

Chapter Seven

I hang up the phone and light a cigarette from the one I'm already smoking and wonder if I have a little dementia coming on, because I'm standing in the middle of Linda's and my backyard on one of the highest pollen count days of the year, smoking a cigarette that I don't know where I found. In my other hand is a bottle of Hendrick's Gin, which is very expensive—too expensive to guzzle directly from the bottle, apparently what I'm planning to do. It's the middle of the day.

The telephone rings. I drop the bottle.

What a waste.

Abigail asks if I'll come pick her up. She's gives me an address near STAPLES Center.

When I arrive, she's waiting outside of one of those drug houses you hear about. She looks haggard, can't weigh over ninety-five pounds. I take her to a park, where we sit on the grass, and I try to convince her to go into a rehab Jessica has researched, called Beit T'Shuvah. I tell her if she doesn't go *somewhere*, where she can get real help, she's going to die. She tells me she's fine, just not quite herself right now. She wants to come stay with Linda and me for a while.

I can't think of any way to tell my daughter she cannot come to my house.

I tell her to get into the car, then drive her to Beit T'Shuvah.

As we pass a strip mall on the way there, Abigail asks if she can have an ice cream cone. We stop, each of us gets one, and we eat them at one of those heavy plasticky tables with an umbrella over it. We don't say a word. We're both crying.

At Beit T'Shuvah, the woman responsible for making the decision asks Abigail if she thinks she can do this, does she have spiritual resources because she'll need them.

Abi glances at me, and with a longing that breaks my heart, says, "My father and I are *very* spiritual."

This is news to me.

CHAPTER EIGHT

I try to reach my friend and agent, Stanley. He's kept me on his list for old time's sake. There's always a possibility someone will remember and think of me for *some* project, and then Stanley might make some actual money from me again. He has a new secretary. So, I tell this guy, the secretary, who I am and that I want to talk to Stanley. He asks me, is it important? I say, "As a matter of fact, no, it's trivial, in the scheme of things." He hangs up on me.

I dial again and tell him that indeed it is important, that in fact it's sort of an emergency. He asks me if there's been a death or sudden illness. Stanley's new secretary doesn't handle authority well. I say, "No, I've just got a little … difficulty I'd like to talk to Stanley about." I guess there's a note of anxiety in my voice because he seems more attentive than before and asks me what kind of difficulty. I tell him it's personal. And so help me, he asks if I'm having a seizure, and that if that's the case I should hang up and dial 911. I say, "No sir, it's nothing like that, nothing physical. It's spiritual, only spiritual, a matter of the soul, my soul." Then I say thank you and hang up. Stanley calls me back a few minutes later and tells me to stop the childishness. Bright fellow. Knows the name for it.

However, he isn't bright enough to know how to respond to my problems, or for that matter to get me a damned job.

My longest-lasting job is *Hec Ramsey*, an NBC series of television movies that alternates with *Columbo, McMillan and Wife,* and *McCloud* under the *Sunday Mystery Movie* banner. The star is Richard Boone, most famous for playing a handful of menacing movie heavies and for the television series, *Have Gun—Will Travel*.

In this one, he plays an aging lawman who discovers modern crime-solving forensics techniques, circa 1901. It's a Theodore Roosevelt-era *CSI*. As Oliver B. Stamp, I fancy myself a modern crime fighter, but what I really am is a cane-up-the-ass neurotic, set down in a little town in Oklahoma and given the title of Chief of Police. The character is so stiff and uncomfortable in his skin that as soon as Boone bails out of the series and we wrap it forever, I go directly into psychotherapy, struggling with—I apologize—"self-esteem issues," a troubled marriage, and an all-purpose wrong-career-track depression.

I took the job, hoping to demonstrate my versatility. What I've really done is once more make the crucial error of wandering away from light comedy; most of the laughs I get are unintentional. I get a good one off-camera when they have to fire my stunt double because he refuses to ride my horse as badly as I do. George Marshall (*Destry Rides Again* and *How the West Was Won*), director of one of the first episodes, says to the guy after he's ridden into a scene at a nice, even gallop, "Damn it, kid. Now we gotta go back and shoot it all over again. The Chief don't ride that good."

Boone is an interesting man to work with, but he is a serious drinker. When I see him before he's been made up most mornings, his face is barely recognizable as a face—it's just sort of a pulpy lump of red clay. One day, as we're waiting astride our horses for a trot-in, he says, "What the hell am I doing sitting in the weeds on this flea-bitten beast? I'm a teacher." (He was a sometime acting teacher off-season—and for a while, head of acting at The Neighborhood Playhouse in New York). He takes a slug of bourbon, leans back to reinsert the flask in his pocket, and falls off his horse. He's so relaxed from the booze he doesn't hurt himself at all.

As an actor, he's often way over the top or mannered, but in his over-the-topness, he's sometimes brilliant and it's a painful treat to do scenes with him. His overall film savvy is extraordinary. When Marlon Brando could no longer live with what he considered the incompetence of the original director of *Night of the Following Day*, in which Boone also starred, one of the producers asked Brando in understandable frustration whom he wanted to take over. Some of the cast and production people were gathered together, puzzling over their predicament. Finally, Brando, sitting on the floor, not even looking up, raised a hand, forefinger extended, and said, "Him." He was pointing at Boone. They had been in class together fifteen years earlier at the Actors Studio, along with Julie Harris, Karl Malden, and several other greats, including Paul Newman.

One day when they were making *Hombre* together, according to Boone, Newman walked by him, stopped and turned to him, pointed at his own face, flashed his matchless grin, and said, "Bluest eyes in the business."

After the first season of *Hec Ramsey*, Boone tries to get me fired because, I believe—in his mind, and maybe mine too—the frequently adversarial aspects of our characters' relationship are bleeding over into our personal one.

But viewers apparently *like* adversarial and NBC is aware of that, so after I'm fired by Universal Television (the production company),

NBC tells them they won't continue the series without me, and my killer agent is in the catbird seat with Universal and gets me a sizable salary increase. He has them where he would have the world if he could work it—Caligula in denim and madras.

Later Boone and I become buddies, at least drinking buddies. Sometimes it seems closer, but that's the way it is with drunks: "I love ya, ya crazy bastard."

Stanley comes through. He gets me an audition and I'm booked for the job. It's a part on one of the current batch of lawyer shows, as opposed to the current batch of doctor shows or crime scene investigator shows. Thank God not everything has become bickering *reality*. I'm to be a high-level functionary with some large corporation, one of the bad guys in this episode. It's the kind of role I've gotten in recent years. My most recent theatrical movie was as a governor of California whose daughter has been kidnapped, which really pisses him off. So he hires a posse of karate fighters to go to the desert, where it's cheap to film, and miraculously, they rescue her and one of them falls in love with her and brings her safely home to dad—who gives them his blessing because what governor wouldn't want his daughter to marry a Hollywood karate bum? And it's a happy direct-to-video ending.

We shoot my new job in downtown Los Angeles in an empty warehouse. I walk outside into the August heat, my asthma kicking up from all the particulates in the LA air. I look up at an apartment building across the street that in other days would be on the brink of demolition. Now, it's being renovated into luxury condos and in a few months I couldn't afford to live in this slum.

There is something nightmarish about this moment, staring at the urban desolation around me. It's the kind of déjà vu that gives you the

Chapter Eight

chills you get when you're not sure if you're looking at the Ghost of Christmas Past or the sickening specter of something yet to happen.

I remember rehearsing a stage production of *The Cocktail Party* by T.S. Eliot. I was playing an English aristocrat. I didn't love the role but I tried to. A friend once told me, "In this business you do things for love or money, but not for neither." Also, I wasn't exactly made for the role. The LA Times drama critic called me "about as British as a Dodger Dog." As I rehearsed, thinking I was going to be lousy and seeing myself as the center of the universe, I pictured the headlines: LENZ LAYS GIANT EGG; MILLIONS FLEE CITY. Or: LENZ PASSES GAS; BREAKS UP COCKTAIL PARTY. Or this:

> *At the gala premiere of "The Cocktail Party," for the first time in the history of the American Theatre, an actor was condemned to death for his performance. The actor's family appealed for clemency to President Reagan, who instructed that a command performance be played for the first family at the White House. At the final curtain, Reagan, who can't bear bad acting, carried out the original sentence of death by execution by shooting the purported actor, Richard Lenz, thus finally avenging the assassination of Abraham Lincoln. The President's only comment was, "I know what I like."*

Ann Stuart's diary is sadder than I remember. I think I'm starting to get a little obsessive about this. I read it again (still stopping to gawk at accidents). I study the remains of her calamity of a life. It's sort of like examining sheep entrails for omens. There's got to be something here that can lead to a little understanding, some clue in the persistent entries of "too hot" and "feel discouraged" and "disgusted." Most nights it was: "Got take-out" from Popeyes or KFC or H. Salt Fish and Chips and her favorite, Yum-Yum. (It's a donut shop. She loved their sandwiches.)

Often, she noted driving—in her twenty-five-year-old Dodge—to liquor stores or markets for sales on vodka and cigarettes. She went to banks almost every day to make deposits of Michael Curtiz's movie royalties or to shift the money from one bank to another in order to get better interest (that was the centerpiece pursuit of most of her days). Then she would move on to various malls and stores to replace a broken toaster or an age-shredded window shade, one of those chores that are endless for lonely people. Then she went back to her house—exactly as it was in 1962 when Michael Curtiz died, not a knick-knack moved from its original position—and recorded how disgusted she was at the prices or that some store wasn't the way it used to be or that something else was not what she wished it were.

And again she documented that it was hot; she recorded a stifling high temperature, adding with apparent pride that she didn't use her air conditioner all day. It was the San Fernando Valley, the desert for God's sake. She had a heart condition from all the smoking and drinking. She recorded proudly that she didn't turn on the air conditioner in her car either.

She had a tortoise named Tewsie that lived for thirty years. She fed the sparrows that landed in her backyard every day and jotted these notes in her diary: "The birds didn't show up today. I hope they're okay." She never realized that the tenderness she felt toward those birds and a pet that hibernated all winter was just the tip of the iceberg of what she had to give.

Ann died at seventy-eight with several hundred thousand dollars in the bank, not guessing that inside her was nothing less than grace or that

Chapter Eight

inner God the Buddhists and rock and roll singers are always giving their little bows to. I mean, doesn't it seem the height of egoism not to at least open your mind to the *possibility* that all those people with that caught-in-the-headlights look on their faces—because they think they've got a soul inside them struggling to have its say—may just be right?

Linda and I asked her over for dinner several times, but there was always laundry to be done or a crossword puzzle that needed to be finished. She played the piano, so she had to practice every day. For forty-two years after Curtiz's death, she lived a life of near solitude—penny-pinching, smoking, drinking, wrapped up in a routine so discouraging and loveless that the high point appeared to be practicing a piece on the piano so she could perform it for her turtle. I think she lived in fear full-time, given the pattern she'd hewn for herself, knowing that her life would never be more than that. And maybe that fear finally turned into an unwitting plea that her life be brought to a merciful end. Linda was with her at the hospital every day for her last two weeks. Her end wasn't so merciful.

I mention these thoughts to Linda, and she looks at me as if I've lost my mind. She doesn't think I should be "invading the woman's life." She says it has nothing to do with me, that it was *her* life and that it ought to be sacrosanct. When I point out that the woman is dead and that she doesn't have friends or relatives to hurt, she says it doesn't matter, that her life should remain *her* life, and why am I bringing myself down with it?

I say, "But she was a case study of a way of life worth understanding and learning from. I always sensed, between the lines of what she told me, something she was too afraid or embarrassed to say in person."

"You told me you wanted to learn about *Curtiz*, but you're not going to. They were different people. You shouldn't have her diary in the first place."

Surrendering the point about Curtiz for the moment, I say, "Why not? Roberta (the woman who was executrix of Ann's estate) said I could have the diary. And I feel like it was meant to be—that finally, if I can figure out what was going on with Ann, maybe she'll have the chance to say what she always wanted to."

"And what would that be?" says Linda. "That life can be pathetic if you live it pathetically? Anyway, who said she wanted to say whatever it was to *you*? It sounds to me like all you're getting out of this is a close-up of her misery. Why? *Why* do you periodically dive down into places like this?"

I don't have an answer for that, so I tell her she has a point and then I go take a shower—to clear my mind and relieve the tension in my back.

She's right of course. Occasionally, I still gravitate toward the dark side.

There's a rare eastern type of spring rainsquall and a rainbow that follows. We take our dog Dash for a walk around the neighborhood, stopping to watch the work being done on Ann's house by the new owners. They are a friendly young couple with no visible baggage, very few old pictures, and with diaries mostly full of blank pages—at least that's the way I imagine it. They chat cordially with us and are as fresh as the air.

Fresher, when you think about it.

I call my friend Jimmy Karen, professional name: James Karen, an excellent Broadway and Hollywood character actor (*The China Syndrome,* the first two *Return of the Living Dead* movies, *The Pursuit of Happyness*, etc.). He probably could have been a Hollywood leading man if he'd decided to move west earlier, but he liked New York life and acting on the stage and didn't make film his goal until that ship had sailed.

He's had a long, successful career, but like every other actor, he's out of work most of the time; it's the way it goes. The difference between Jimmy and most actors is that he's cheerfully adapted himself to that aspect of the life and gives all appearances of being good at it. He keeps busy and is gregarious. In fact, his terrific personality—including his never being desperate for the job nor overly concerned with anybody's judgment of him—is sometimes, perhaps, the key thing in getting him work. He's an old pro of an actor, but it never hurts to be extraordinarily likeable on top of it.

One of the reasons—I've persuaded myself—I didn't take off after my initial success was that I didn't understand that if I need those people's approval too much, it threatens their psychic underbellies, and they want to get rid of me as fast as they can. They're looking for me to give them what they want, but I'm lost, so they feel lost. And they *hate* that. The number one thing a person has to do to fit in and make everybody happy is act like all his internal machinery is working just fine. Then the people doing the hiring want to attach themselves to that because most of them are lost too.

Jimmy always makes people believe all of his machinery is working perfectly. He puts them at ease. He has that gift. And God they love it.

It's late afternoon. I've had a couple of small drinks. It's okay with Jimmy. He doesn't judge; in fact, he's a pretty good drinker himself. I remember at my house one night, he came into the kitchen where I was putting hors d'oeuvres together and said, "Ricko, could I have a little more gin in my gin and tonic?"

Today I ask him, "Jimmy, man-to-man, what do you do—*you* know—with your day, now that you don't have kids around and you're ... of an age."

"Man-to-man, Ricko, I don't understand the question."

"That's glib."

"You're right. Okay, I contemplate the universe and my place in it."

"You do not." He knows me well enough to know that's the kind of thing *I* do.

"What do you *really* want to know?" he says.

"I want to know what you do all day."

"A thousand things."

"But *what*?"

"How do *I* know?" He sounds genuinely perplexed. "There's way too much to do for me to answer that. I read. I try to keep up with the world. I do all the things Alba [his equally charming wife] and I need to do to keep life working. We travel ... You know all this. What's going on?"

"Nothing. Abigail's giving me fits. I don't know where she is half the time. She's still doing drugs ..."

I sense I could slip over into seeming a bit peculiar. "Before I met Linda, I kept a diary," I say. "But at least I *identified* my loneliness. I never let my life force get so drained that I found even the thought of *breathing* too expensive."

There! I've done it. I'm coming across as mad as a hatter.

"I mean, I don't work anymore. I write, but nobody buys it. I get a play done here and there, but then it closes and the play hasn't gone anywhere. Not really." He's quiet for a while. "Jimmy?"

"This is a killer business. What did you expect?"

"I don't know. ... *Something*."

"Are you getting out—into the world? Or are you using your

Chapter Eight

asthma as an excuse?"

"Fuck you!"

"Are you reaching out? Doing things?"

"Sure!"

"What?"

"Trying to keep sane."

"That's not a plan. Just because you're not in the conventional planning stages of life doesn't mean you don't need a plan."

"Like what?"

He takes a deep breath. "Like understanding where you're trying to go."

"Where's that?"

"I have no idea. I'm not you. Hey, Ricko," he adds, "it's too early in the day to be drinking that way. You're not a kid anymore."

How the hell did he get so wise?

Ann Stuart's diary:

> *7/1/04: Went to Dr. VanPeenan's office 11:30 and got lost. Couldn't find it. Everything has been repainted—was ten minutes late. Shopped at Ralph's around 1:30. Later, got fish at Popeye's for dinner. 78 degrees today.*
>
> *7/5/04: Slept late. Didn't feel like doing much. Went to Rite-Aid for vodka on sale, used $20 Florence gave me for my birthday. Got chicken at Yum-Yum for dinner, then killed weeds in azaleas. Wish I didn't feel so tired all the time. Temp: 85 degrees. Didn't use the air.*
>
> *7/9/04: Gardeners came* [they'd given her a bargain rate "because she's poor"—we had the same mow-and-blow gardener; he

told us this], *went to Yum-Yum, Ralph's and Gelsons. Harriet called, said Clara has pancreatic cancer. Tried to get her on the phone but her line is busy all the time.*

7/11/04: Stayed home most of day. Read papers. 98 degrees today. Turned air conditioner on. Went to Weinerschnitzel for chilidog and was disappointed. Hardly any chili on it. Did personal washing this A.M.

7/14/04: I still have my bowel problem. Went to Sally's Beauty Boutique this A.M. They aren't like they used to be. Went to Target and looked at toasters. They aren't like they used to be. Went to Washington Mutual, then Wells Fargo, transferred $140,000.00—one point improvement in interest. I'll try the May Company for toaster tomorrow. 95 degrees today. Didn't use air conditioner.

7/19/04: Harriet picked me up, went to Smoke House for lunch. I had a Monte Christo sandwich, which was awful. When I got home, I vomited.

7/22/04: All day, I laid down a lot. Medicine I took last night didn't work. I'll try again tonight. If only my bowels would work I know I would feel better. Watered my roses tonight. Cooler today, 92 degrees.

And that was the end, except for one more sentence. The last recorded words of Ann Stuart, aka Anitra Stevens, aka Alice Ann Yoder, were:

"Didn't use the air."

CHAPTER NINE

This morning I stumble into the kitchen, feeling happy to be alive, a sensation that crops up from time to time lately. I don't know why. It connects to a peculiar intuition that the world—at least the world immediately around me—is having moments of being quite fond of me. It's puzzling, because as Linda points out, occasionally I let myself get a little downcast. But this cheerful feeling, when I get it, does seem more intense recently. I wonder if, despite my fear of the similarities between Ann Stuart and me, I'm so relieved at the contrast between her life for most of her years and mine right now, that I'm seeing the rewarding moments of mine for what they are: gifts, or even—and it's a word I trip over because of its association in my mind with much of the church industry—"blessings." Maybe it's the God-is-inside-you books Linda has recently left in my path. I am becoming increasingly intrigued by the idea of a window into the formless.

My cynical side wishes to interject himself at this point, but sometimes I'm able to draw the line; smack him into submission with my coffee spoon.

I make another pot and put a cinnamon-frosted rice cake into the toaster. I occasionally decide I want to try various calorie-and-cholesterol-saving items like this and Linda kindly humors me. As I'm taking it out early and throwing it on the plate (the cinnamon-and-sugar goo on top gets hot very fast), I look out the window and see a white butterfly. It's two and three days, respectively, after Thanksgiving and my birthday, and I might otherwise be feeling old and burdened by the coming Christmas season.

But instead, I see this butterfly, which may not even be the last one of the year, fluttering over the kitty Taj Mahal. There's a squirrel on top of the Taj, eating the unsalted peanuts Linda has placed out there for his pleasure (he will have nothing to do with salted ones), and nature is very happy outside my kitchen. I don't even need to go out there to appreciate it.

I hear humming and turn around to find Linda wiring up a Christmas tree ornament that must have been a gift from last year, one of those things you get on Christmas Day and think, oh hooray, a brand new bauble for *next* year's Christmas tree. Now, I notice this is really a surprisingly beautiful ornament, covered with enameled birds and flowers. Linda asks me is there any particular place—not on the Christmas tree—I'd like to see it hanging. I say "Just a second," because I'm scribbling some notion on a legal pad having to do with this very moment and she says, "Well!" in a comic way, which I recognize as her impression of Jessie Royce Landis as Cary Grant's mother in *North by Northwest*. It comes with a funny shrug that Linda does nicely, and that indicates she will have to proceed without me in this matter.

And she does; she hangs the ornament in a ray of sunshine above and to the right of the toaster, and just before I turn to head off toward my office to go to work, I notice that my white butterfly is right in front of us, dancing in the sunlight.

On the road again—just can't wait to get on the road again …

Chapter Nine

I remember being in a motel room in Portland, Oregon. I was there doing a TV movie. It was the early eighties and they were starting to do lots of "Women In Jeopardy" stories. I was between marriages again and the vigorously sexy Joanna Cassidy (*Blade Runner, Six Feet Under, Who Framed Roger Rabbit?*) was in the cast. I developed a crush on her and for a moment thought she had one on me too. When I saw her again recently and approached her with a shared-history kind of familiarity, she was distinctly cool. (Jeez! I wasn't coming on this time. I'm married now.)

My room in Portland was on the ground floor. The guy who ran the place had a calico cat that took a liking to me, possibly because I always gave him shrimp from my salad bar dinner. He was actually my best friend in Portland. I can't count Joanna Cassidy.

When I got back from Portland I called Linda, whom I'd had my first date with a couple of months earlier, then had broken up with before I left for Oregon—I'm pretty sure the reason was that I was confused by her alarming lack of dysfunction.

It was the luckiest moment of my life. Linda answered the phone and said yes, she'd see me.

I think of her cats at the time, Panther and Willoughby. Linda taught me to understand feline love. We had to have Willoughby put to sleep quite a few years ago. I felt like I was dying, or Linda was.

I realized for a split second as I was calling her, that it was the first time in my life I was doing the right thing and *knew* I was. That call brought her as permanently as time allows into my life. The thought of her not being there, or by then being involved with another man, gives me chills I can't possibly put into words.

I'm one of the emcees for the IBM Pavilion at the New York World's Fair (not the 1939 one that E.L. Doctorow wrote about—I hadn't *quite* been born yet). Sarah and I are living on Riverside Drive in an apartment with a view of the Hudson River and the George Washington Bridge. Charlie and Scott are two and three years old. We have this classy place because this job pays far more money than I've ever gotten before. We buy the boys toys and games and go to great restaurants, drink good wine, and Sarah and I pipedream about the ritzy life ahead of us.

Five days a week, I work a six-hour shift. I descend from a huge flattened sphere that looks like a giant mushroom. I'm standing on a one-man elevator, like Sean Connery as James Bond on his one-man gyrocopter in *You Only Live Twice*, except I'm wearing white tie and tails. I say a few introductory words to about four hundred visitors who've waited in line to get on the pavilion's People Wall, which is canted like stadium bleachers.

After I've completed the general greeting, I acknowledge any celebrity guests in the group. Danny Kaye comes to the show one day and because it's stuck in my head forever, I remind him of a line from *The Court Jester*: "The vessel with the pestle has the pellet with the poison." He gives me a lame smile—the one you give a hapless colleague who's "dying out there."

I tell the audience what's going to happen, then rise up into the sphere as the entire People Wall also ascends hydraulically into it.

Once the guests are in place in the darkened theatre, the show begins. It's a simultaneous-action series of films, shown on multiple screens, big and little, all around the inside of the squashed IBM sphere that dominates the exhibit. I pop out from between the screens from time to time and speak the narration.

When I'm outside addressing the guests from my open-air elevator, I'm doing it live. Up in the theatre, my spiel is lip-synched. This is so that if something happens to my little module, the show can go on without me.

Chapter Nine

One day something does happen: The mechanism that powers my one-man elevator fails and I'm stranded, stuck in the down position, but too high above the ground to dismount. I watch as the People Wall ascends. The rest of the show—up in the mushroom—goes on without me, except there's no spotlight on the narrator between the movie screens, because there *is* no narrator for this show.

Forty-five minutes later, the wall has descended again and been reloaded with its human cargo. I've given my speech, and it's gone back up, leaving me outside on my broken perch, in a drizzling rain that's trickling onto me through the girders high above. We do four or five shows this way.

It's early evening when my workday ends. I'm *still standing there* in my fancy feathers, waiting for International Business Machines, Incorporated, to get their deluxe one-man doohickey working again so I can rise up like a drenched phoenix out of the rain.

Around midnight, with the Fair closed down for the day, they finally get the machine fixed. I go change out of my sopping monkey suit and head for the IRT platform to catch the next 7 train back to Manhattan.

Kansas City, twelve years later: *The Owl and the Pussycat* runs for thirteen weeks, plus one week of rehearsals. They don't spend much time rehearsing in dinner theatre because no money is coming in while you're doing that. The girl they've cast in advance to play opposite me in this two-character comedy isn't really right for the part (she's lovely and a good actress, but not believable as Doris the hooker), so after the first day, the director gives her notice and we have casting sessions.

I especially like a young woman named Carol, whom I convince them to cast. I like Carol so much that I fall in love with her—I'm between marriages—and a few weeks after the show closes on December 19th, she moves to Los Angeles and we go on with our relationship until she shocks me by moving out of my little house into a much nicer one with Dudley Moore. I don't know how that comes about. She doesn't want to tell me.

He plays the piano, is funny and charming.

I'm taller.

I stay in the Ambassador Hotel while I'm in Kansas City. My pleasant little suite looks out over a park. It's Indian summer, beautiful. I love playing Felix, and I love the sexy, affectionate Carol. It's the second time I've done the show. The audiences seem enthusiastic. The director and the producers have only the nicest things to say to me—and, as far as I know, about me.

There are only two built-in negatives: I miss Abigail and suffer a lot of hangovers, for the usual reasons. I film a commercial for a local department store one bleak, early Monday morning at four a.m. when the store is empty. It's the most painful work experience I can remember. The dialogue has something to do with happy penguins, presumably Kansas City penguins. I don't bother to ask what penguins are doing in K.C. and what makes them so damned cheerful. I play several scenes with them, even though they aren't there (they will be animated in later). My hangover may be the worst I've ever had. I'm amazed they don't fire me—except where do you find someone in the middle of the night to come down to your department store and chat with your hypothetical penguins?

Another morning, near the end of our crammed-together rehearsals, I've gone into a radio studio to record a publicity spot for the play. In addition to my drinking, I'm taking two or three Darvons every four hours for back pain. I'm between surgeries. I couldn't actually swear it's my back that needs relief. Something does.

Chapter Nine

I go through take after take for two hours to get a thirty-second spot right. I don't talk well in the mornings. I can barely say my name. I see a contemptuous look on the technician's face I'll never forget. I think it's that look that finally convinces me to quit the Darvon—but not until later, after I've gotten home from Missouri.

One evening before I go to the theatre, I call Abigail at her mother's house. We have a good talk, and then Jessica wants to speak to me. She seems a little breathless, talks about the therapy she's been doing, then abruptly tells me she's not scared of me anymore. I'm startled by that although looking back, I shouldn't have been. I already have a sense that the same man Linda won't take any crap from is terrifying to some people with his barely under-the-surface anger—people who, in their own ways, are as frightened as I am.

I watch the seasons change in the park. I'm crazy about Carol, and I'm still enjoying playing *The Owl and the Pussycat*. I'm in fairly high spirits every day, after I've gotten through the tricky mornings. Only once or twice does it cross my mind that the reason I'm here, doing dinner theatre in Kansas City, is because I made a decision not to live in my cozy house in the Hollywood Hills, see my daughter on a regular basis, and work with Michael Gordon and Eugene Ionesco on a new version of *Rhinoceros* that will be seen by the whole Hollywood community.

Instead, I've come to Kansas City, where no one from the Hollywood community ever sets foot, to *try* to get away from the banshees in the back of my brain and the narcissism I'm employing to steer my life.

My out-of-control gyrostat throws me back to 1965, near the beginning of my career: I leave the IBM show a month early to do my first Broadway play, *Mating Dance*, at a great reduction in salary. On the other hand, this show could run for years. Eventually, as I picture it, I'll take over the role I'm understudying. After that, it's name over the title, and—*shazam!*—I'm *All About Eve's* eponymous Eve Harrington. The performer I'm understudying is Richard Mulligan, a brilliant comedic (and otherwise) actor (*Soap, Little Big Man*). I'm also playing a very small role. The name-above-the-title star is Van Johnson. After New York rehearsals, we will tour New Haven, Boston, Philadelphia, and Wilmington. Then we'll open on Broadway.

Among my fellow cast members is Paul Sorvino. He's entertaining, a non-stop talker, who, when he's not down the hall singing a Puccini aria, is filling in any gaps you may have about the meaning of life. He is also charming and sweetly human. When his daughter Mira wins the Academy Award for *Mighty Aphrodite* and they cut to Paul in the audience, he's openly weeping. It reminds me of *Moonstruck* and Italian families I've known. I love Mediterraneans and big, animated, happy families. Anyway, they *look* happy.

In New Haven, *Mating Dance* is a disaster. Same in Boston. Not much better in Philadelphia or Delaware. As the show is rewritten again and again, three different actors end up winning the leading lady, Marian Hailey: Van Johnson, Richard Mulligan, and J.D. Cannon.

One day, Richard and I are sitting backstage at the Eugene O'Neill Theatre during rehearsals. He's waiting for his next entrance. Since, as his understudy, it might be important to me, I ask him if he thinks he'll end up getting the girl.

He shrugs glumly and says, "Dunno."

"It's the most sensible thing. Van and Jack [J.D. Cannon] are too old for her."

He shrugs again.

"I mean, who wants to see *Funny Face* all over again—young Audrey Hepburn ending up with ancient Fred Astaire, for cryin' out

Chapter Nine

loud? They really ought to know by this time who the romantic couple is in a romantic comedy."

He says nothing again, and now a rat the size of a Portuguese water dog ambles out from behind the light board and strolls past us like a boulevardier, across about twenty feet of backstage and into a pile of platforms and flats up against the back wall.

We both watch him the whole way. After a perfect pause, Richard says, "That's the only stiff around here with a little savoir faire. They oughta let *him* get the girl."

The night before our opening, having read something about Richard Burton walking the streets of London all night before he opened in *Hamlet*, I do the same thing. I walk through Riverside Park, then fifty blocks down to the show district—then back, contemplating my destiny. What I'm actually doing is trying to deal with my nerves, insomnia, and fear. Anyway, it doesn't matter; an eight or nine mile all-night walk doesn't make a lot of difference when you're twenty-five and doing a six-line role.

At the end of the first act on opening night, the curtain doesn't come down. The Local One Union curtain-puller is in the basement of the theatre playing poker.

Van, as likable an old-time movie star as you'd ever want to meet, is on stage alone. He holds character for five or six seconds when the curtain doesn't fall, then throws one hand in the air, grins broadly, goes, "Da-da-da-da-da-da—da-da-da-da-da—da-da-da-da-da—dyaaah." And he song and dances himself off the stage.

He gets a huge round of applause.

The next morning, I find the following telegram under my apartment door:

> *Pursuant to Equity rules with regret we must inform you that the performances of* Mating Dance *are terminated as of this*

date. Payment due will be available tomorrow afternoon at my office. Please call.

Elliot Martin (Producer)

That's my Broadway debut. If you look up *Mating Dance* on the Internet Broadway Database, it says, "Opened November 3rd, 1965, closed November 3rd, 1965. 1 performance." Van's impromptu song and dance turned out to be the single highlight.

In 1968, Hollywood will make a Doris Day movie called *Where Were You When the Lights Went Out?* It's based on the Northeast Blackout of 1965.

On a Tuesday evening, six days after the opening and closing of *Mating Dance,* Scott and Charlie and I are looking out of our tenth-floor window at New Jersey across the river. Like Manhattan, it's black as a rock quarry on a moonless night. Over twenty-five million people are without electricity—from New York through Ontario, all the way up to Hudson Bay, north of Canada.

Sarah hasn't arrived home from her receptionist job in midtown. I tell the boys not to worry, but I'm nervous. They don't know it, but their very young mother has *three* children to cope with and it's a dark, cold city out there.

When she gets back around nine o'clock, we're all relieved and after the boys go to bed, Sarah and I have drinks and talk about our lives and how exciting it is to be young, with two beautiful sons, living in Manhattan.

In a few months, I will leave her and the boys without the lamest excuse.

Chapter Nine

Years later, Sarah comes out from New York for Scott's wedding in Linda's and my backyard. As I drive her to our house where she'll be staying for a few days, she tells me out of the blue that she forgives me.

I turn and look at her dumbly. Finally, I mumble, "Thanks. That means a lot to me." It's the truth, but it's hard to say anyway. It's such a paltry response; seven crummy words, years after the fact, to make amends for something so *shabby*.

I'll never know how hard it was for her to say she forgave me. Maybe she was just doing what she had to for her own peace of mind, but I don't think so. I think she meant what she said. I didn't even begin to recognize how elegant she was until long after our marriage was over.

CHAPTER TEN

Sarah was married twice to Jim Zimmerman. There came a time in the first go-round when—according to the boys—his somewhat autocratic ways got to be too much for Sarah and she let him go for a while (the "somewhat" is mine). Then, apparently, he remade himself in a kinder, gentler form and Sarah, who still loved him, rethought things and they remarried.

But before the divorce, Sarah is understandably concerned about the settlement. Charlie is living with Linda and me. He and his brother are both attending UCLA. Sarah asks them if they'll put their heads together and make a list of some of Jim's shortcomings.

One evening, Scott rides to our house on his bicycle (fifteen miles over the Santa Monica Mountains—the kind of thing he still does; he routinely rides a hundred miles a day on non-school days). He and Charlie start to make a list of Jim's flaws. They're working to put themselves through UCLA—I'm of no financial use—and they're both tired from another long day of school, studying, and work. They have a couple of beers to relax.

I'm in another room, staring at bills, wishing I'd taken a sitcom when they were still being offered to me. I hear Scott and Charlie giggling. I go into the den and ask what's going on.

They look up at me, beers in hand, and giggle some more. Charlie looks a little like me, but handsomer. He's got chocolate-brown eyes, an engaging sense of humor, and an appealing modesty about him. Scott's Scottish/Irish good looks favor his strawberry-blonde mother. He's an inch or two taller than Charlie at about six feet and has an analytical intelligence that matches his penetrating blue eyes.

"Seriously. What's so funny?"

Scott shows me his great, always surprising, goofy grin and says, "We can't think of anything."

"What do you mean?"

"He means we can't think of anything," says Charlie, chuckling.

"Well, you've told me about things you didn't like."

"Yeah, but none of them are going to help Mom."

I try to assist them in regaining concentration. "Well, like what do you have so far?"

Scott looks down at their list. "How about this? 'He's got a shitty personality.' Do you think that's grounds for divorce—if one of the parties has a shitty personality?"

"But you're not looking for grounds," I say. "You just want to make sure your mom gets a fair settlement. Right? I mean how shitty was he? What did he actually do? He didn't ever hit you, right?"

They both chortle. "Right."

"Well, what did he actually do?"

"I don't know," says Charlie. "He was mean."

"Like what?"

"He wouldn't talk to anybody for days."

"Well, that's hardly a good reason for—"

"I know!" They both giggle all over again. "I was always *glad* when he didn't talk." More laughter.

Chapter Ten

"Well, come on," I say. "You've got to be able to help her more than that. What do you have written down here? Can I look?"

"Sure," says Scott.

I look at their list. At the top it says, "Won't do his fair share. Is stingy. Has Muzak on every hour he's awake."

They've written down several similar items. "I admit he doesn't sound like a bundle of fun," I say, "but these things are hardly going to win your mom any points with a judge." I point at one of the entries. "'Always takes the biggest half.' What's that mean?"

"It means he always took the biggest piece," says Charlie. "If you had part of a pie left, he'd cut it, then give himself the biggest half." They're both laughing again and now tears are rolling down their faces.

It turned out that Jim settled fairly. Perhaps it was the beginning of a new pattern between Sarah and him, and might have been responsible for what in the end turned out to be what I gather was a satisfying marriage.

I pick up a copy of *Variety* today and see that some group is honoring Angela Lansbury. I did a couple of *Murder, She Wrote* episodes with her. Before the first one, I had feelings of foreboding, which, like many such experiences, I didn't recognize for what it was until after the thing that was worrying me had faded away.

My first memory of Angela is as the evil mother in *The Manchurian Candidate*. That character had always reminded me in a visceral way of my own mother. Maybe, before I was born, I saw the mother I wanted, but God—understandably preoccupied with all the craziness we keep handing him—didn't notice that I was pointing at Angela and instead, gave me the mother who kind of *reminded* Him of her. Unfortunately, it was the one from *The Manchurian Candidate* (to her credit, Mom never made me assassinate anybody).

The first day I worked with Angela (we were in Mendicino, California, which doubled as the fictional Cabot Cove, the hometown of Jessica Fletcher, Angela's character), I was sitting in a make-up chair, wondering if I was coming down with something. It hadn't yet dawned on me that I was *afraid* of Angela Lansbury. Later, the second assistant director came to my dressing room and told me Angela would like to see me. My heart began to pound.

She opened her dressing room door to me. "Hi, Rick. I'm so pleased to be working with you." She wore a welcoming smile. She wasn't at all like my mother. She is a kind and generous woman. Discord seems to melt wherever she goes.

The reason I'd been summoned to her dressing room was to run lines for our big scene together. We chatted about other things, and I was immediately comfortable with her. She listened to everything I had to say as if there were hidden value in my words, in *me*. She reminded me of a lady on my paper route who used to give me cookies and ask, "How ya doin' today, honey? You keeping warm enough?" She also reminded me of Ingrid Bergman. (They worked together in Angela's first film, *Gaslight*. They both had warm things to say about each other.)

Later, Angela suffered a serious illness. I sent her a get well card. After she'd recovered, she wrote me a note back, thanking me for my thoughtfulness when all I'd done is be a fraction as nice to her as she's been, I assume, to every actor she's ever worked with.

Linda and I went to a party, a celebration of the one hundredth episode of *Murder, She Wrote*. A lot of the guest actors on the shows were former movie stars. It was funny to see all these old contract movie players—many of them very big in the business in their day—lined up like fans to say "hi" to Angela. They all had something like the feelings

Chapter Ten

I had about her. When she won her fifth Tony Award, this time for Best Featured Actress in a play (Madame Arcati in *Blithe Spirit*), she said in her acceptance speech to the other nominees in her category, "It's not fair." The award was given to her—I think—out of affection and maybe nostalgia.

And she was right; at eighty-three, she was superb as Madame Arcati, but not *quite* at the peak of her consummate game anymore, nor any better than the other nominees, and had the grace to say so. It would have meant so much to one of those other actresses and she knew it. Classy.

I'm in another older actress's dressing room a few years earlier. It's an episode of a series called *Masquerade* that stars Rod Taylor (*The Birds*), co-starring Kirstie Alley, when she was young and knockdown gorgeous. I don't remember the plot of my episode; it's routine adventure stuff. We're on a fake airplane for a few scenes. My seatmate is the great character actress Eve Arden (born Eunice Queden).

One day I knock on her door. We're going to rehearse the short scene we have together. It's a good thing; I need it. Linda and I celebrated a wedding anniversary yesterday—spent the night at a motel in Malibu; had dinner out, then went to bed late, and I didn't spend the time I should have working on the scene.

I'm surprised to see Eve has a guest, a woman about her age, wearing a blue and gray scarf, nondescript slacks, and a green silk blouse. Eve introduces me to Dianne Belmont, although what she says is, "Lucy, do you know Rick?" Dianne Belmont is the name Lucille Ball was born with.

Lucy glances at me and shakes her head as I go red in the face and say, "I met you briefly at the Hilton in Las Vegas." I was there to see

Liza Minnelli's show (if athletes at their best give 110 percent, Liza gave 150 percent. I don't know how her body survived the punishment she inflicted on it). Liza had been going with Desi Jr. at the time.

Lucy just looks at me. No expression.

I say, "I know Desi." Her expression doesn't change. "*Junior*," I add.

With the dry, smoky voice of her later years, she says, "I hope so." Her marriage to Desi Sr. is long over.

"I did an episode of *Automan* with him."

Her look gets even dryer. "Oh. *That*."

I glance at Eve for help, but she's giving me her trademark wry half-smile, indicating I'll have to get out of this myself.

"I also did a *Medical Story* with him."

"A *what*?"

Medical Story was an anthology series that ran for a year or two, then folded. "Meredith Baxter was in the one we did," I say, trying to not fail in front of Lucille Ball *and* Eve Arden. I name a couple of other cast members of the episode, ending with: "John Kerr was in it!" Then triumphantly: "He was in *South Pacific*!"

Now Eve steps in with her best *Our Miss Brooks* vocal shadings and says, "And *Tea and Sympathy*."

"That's right," I say. "And *Tea and Sympathy*. Why don't we rehearse a little later? You know, when you don't have company. A little later. It was nice to meet you, Ms. Ball." I turn to go.

Eve says, "Lucy, this won't take more than two minutes. Do you mind if we just run it once? We're going to shoot it in a half hour or so, but I don't want you to go till you have to."

As Lucy says, "Sure," I turn back and say, "We *are*? I thought we weren't doing it till tomorrow."

"No," says Eve. "It's on the schedule for today." She produces two pink pages. "There's a note here on the top of the pages."

Chapter Ten

"*New pages?*" I open my script. My pages for the scene are still white, the originals. "I didn't get any new pages."

"They sent them to you last night."

"I wasn't home last night. I was …"

Both women are scrutinizing me. "Well," says Eve, "you'd better go find the A.D. [assistant director] and tell him you need the new pages for scene forty-seven. They've re-numbered it. It's a whole different scene."

I suspect I've gone ashen beneath my makeup.

As I collapse back toward the door, Lucy gives me a smile for the first time; her familiar, mischievous one, and says as if speaking to someone not quite bright, "Ricky, you got some 'splainin' to do."

My mind is still young and fairly supple. I learn the lines and make it through the scene.

Another time, I'm doing an episode of *The Greatest American Hero* with star William Katt, a solid actor. This time, I *don't* make it. They hired me the night before and sent me the script at midnight. Maybe somebody got sick, I don't know. I only have one big scene. They shoot it in the late afternoon.

What my role consists of is every single bit of exposition for the entire story, all spoken in one dense-with-information scene: names, places, animal names, local history, and statistics—lots of them. It's dizzying. It might as well be in Aramaic.

When it gets to my close-up, the director says, "I hope you've got this cold. We're losing the sun."

A few years earlier, or even if I'd had all of last evening with it, I probably *would* have had it cold, but not today. A couple of other actors and Bill Katt are off-camera, feeding me my cues. I get about halfway through my second long speech and start to go blank. I feel myself begin to sweat and lose all the confidence I've been pretending to have—trying to be a local veterinarian, who knows all of this stuff like he lives it every day of his life.

As the words evaporate from my brain, I'm looking at Bill Katt. He sees what's happening and his eyes roll up in an unsubtle expression of contempt.

Then all the Aramaic I've struggled since last midnight to jam into my brain turns upside down and backwards and I haven't the faintest idea who I am, let alone what any of this stuff means or why I'm saying it. And my character is now a puddle of sweat trying to hide his anger at Bill Katt, who's looking at me like he just caught me feeling up a kindergartener.

After I get back from Kansas City and have hugged Abi until I'm afraid I'll injure her, I settle back into the craziness of LA, living my bachelor life in my "bachelor pad," wondering why no one's requesting my acting services. It hasn't hit me yet that disappearing from the job market to do dinner theatre for three months is an aggressively dopey career move, about as clever as a prizefighter biting off his opponent's ear.

Out of work, out of confidence, I think about that look on the radio technician's face when I was trying to get the words out for the *Owl and the Pussycat* commercial and decide I should quit taking Darvon. My girlfriend, Carol from Kansas City, hasn't moved to LA yet.

I don't seek medical assistance, or even cut down sensibly, little by little; I do it all at once—quit the pills I've popped every four hours for eight years. I feel like Gene Hackman in *French Connection II*, getting off the heroin, or Frank Sinatra in *The Man with the Golden Arm*. Deprived of their narcotic, snakes with razor blade scales show

Chapter Ten

up. They slither through my innards, gouging raggedy tunnels, and it feels as if the pain and self-pity will never let up.

I'm living in a bungalow at the top of Barham Boulevard, in the hills above Warner Brothers. For ten days I don't even go out for groceries. I pass chunks of the time by shouting at the top of my lungs all the Shakespearean soliloquies I know. They're great vocal exercises, plus if I'm ever at a Royal Shakespeare performance and both Richard Harris and his standby are too inebriated to say their names ("If you think I'm drunk, wait till you see my understudy."), I'm ready to go on.

The producer says, "Ladies and gentlemen, I'm sorry, but we have to cancel this evening's performance." Then, from the audience: "I know the lines!" shouts the drug addict. "I can take over!"

Toward the end of my withdrawal, I feel the first waves of exhilaration. It feels as if I'm dog paddling toward the shores of sanity. But as I swim on, the features along the shoreline remain tiny, far off in the distance. I keep paddling. It's still as far away as when I began. I lose hope. I'd like to turn around and go back, but that's no longer an option. It's harder than I thought to be sane. You could drown trying to do that.

Sometime later, thumbing through my copy of Bartlett's Quotations, I come across William James's line: "The greatest discovery of my generation is that man can alter his life by altering his attitude of mind." It's one of those nuggets of wisdom that, if you look at it in just the right way, can change your life for the better. *I love that idea.*

My only little problem is that *my new* attitude of mind—at least so far—doesn't feel *that* much different from the *old* one. And my old attitude of mind is a lot like Wile E. Coyote's as he plummets out of the sky—just before he hits the canyon floor.

It's clear there's no point in swimming on. I'll just forget about sanity. There's no such thing.

On the other hand, I am sane enough not to fancy the idea of drowning.

Or smashing into the canyon floor.

The late, sad Queen Nefertiti, down the street, only has one subject: Michael Curtiz. His name is in every other sentence she utters.

From my conversations with her and from reading her diary, he was a demanding, devoted paramour. In his later years, other than his work, he had only her. He expressed dedicated affection during this time—if Ann is to be believed—for only one other woman: his mother.

I watch *Captain Blood*, starring Errol Flynn, a Curtiz film from 1935. *Leonard Maltin's Movie Guide* gives it three-and-a-half stars, but it's nowhere near his best work, which is to say it's nowhere near *Casablanca*. And although nobody asked me, here's my opinion of how *Casablanca* got to be … *Casablanca*. I've revisited it regularly since I was six years old. I almost suck my thumb when I watch it.

One of the most startling things about it is that there were so many irreplaceable creative forces behind it. You could never use the word auteur about *Casablanca*. Its combination of influences includes writers Julius and Philip Epstein and Howard Koch—without their distinctive contributions, it's only another studio movie, loosely based on a failed Broadway play (*Everybody Comes to Rick's* by Murray Burnett and Joan Alison).

Jack Warner bought the film rights. Irene Lee, head of the story department at Warner Brothers, was responsible for getting Hal Wallis, who ran the studio, to make it.

Without Wallis's experienced producer's perspective, it's unlikely the matchless cast would have happened. All of the actors made the ambiguities built into their roles work like God was whispering in their ears. Wallis made a thousand contributions, including the last line of the movie, spoken by Bogart to Rains: "Louie, I think this is the beginning of a beautiful friendship." (The line was dubbed in several weeks after shooting had been completed.)

But maybe the most important gift Hal Wallis brought to *Casablanca* was his uncanny knack for assembling exceptional filmmaking specialists. Without Arthur Edeson, the director of photography, the look of the sets would have been Warner Brothers' standard—good, but too flat for this work of art. The same applies to Max Steiner and his musical score, Owen Marks's film editing, and so on.

Without *Curtiz*, there wouldn't have been the invariably impeccable composition and seamless camera movement—never calling unnecessary attention to the photography. The camera was always perfectly placed, scenes always shot from the perfect angle, in the perfect light, always realized at the perfect moment. He had an uncommon eye for comedy, and one of the many things that make *Casablanca* so magnificent is the undercurrent of "chocolate-box humor" (Aljean Harmetz's phrase), despite the unfolding tensions of the plot.

But again, the film had to be perfectly cast. English was Curtiz's second, arguably third language (after Hungarian and German—he directed his first films in his native Hungary, then moved to Vienna). If he hadn't had such skilled actors, even given his strong directorial suits, it would have been like eating Oreos without the filling or watching George Raft play Rick, which Jack Warner suggested at one point. Being dealt the ideal, inspired cast, Curtiz knew exactly how to use them—despite his often peculiar use of English. (Memorable Curtizisms: "Send in the empty horses." "It's dull from beginning to end, but it's loaded with entertainment.")

None of the overview bosses of *Casablanca*, including Curtiz, could have made it work without the others. Studio head Jack Warner,

Hal Wallis, and Curtiz each had a confidence that bordered on arrogance. They didn't agree most of the time. But when it counted, they did. It was as if three Napoleons had dug themselves into a hole and despite their colossal egos, had no choice but to work together to dig themselves out. If you were a spiritual type, you might say the movie was put together by a higher power. Howard Koch said, "I've got almost a mystical feeling about *Casablanca*, that it made itself somehow."

Reading what Wallis, Warner, and Curtiz said at the time, each of them came away from it, adamant that it was *he* who had made *Casablanca* flawless.

In a way, they were a *team* of auteurs, *more* than just supported by a team of inspired artists and craftspeople.

Ann told me she never argued with Curtiz. He, in turn, had a helpmate in Ann who never disagreed with him. I'm sure he loved her in his way. He was a sentimental man. Julius Epstein said Curtiz made the Paris sequence more romantic than he and his twin brother Philip had written it.

From the reading I've done about Curtiz and from listening to Ann, they both came from emotionally volatile backgrounds. Despite the smile on Curtiz's mother's face, Curtiz loved his mother (Ann used this word) "*dutifully*," implying, I imagine, there was something sterner beneath that smile. Ann's own mother had been a tyrant who lived with her and told her what to do and how to do it until Ann became involved with "Mike."

Shortly after Ann moved into the house down the street, her mother was redistributed into a nearby apartment. I don't know it for a fact, but I assume Curtiz was the primary influence in that. Quoting

Chapter Ten

him again: "The next time I want some dumb sonofabitch to do something, I'll do it myself."

In Curtiz, Ann had found someone who kept her safe and whose authority was constant. After his death, she continued to run her life according to his rules. He was the only man she'd ever loved. He was "the best director on earth," she said.

But the unbending ghost was jealous of his authority. He allowed no leeway. His directions were doting but rigid. There was no Wallis or Warner to shed contrasting light and soften his edicts. When he was gone, Ann had to fill in the gaps for herself. To keep safe, the faithful servant of an autocrat had to make her ghost's decisions for him. She made them carefully and inflexibly, as she imagined him doing it, and in the end she never came to know herself with any moderation. I'm beginning to think Ann's between-the-lines portrait of Curtiz was probably accurate. I don't know why I've ever been surprised that highly creative people can be tyrants.

One night, I walked Ann home after an evening of drinking and talking about movies. When we got to her door, she regarded me warily, as if I might be about to make a pass at her. She said, "You know, sometimes I still hear his voice." She was most comfortable with people when she'd had a few. It made her sardonic, wry. Now, on her front porch, after the drinking was over, I was an unforeseen element that didn't fit, and it was making her anxious.

I rarely had trouble being with people anymore, especially if I'd had a few, but now I felt awkward too. "That must be nice," I said. "To feel like he's still … here."

She was right. Our casual friendship and the intimate feel of this moment didn't go together. Her discomfort—and now mine—was doing most of the talking. "Yes, it's … *nice*," she said, almost stammering. "I wish he hadn't …" She shook her head, frowning down at the house key in her hand.

Then she turned, unlocked her door, and was gone.

It was the summer of 2002. Michael Curtiz had been dead for forty years.

CHAPTER ELEVEN

Jessica and I (she is by now my ex-wife) are both cast in the remake of *Little Miss Marker*, starring Walter Matthau, who promises me a nice payday for the small role of Little Miss Marker's daddy.

But Walter no longer has the clout he had when we did *Cactus Flower*, so instead I take a job for Jonathan Demme in *Melvin and Howard*, which has a better script by far, and anyway I believe Jonathan is a genius. He's started to develop a body of work, is daring in all his choices, and very grounded in the skills that make a great director. He saw me in a stage production of *Once in a Lifetime* at the Mark Taper Forum in downtown Los Angeles three or four years earlier, and tells me he's been looking for the right role for me.

I don't know if it's right or not. But it's *small*.

No, it's *not* right. Or at least there's not much I can think of to do with it. It's a one-note character. I play Melvin's lawyer.* In my single big scene, I try to convince Melvin (Paul LeMat) that everything has

---

* The movie's plot centers around a real-life incident in which a Utah man—Melvin Dummar—picks up a bedraggled stranger in the Nevada desert and later produces a handwritten will naming Dummar as heir to Howard Hughes' vast fortune.

turned out well, that he's won his suit for a share of Hughes' estate. But Melvin doesn't believe me.

There's so little substance to my role that I grab on to kind of a Jimmy Stewart impression as I play it. It's unconscious, I swear. I've never been happy about the Jimmy Stewart thing people have accused me of. I never *tried* to do Jimmy Stewart. I don't in *Melvin and Howard*. But that's the way it feels even to me and I hate it. No actor wants to remind people of another actor. It's death. My voice comes out sounding a little like Stewart's did, accompanied by a hesitant speech pattern that was natural to me and vaguely resembled his. I haven't let myself fall into that trap for years, but I do in *Melvin and Howard*.

During the shooting, Paul LeMat makes some hinky "star" trouble. He's persuaded himself—God knows why—that he's a likely sniper target, and gets down on the floor of the limo as he's driven to the set. He's also late several times. Finally Jason Robards, who plays Howard Hughes, tells him, "You haven't paid enough dues to behave like this."

On the other side of the scale from the extremely functional people like Angela Lansbury, Tom Hanks, Meryl Streep, and the many other performers who make artistic lives mesh with productive personal ones, are the personalities without boundaries. I used to study with Milton Katselas (teacher, director, artist, and love of a man). One Saturday, Tovah Feldshuh was doing a scene from *Dylan*, a drama about Dylan Thomas, opposite an actor playing Dylan, who in the scene is just getting up after a knockdown hangover. The class watched as he stumbled to his feet, went upstage, and pissed into a bucket.

After the scene, Milton told him there's a difference between theatre and—well, pissing in a bucket. Pissing in a bucket can't really be considered something to be observed by others. It doesn't serve as entertainment or education or anything other than what it is. A few years later I did *The Fourposter* in Chautauqua, New York, with Tovah

Chapter Eleven

(a life force of an actress). She reminded me that Milton also said to that class: "Theatre is life with the dull parts left out. That doesn't only mean not asking the audience to listen to dull dialogue," he went on. "It also means not asking them to watch things civilized people don't—or *shouldn't*—want to pay to see, like: shoot drugs, fornicate, torture animals, or urinate on stage." Then, with a twinkle in his eye, he quoted the late British comedian Peter Cook: "'I go to the theatre to be entertained. I don't want to see plays about rape, sodomy, and drug addiction. I can get all that at home.'"

I have a dream last night that I'm on a pirate ship—maybe *Captain Blood* is still on my mind. In the dream, people who have gotten along up till now begin a wholesale slaughter of each other. They're tired of *waiting*, fatigued by anger that's boiling over. Then the hold of the ship turns out to be full of writhing snakes. Awake, I try to figure out what all this means. All I can come up with is that I want my plays to be performed. I'd take some white male functionary (dull part left in) acting role. Anything.

As I often do lately when I'm feeling this way, I go for a drive, turning on the air conditioning and the portable air purifier we keep in the car. When Linda's not with me, I put it on the passenger seat. If it were a few inches taller I could put a hat on it and drive in the diamond lane.

The theme park called Metropolitan Los Angeles extends from the ocean on the west, north up to the San Bernadino Mountains, and east to Riverside. When the Spanish first showed up from the south, they found all of it harsh and inhospitable and wanted as little as possible to do with it. It was essentially a coastal desert, populated by a delicate balance of Indians and bears. The Indians were mostly peaceful. The bears were not. Also, the basin is covered with desert chaparral that burns itself off whenever it feels like it, and when that's not happening, there are the periodic flash floods, or else some subterranean region is hatching its geological plans for the next earthquake, and will soon turn a large chunk of the countryside into a monster vibrator, a continental divider.

In modern times, LA has captivating riches to offer. You can swim in the ocean or a cool lake or one of tens of thousands of pools in the morning, ski in the afternoon, dine in gourmet splendor in the evening, and step out to some of the most diverse nightlife on earth after dark. And if you happen to be here during May and notice a sea of lavender, those are jacaranda trees, frequently accented by exploding cascades of bougainvillea and star jasmine.

It's true, the basin, and even more so the valleys, are dry most of the year. Mark Twain said he "fell into the Los Angeles River and came out dusty." But a few generations ago some local honchos (see *Chinatown*) worked out a way to siphon millions of gallons of water out of the Colorado River (and pirate more out of the Owens Valley—under the heading of what they liked to think of as a kind Manifest Destiny). And now, despite geographical definitions of the Los Angeles area as being semi-arid, major portions of it resemble the Garden of Eden.*

The cultural advantages of Los Angeles are exceptional—from the LA Philharmonic, one of the world's best; to the world-class LA Opera, long under the leadership of Placido Domingo; to the museums, which challenge in scope and variety the best in the country, excepting the great New York galleries and the National in Washington, DC.

---

* UCSD professor Steve Erie says in his book *Beyond Chinatown*: "*Chinatown* was a great movie but lousy history," and adds that The Metropolitan Water District is one of the greatest and most important public water agencies in the world.

Chapter Eleven

And then there's Chicago and … Still, LA has broad and beautifully displayed collections of terrific art.

There are more professional plays performed nightly in LA than in New York or London. True, a lot of them are staged in dilapidated, grungy little theatres, but plenty of creativity comes out of such untidiness. Some LA stage work does begin in vanity and with the desire to draw attention for the sake of creating or advancing film careers, but that doesn't work nearly as well as it used to—mostly because of the overkill of Equity Waiver theatres—and what remains is the shape of the thing: actors, writers, and directors doing their single-minded best because it's their passion.

Los Angeles can be physically dangerous. It's possible to die in the wilderness in this city, to plunge off a cliff if you're not paying close attention to your driving, and not be found for months. Or you could collapse from exposure if you get too far off the hiking path and, because LA is an automobile city where you don't necessarily expect to see people for gaps of time, you could rot before anybody finds you. Or you could simply wander out into the desert and run into some dead-eyed old Charlie Manson disciple or one of Sam Peckinpah's leftover cowboys and never be heard from again.

Los Angeles can be a prettified chaos of greed and shallowness, imagined and real, and sometimes the imagined is the worst. Most of the rest of the country revels in disparaging LA and then people start accepting it almost as a defect of the state itself: "Don't Californicate Oregon," the stereotyped Southern California fizgig blonde, the Venice Beach bodybuilder, the wildly-caricatured Hollywood dealmakers, and the whole array of narcissists and hedonists—no more solely California phenomena than most of the rest of America's bottom-feeding fringe of egotists, crooks, degenerates, freaks, zombies, pederasts, gerbil-stuffers, looney toons, public masturbators, and heartrending homeless schizophrenics.

Maybe all the vanity stage plays evoke the worst you can say about LA: that it's a little fuller than most cities of idealists, romantics, and fantasists, dreaming the nearly impossible dream. Maybe they come here or, if they were born here, stay here because without really thinking about it, they imagine they'll be able to put right all the wrongs ever done them—that in some unforeseeable way someone who matters might end up saying, with more tenderness than they've ever expressed before: I had no idea you've suffered like this.

I go to a local bar called McRed's, in days not as long ago as I wish they were. It's up on Victory Boulevard in Van Nuys. This is a bucket-of-blood joint where I played pool a few times with a biker who ends up in the tabloids and on all the local "action" news reports because it turns out he's a serial killer wanted in several states. I wonder if I'm just naturally drawn to the lairs of murderers.

Everybody is forever laughing and hooting in McRed's. Linda goes in with me once and says, "I'm sorry, life is too short to drink with these morons." Linda rarely says anything bad about people.

On this night, an alcoholic teacher from Valley College, a pretty good two-year institution a mile or so away, is sitting on his usual stool, watching the snake-pit world of McRed's with his characteristic condescending eye. He casts his gaze at me. As an actor who works from time to time, I'm sort of a *somebody* in this place.

The college teacher says to me, very quietly, "You know what you are? You're a loser."

My fight-or-flight mechanism kicks in. What a ferocious thing to say to anyone.

But I don't fight and I can't just run out of the bar. A loser is calling me a loser. I've never been one of those people who can snap back a

Chapter Eleven

clever retort that silences the offender and all the bystanders are awed by my wit. The teacher makes his observation with smug composure, a doctor complacently prescribing medicine, except the medicine doesn't make you better; its *aim* is to kill you. Also, I'm pretty sure he wouldn't have said this to the psychotic biker. Am I so harmless he feels no danger in saying something so calculatedly evil to me? Should I beat him up? I *might* be able to. If he'd stand still. I manage a phony smile and tell this arrogant jerk that maybe he's had a couple too many and that he ought to go home.

He smirks at the lameness of that and turns away. I think about *my* home—in Jackson—where I'm safe, and where I would very much like to be right now. Maybe I'll stagger back to North Hollywood and tell Linda I think we should move to Michigan. She'll jump at that all right.

Later on, hating myself not only for being a pussy, but an inarticulate one, it strikes me that maybe this teacher is *partly* right—*for the moment*. Maybe this experience has been a good thing—toward *finding myself*. Maybe his diagnosis *is* curative. Most medicines don't taste good.

But your stronger realization is that an ice pick between his ribs might have been more curative.

The stage is in semi-darkness. The set is a hazy indication of a tacky hotel room. There is a linoleum-topped table, and a straight-backed, vinyl-covered chair; a vanity with mirror attached; another chair, and an old iron-framed bed with a saggy mattress.

I wander uncertainly onstage because I don't know my cue. Also, I've gotten older. The audience used to be fond of me, but now I'm scared to find out what they think. I've been away so long that instead of being a familiar face people are glad to see, I've grown unrecognizable, shadowy, suspiciously mortal; and now that they've fully taken me in, they know for sure they don't want to watch me for one more second. I'm "dying out there," and although I can't quite explain why yet, it feels as if I'm beginning to understand.

I go to the window, open it, and take a big breath. The air feels surprisingly fresh. It's dim early light, just before daybreak, the magical moment when the mist rises from the street. The veil between substance and rarefaction is a little thinner, and somehow things hard to see in the dark are clearly illuminated.

If the audience could just see inside me—at least as well as I can see out the window in this extraordinary light—they might realize that I'm youthful and charming; and, Jesus, far more importantly: that if I weren't absolutely convinced there was something better than I am waiting around the corner in my story, I wouldn't dream of telling it.

Then, I remember how my daughter struggles one day at a time, and that trying to see the top of the mountain before you get there is madness.

CHAPTER TWELVE

Time and orderliness are inconsiderate the way they slam around with no regard for your feelings—such as you might like to linger a little more here and zip through this other part instead of the other way around, the way time in its pigheaded tenacity chooses to do it.

And orderliness—**fuh-geddaboudit**.

I go to one of the last love-ins in Central Park—a huge demonstration against the war in Vietnam—the peace children, the flower children. There are 250,000 people there, the air heavy with the sickly-sweet perfume of marijuana. I've been there just a short time when a guy with the word "peace" on his chest—not his shirt, his chest—sees a little boy with a plastic toy gun. He grabs it out of the kid's hands, scratches him on the forehead as he does it, smashes it and screams, "Don't bring a fucking gun to a fucking love-in, you fuckin' little fuck." And now the poor disarmed kid is bawling and I guess his father has seen all this because he yells at the guy, "What'd you do to my kid, asshole?" Then he kicks the guy in the knee. Then there's a fistfight. Finally, the guy who'd taken the gun away from the kid holds up the peace sign and the other guy grabs his peace *fingers* and snaps them apart like a wishbone.

As soon as I get to New York I begin to see celebrities.

I see JFK coming down Broadway. He's in a covered limo. I'm at the curb behind a line of those wooden sawhorse things and a seemingly endless row of police, but I see him very clearly. He's looking out at the people lining the sidewalks. He has his warm smile on, but it's preoccupied. He's well into the last year of his life.

Later, near the Kennedy sighting, I see the Beatles make their getaway from the Ed Sullivan Theatre after their first American show. They seem to be afraid for their lives.

Both of these encounters happen near the Americana Hotel, where I'm night clerking. For three weeks in a row, I manage to work my break so that it comes in the middle of Ella Fitzgerald's show in the Americana Room downstairs, so I get to see her every night.

One night after her show, she stops in the lobby and says, "You come down and see all my shows. What's your name?" I tell her. From then on, when she sees me, she says, "Hiya, Ricky." Finally, the last night of her engagement, she stops and says, "I do believe you're a music lover." I swallow hard and say as coolly as I can, "I'm an Ella lover." She grins and says, "Where'd you learn to talk like that to a woman?" I just grin back at her.

She smiles and says, "Thank you, Ricky. I'll miss you."

I realize I'm beginning to feel frenzied by my proximity to all these iconic and famous people and that I'm drawn to get even closer.

And it's as simple as that: I'm a *fan*—not just in the sense of liking a certain politician or performer, but in the feeling of being one of *them*: the spellbound throng.

I see Alec Guinness in *Dylan* (no peeing in a bucket in *this* version). In the play's final moments, Dylan Thomas makes a pyramid out of

Chapter Twelve

the shot glasses he's been drinking whiskey out of. He's piled up so many glasses that he ends up dead. He's finally drunk himself to death. I'm spellbound.

I watch James Earl Jones in *Bohekee Creek* and later, *The Great White Hope*. I see *The Fantasticks* at the Sullivan Street Theatre, still near the beginning of its record setting run.

I see Uta Hagen and Arthur Hill in *Who's Afraid of Virginia Woolf*, Zero Mostel in *Fiddler on the Roof*, Peter Cook, Dudley Moore, Jonathan Miller, and Alan Bennett in *Beyond the Fringe*, and Barbra Streisand in *Funny Girl*. I watch Charles Aznavour perform solo on the huge stage of the Alvin Theatre, a bantam cock who owns the world.

I go to one of my first auditions. It's for an episode of George C. Scott's only television series, *East Side, West Side*. I'm to meet the producers on the top floor of a building on Madison Avenue. When I arrive, no one is there. I poke my head in another office and see two men, sitting at separate desks. One of them is Mel Brooks. I know who he is right away. I've nearly worn out my *2000 Year Old Man* record that he made with Carl Reiner. It doesn't really surprise me to see him here in this office high above Madison Avenue. I've learned by now you see all kinds of people you recognize in Manhattan. I ask him and the other man if they know when the people across the hall will be back. Brooks looks at me with a world weary smile, then begins a riff that will last at least twenty minutes on the possible doomed fates of the producers of *East Side, West Side*. Finally, he sighs and shrugs at the thousand natural shocks that flesh is heir to, gets up, strolls to the window and looks idly down at the street below.

His whole body convulses. His hands fly up. He clasps his forehead and turns to the other man and me, his eyes wide with horror. "Oh, my God!" he cries. "They leaped!"

This is *way* better than drinking Hendrick's Gin in a penthouse.

A few months after I arrive in New York, I see Richard Burton do *Hamlet*. Somehow, I've gotten a box seat—good theatre seats are affordable to the non-wealthy in these days. I'm not too high up, right above the third row of the orchestra, leaning forward, resting my elbows on the railing.

Seated in the middle of the fifth row is Elizabeth Taylor. It's not long after *Cleopatra* and they are still the most frantically followed celebrity love story since Edward VIII and Wallis Simpson. I'm watching both of them at the same moment, from the far corner of an isosceles triangle.

Burton is good that night. It's a solid, pulsating *Hamlet*. But that's not the show from where I'm sitting. The focus-puller is the passion play that's going on between the actor downstage-center and the movie star in the fifth row. Taylor gobbles him up with her eyes, and he's feverishly emoting for an audience of one.

There's no going back. I *have* to do this—get into show business, which is, after all, what I came here to do.

My first professional job is at Bucks County Playhouse, where a year later I'll be doing *Sunday in New York* with Alan Alda. *This* play is by Jean Kerr and it's called *Jenny Kissed Me*, based on the title of a poem by Leigh Hunt.

After I audition for the role (a peacock teenage Lothario), the producer, Mike Ellis, asks me if I belong to Actors' Equity, the stage union. I say, "Yes." And he says, "No, you don't." I go home thinking

Chapter Twelve

I've blown it by auditioning badly, then lying to the producer. But I get the job anyway, plus an agent, and with a job in hand I get to join Equity. It's a perfect day.

The star of the show is James Daly, a popular Broadway and television performer of the time (he was later one of the two stars of *Medical Center* on television). He is an actor's actor and a gentleman. Most of his family is in the cast: his wife Hope, his daughters Glynn and Tyne, and his son Tim. The latter two, I'll work with years later: Tim, on an episode of *Wings*, and Tyne on her series, *Cagney and Lacy*.

Tim is eight when we do *Jenny Kissed Me*, Tyne about sixteen. Tim is a juggernaut of energy, cute little kid. Tyne is an awkward teenager, already very ambitious, but friendly, full of joy, endearingly vulnerable. After opening night, her father proposes a toast to her and me on the occasion of our first professional jobs.

When we're adults with children of our own, Jessica and I will be in a carpool with Tyne and her husband, Georg Stanford Brown, trekking our daughters up to the top of Mulholland Drive to Westland School. But Tyne and I will never come anywhere near recapturing the unique intimacy we had when we did our first pay-for-play jobs together and a roomful of people toasted our commencement.

When I do that episode of *Wings* with Tim and remind him of *Jenny Kissed Me*, he just smiles. My guess is that the smile means he doesn't remember very much about *Jenny Kissed Me*. Or it's possible it's just *me* he doesn't remember.

He comes across as kind, like his father and Tyne and the rest of his family.

Abigail finished her most recent rehab about six months ago. She calls about noon on a Saturday. She's been in a car wreck. I drive down and find her at the side of the street in her badly dinged-up Jeep. She didn't stay at the scene of the accident or exchange telephone numbers or insurance information. She tells me the other person took off too. I don't know whether I believe her or not. It doesn't matter. Her Jeep still runs; she follows me home, up Lankershim.

The Jeep is lurching badly. She stops, then weaves-and-wobbles forward again. It goes that way for a couple of blocks.

I pull over, get out, and tell her to pay attention to her driving. She screams, "Don't yell at me!" I try to calm her, and myself, and once again lead her, slowly, toward my house. She floors her scraping, staggering Jeep, veers around me, and speeds the rest of the way home, where she slams into the house and heaves herself onto the sofa, sobbing.

Trying to figure out what to do, I circle her like a nipping sheep dog. I can't call the police. I sit down next to her and see she's got a large bump on her forehead. I have to do something—it could be a concussion. I take her to the Valley Presbyterian Hospital emergency room. The triage nurse asks if she's taken any drugs. "No," Abi tells him. "Nothing."

Three hours later we see a doctor. She's a heavy black woman who looks like she has high blood pressure.

She stares daggers at Abi and hands me the blood test results.

Abigail Lenz: Cannabinoids: positive.

Cocaine metabolite: positive.

Opiates: positive."

Shit. Shit shit shit.

I tell Linda: "Somebody said—I read it—that we have a stream of sixty thousand thoughts a waking day, never mind our dreams. That

Chapter Twelve

means I've had well over a *billion thoughts* in my lifetime. Most of them have had to do with how can I *promote* myself—to better billing, a better position, to having better stuff, better food, nicer vacations, etcetera, etcetera. What futility. And Abigail is out there, wasted, risking her life, but maybe with luck, crossing some major river. And all I have to show for my life is an irrelevant North Hollywood existence. What the hell big river have *I* ever crossed?"

I think of the Valley College teacher at McReds. I know what I should have said to him: "*You're* the loser. Your very existence makes the world a meaner place." I start to get sidetracked by other great retorts I could have made to him, but I remember that I'm still talking to Linda, and explain to her that I'm trying to boost myself up to a whole new plateau of honesty.

She gives me her about-to-charge bull's eyes and leaves the room.

I manage to hang on to my thematic compass: Just because you've fooled around with a few constructive thoughts on Friday and Saturday, it doesn't necessarily mean you'll be safe on Sunday. It's not what you put your mind to *this* Friday and Saturday, with all your noble intentions; it's what you *thought* and *did*, and the damaging words you *said* all those Fridays and Saturdays when you didn't know any better, that's playing unkind tricks on your day of rest.

A month later, Abigail telephones at one o'clock on a Saturday morning. She's in a phone booth, weeping, gasping to get her words out. I can barely understand her. All I can make out is "Cahauenga exit." I'm a half-decibel away from not being able to understand where she wants me to come get her. The line goes dead. I tell Linda what I think I heard her say, what I'm going to do, then get in the car and drive seven miles to the Cahuenga exit off the 101 Freeway, in

Hollywood. I see no phone booth near the base of the off-ramp, so I keep on driving a couple of blocks.

I see a gas station/convenience store and pull in.

Abigail reels out and gets into the car. She's still crying, but there's something very odd beneath the tears.

"Where's your car?" I ask her.

"In Venice."

"How'd you get here?"

"I walked." Venice is about twenty miles away. She's wearing once-pink rubber sandals; the sandals and her feet are black with grime. I believe in some unlikely way that it may be true.

"I'll take you home."

"Okay." She doesn't look at me, just out the passenger-side window—down at the pavement disappearing behind us. "I've got to get out of this. I saw God."

"Out of what?"

"*This*! *I saw* God. *I talked to him*!"

"You *saw* him?"

Still not looking at me: "That's right."

"What'd he look like?"

"Jesus."

When I ask her, she doesn't tell me what He said, but I don't think I'd have taken it very seriously, whatever it was. I don't believe in visitations from God.

At home, I bring up the notion of rehab. She does a fifteen-minute rant on how she doesn't want to "talk about all this shit anymore," says it only works the opposite way it should with her.

After several stop-and-go conversations, I give up, go into my bedroom, close the door and start making calls to see if I can get her into her third rehabilitation center. There are people out there who care about her and want to help her.

A therapist who's been working with her recently tells me about a place in Mississippi that has a very good record of resuscitating people from the near-death state Abigail is in and puts me in touch with a guy whose business it is to escort addicts to treatment centers. He's a private contractor at that kind of work. He'll be here tomorrow morning. I imagine tying my daughter up if necessary to keep her here until the escort guy arrives.

After dinner, which Abigail doesn't touch, she asks Linda if she thinks Jesus is the Son of God. Linda says, "I think we're *all* the Son of God." Abi seems to like that answer. I wonder from my recent reading if something like Atman from the Hindu school of Dvaita is involved, or one of the other Eastern forms of that deity. Or maybe it's the Holy Spirit that turns up for that exchange between Linda and Abigail. Some Hebrew scholars refer to the Holy Spirit as feminine and students of the Dead Sea Scrolls speak of it as the "female vehicle."

Anyway, it's a moment distinctly between my wife and daughter.

Later, Abigail asks me, "Why isn't there some nice practical set of rules about how to live your life?"

"There *are* rules," I say. I'm thinking of the Ten Commandments and the Golden Rule, things like that. But I *know* that's not what she means, so I tell her that in the end, you have to make your own rules.

"I'm not qualified."

"Maybe your mom wasn't able to give you enough guidance." Jessica had legal custody of her.

"What would *you* have done?" she says.

"To begin with, seen to it that you were in school every day."

"What about your work?"

"Most days, I didn't work."

"Then I would have limited my truancies to the days when you *did*. Except I would have done whatever I was doing twice as hard."

"Why?"

She stares at me for several seconds, as if trying to decide whether I'm mature enough to hear this. "To get back at you."

"Me? Why?"

"For leaving."

"I spent every moment with you I could."

"Not good enough. You left."

The counselor calls and Abigail says, "Is that her?"

I nod, she reaches for the phone, takes it from me and says, "Hi. I want to go to that place in Mississippi."

I wonder if maybe God did show up and talk to her.

CHAPTER THIRTEEN

We're going through a disconcerting run lately. Debby found out she may have cancer, and Linda's mother is doing poorly. Linda's mom Grace is eighty-seven, but you forget that when you don't see her for a while. She doesn't sound old on the phone. She's not old in spirit. Her name fits her. She is graceful and kind—the opposite of all the mother-in-law clichés. She loves Linda, Linda's sister Morgan, with whom she lives, and her granddaughters (Morgan's grown girls), Alison and Ashley.

She loves me too. We talk often, which is saying something because Grace is not really a talker. She's got aches and pains, but she doesn't speak of them except when Linda questions her, trying to figure out how to make her feel better. Grace has macular degeneration, among other problems, so Linda calls her almost every day and reads to her. Grace is a big part of our lives. I will miss her when she goes—her sweetness, the niceties of her mothering, her soul. I can't even imagine what Linda is going to feel.

My sister has never passed along the pain she went through growing up and is also a positive force. She had breast cancer in her twenties. As a nurse, she took an accidental stick from a needle somewhere along the way, got hepatitis C and survived that. Now, in preliminary tests, they think she may have ovarian cancer. I can't yet take this in; it freezes my blood. Debby is scared, angry, and a kind of quiet I can't read. I talk to her, send her copies of some of the same spiritual books Linda keeps around the house, ask my friends to pray for her, which by now I *sort* of believe in—from a distance.

But I can't be distanced anymore. Since I've asked other people to do it and since I don't *know* that it might not be important, I have to try to talk to God, too. So I've begun to make a habit of my awkward prayers. To be truthful, talking to *Him* embarrasses me. If He's there, I'm uncomfortable about a million things I've done—or haven't done. If He's not, then I just feel silly. Also, if He's not there, I guess *that* pisses me off—mostly because Debby's sick.

I tell this to Linda, whom, even though she makes me angry along with everybody else during times like this, I can't really blame my problems on any more than I can blame them on my dead parents.

She says, "Get out of yourself."

"And go where?"

"Anywhere! What's wrong with you lately? I know things are a little rough right now, but nobody's dead; nobody's going to *be* dead for a long time. Somebody tell a joke."

During my tapering-down acting years, I begin to freeze up at auditions. Years ago, I was offered a role on *Columbo*. I didn't take it because Scott and Charlie were coming to LA during the shooting, which was to be in North Carolina. I didn't want to miss any time with them, so I said no to the job. It was just one of the victims anyway. Who wants to get killed in the first reel?

Years afterward, I have an audition with Peter Falk for one of his latter-years episodes of the show. I want it desperately, and that's how

Chapter Thirteen

I read for it. I've rehearsed it over and over again, bouncing off the walls, driving Linda crazy. I've come up with an absolutely rock solid idea of what I need to do to make it perfect. I map out every moment.

That's the number-one film auditioning no-no. I'm programmed like a robot and that's how it comes out at the audition: mechanical, unnatural, and dead.

I skulk out of the audition room. Both Peter and the casting director, Ron Stephenson—who's hired me several times before—have been as warm as they could be, but I've blown it by a combination of wanting it too much and my Trojan Horse acting.

As I'm about to exit the offices, Stephenson hurries after me and says, "Peter wants you to come back and do it again, but this time, play it a little … looser."

I go back in and do *exactly the same thing* I did the first time.

Peter is his pleasant, unperturbed Columbo self, but it doesn't help—even though it's obvious he's trying his best to set a relaxed tone for me. I've rehearsed so hard, I've welded myself into a groove and can't break out of it.

I know there's a larger lesson in this, but it eludes me. I'm too disappointed in myself. When auditioning goes badly, it's like being a golfer with the yips—you're trying to steady your nerves for a putt but your mind is in the wrong place—not on the Zen of putting, not on allowing your muscle memory to do what it does as sure as you know how to walk, but on your self-defeating need to try to *force* the ball into the damned hole. It's the opposite of being *in the zone*. And you realize that movie cameras are okay, big audiences are fine (it's not that hard to look upon them as impersonal), but a small number of very close human witnesses to your *crime* of forcing what can't be forced is just another way of "dying out there." You can *feel* them breathing on you and you *know*, as near as they're sitting, that—unlike a camera or a theatre audience—they are not only going to send you home without the job, they are seeing every flaw in your character.

I take it back. The lesson doesn't elude me. It's as simple as I'm trying too hard, and trying too hard is trying for the wrong reasons; it's playing to the gallery, acting from your measly intellectual guess of what *they want* and not from the truth. And not looking for the truth is insulting and discordant and the opposite of art or anything else worthwhile.

And if it's strictly money you need, they know it. You might as well tattoo it on your forehead.

In television, I went through ten years when I didn't have to audition. God, I loved that. It was liberating, energizing. But I may have been one of the people who brought to an end the practice of hiring guest stars by reputation, without even a meeting.

I get back from doing a job in Las Vegas, and staying up late and gambling and related adding-years-to-your-age vices. There's a message from my agent that I'm to do *The Mary Tyler Moore Show,* beginning rehearsal the next day. It's the first episode of the season and the regular cast members all greet each other warmly, exchanging news about how they've spent their vacations—which, with successful series actors, are often working vacations.

In this episode, I'm to play Mary's new boyfriend. The conflict is that I'm too young for her. There are lots of cradle-robbing jokes aimed at Mary by Rhoda and Lou and Ted and Murray. We begin to rehearse—me feeling like the outsider I am—and right away it's clear what the real problem is. Mary is only three or four years older than I am, plus I haven't slept for three days and, because of my unwholesome habits lately, I'm looking like Dorian Gray's picture.

Chapter Thirteen

They send me off to make-up to manufacture a younger look for me, but that never works. They can make you older, not younger—you just end up looking like you're wearing a thick coat of make-up, which might make an interesting story, but it's not this story. So they replace me with Peter Strauss (later, of multiple miniseries' fame). He's not much younger than I am, but enough for it to work. It's the only time I've ever been fired and it chills my blood, giving me a virtual preview of the yips to come.

Another time, a few years later, I meet some people on an interview for a movie and my hands feel like they've been dipped in half-chilled consommé. But you can't ignore a room full of five people who have the power to hire you and all have dry hands stuck out to be shaken. You can't nod at them or wink. So, I grab the back of my sport coat, trying to dry my clammy hands, and pretend I'm pulling it down and adjusting it. Only I've worn my old gray tweed—I'm up for the part of a disheveled professor type—and you can hear about ten stitches in the right shoulder rip out.

But we all ignore it and I shake their hands and say, "Hi. How are you? It's nice to meet you. I certainly do like the script." And by this time the elastic band on my underpants is saturated. The sweat is rolling down my legs like I'm a garden fountain, and all the time I'm trying to be myself, I'm wondering what they'll think when the sweat starts to show through my slacks. Nobody likes to hire damp people.

Another time, I'm auditioning for the television series *Picket Fences*. Kristoffer Tabori is directing it. Everybody but maybe Kris is unsure about me. They call in David E. Kelley, the executive producer and Michelle Pfeiffer's husband—which I know for no other reason than that's the kind of junk my head is full of.

I've been okay up to this point in the audition, good enough to call in Kelley.

As soon as he arrives, I fold like an adolescent who's only just realized he's not actually a member of the same species as everybody else in the room, and I give the most nervous reading of my life. Good film acting is like painting on cobwebs. It's impossible if you're shaking like a leaf.

One time, I audition for *St. Elsewhere*, produced by Bruce Paltrow, Gwyneth's father. I'd done an Off-Broadway play with his wife, Blythe Danner, shortly after I got to New York. It was her first role in New York theatre. Her character was German. She spoke not one word of English and was brilliant. Among the cast members was Jim Rado, who was co-writing *Hair* at the time. He gave me the first or second draft of it to read while we were rehearsing—it was just a play then. I told him I thought it (*his cultural watershed show*) needed work. I was sort of right; what it needed more than anything was to be a musical and for the playwrights to be brought together with producer Joseph Papp, and especially with Galt McDermot, the composer.

I digress badly.

I blow my audition for Bruce Paltrow and he hires Tony Bill, so I go home and methodically beat a chaise longue to death with a garden hoe.

Maybe I can just put all the blame on this industry. I love acting, but I don't care much for show business. Dressed in this year's fashion with its tricky accessories, she is not just a heartbreaker: She's a floozy, a flim-flam, a Judas kiss. The profession of acting is rarely dignified even if you're not wildly neurotic. It doesn't matter how good you are, it's a hat-in-your-hand line of work. There are clear, genius exceptions; actors who rise above the normal constraints: Meryl Streep, Dustin Hoffman, Ben Kingsley, Patricia Clarkson, Philip Seymour Hoffman, Cate Blanchett, and all that group of people who've obviously signed pacts with Satan. But for most actors with a modest gift, it's more often than not humbling.

Chapter Thirteen

I co-wrote a television pilot for a short-lived ABC series called *Aloha Paradise*. As Van Johnson said to Debbie Reynolds after she'd had a prima donna moment during the shooting of it, "We're not at MGM anymore, darling. You have to eat a little shit once in a while."

I'm acquainted with stars of all generations. I meet Gwyneth Paltrow a year or two before or after my audition for *St. Elsewhere* at a party given by Blythe and Bruce. Gwyneth is about six. Well, I don't actually meet her. She's playing in the backyard and Blythe says, "That's my daughter Gwyneth."

I try to teach my children and to learn from them. Sometime before her late-night call and her decampment for Mississippi, I catch Abigail at a time when she's open to talking to me. She's not using drugs at the moment, but underneath, I feel the threat of it ratcheting up again.

"It was just a little slip," I say about the only incident I'm aware of right now—even though I secretly fear there have been more. I'm trying to jolly her away from the path she's on, a *real* successful approach with addicts.

"A *two-week* slip," she says, her eyes fixed on mine.

I think I go pale, but either she doesn't notice or isn't surprised.

"Every time I imagined getting up and going out and sitting through another fucking AA meeting with all those fucking haunted people smoking their suffocating fucking Marlboros, staring at me with their fish-eyed smiles like robots with their batteries gone dead, I felt like I was going to puke. So, I stopped going for now." Looking at me, she sighs, but it comes out as a groan. "I'll go again."

I try to feel relief. "You're good with words."

"You wouldn't think so if you could hear me talk in front of one of those groups. I'm fine singing for people. I wish *I* could *still* sing for them!"

I remember carrying her in my arms when she was a baby. Her rib cage felt so narrow, so *fragile*, I was afraid I might damage her.

She breathes deeply. "But give me a bunch of sober junkies who see straight through me, and I get cold sweats."

I look down at her wrists and see the faint scars from self-inflicted cigarette burns. When I've asked her about them, she's never more than shrugged. She doesn't like to talk about it; says it doesn't mean what I think it does. I have no idea what she *thinks* I think it means. It feels familiar, though, as if wounding yourself might prevent you from wounding others, I don't know. Anyway, she wasn't *this* Abigail when she did that to herself.

"I just want to sing the blues," she says. "Why? Can you answer me that?"

I shake my head, partly because I'm confused by such moments of apparent self-knowledge. "What's it like—the crack?"

She studies me, I think wondering if she can trust me. She decides for the moment she's safe to "share."

"It makes the tension *go away*! It's *fantastic*! It's like being on a beautiful tropical beach. The air becomes light and cool. It caresses your skin. It's like the touch of a doctor you feel trust in. It presses … very gently, into your … *deep inside places*." She shakes her head, remembering. "It floods you with a rush of healing and joy and … *hope* that was as far away a few seconds earlier as the sun is from some …" She searches for the right phrase, then, with disdain: "bottom feeder."

This has not bathed me with relief. "Can you tell me the worst part?"

Her shoulders rise slowly. Then, matter-of-factly: "I've almost killed myself a few times. "The last time, this arm"—she holds up her right

Chapter Thirteen

arm and shakes it violently—"was all of a sudden out of control, shaking. I knew I was really fucked up. I looked at my cell phone, but I didn't know what to do with it. I thought of leaving my apartment to go …" She shrugs. "I didn't know where. And anyway I couldn't figure out how to get down the stairs. I was … well, you know a little about this. I was … 'stuck.' So … I just cried and cried and finally, I cried myself to sleep." She looks at me, her eyes glistening, but with no hint of self-pity. "Then … when I woke up, I was sort of okay—physically."

"Jesus!"

She doesn't look me in the eye very much in the last couple of years, but now she does. She gazes at me with the same look of longing I saw when she told the woman at Beit T'Shuvah that she and I are spiritual.

I have a powerful urge to tell her with all the feeling I have that the path she's been on is *possible to change*—that all she has to do is decide to step away from it and then *do it—make the change*!

But I had a couple of drinks an hour or so before she got here, and I'm not sure my tongue might not betray the fact that it was perhaps a drop more than I should be drinking—at my age. I remember my dad telling me something it was obvious he sincerely believed and that he wanted me to try to understand from his point of view. But l didn't want to hear whatever it was because he was one of the two last people on earth I wanted to hear *anything* from. Besides, he was a little drunk.

I don't say a word to her.

One night Linda and I got a call from Charlie's friend Ed. They had flipped over in Charlie's car, landing upside down. Charlie's spine would turn out to have been severely compressed when the car landed. One policeman wanted to move him out of the driver's seat—I'm not sure why. It's not protocol. There was no immediate danger. Ed pleaded that they not do that, to wait for the paramedics. The policeman listened and reconsidered. They waited for the ambulance.

Ed was calling from a hospital in the Northeast San Fernando Valley. A few minutes later I talked to some doctors at that hospital. They wanted to operate right away. I said okay, then I changed my mind—had second thoughts. I talked to one doctor and then two more to find out if it was life or death. The consensus was that the operation could wait for a couple of days. I talked to Sarah in New York and she booked herself on the earliest possible flight to Los Angeles.

The next day I made about a dozen phone calls until I finally managed to get the head of orthopedics at UCLA on the line. I asked him who he would have operate on *his* son. He gave me the name of two surgeons at Rancho Los Amigos National Rehabilitation Center in Orange County. When Sarah arrived, we drove to Downey and had a talk with those two surgeons. They had seen the x-rays of Charlie's spine and wanted to operate as soon as possible.

Charlie was transported to Downey and the two surgeons performed the surgery.

The damage had come to within *one millimeter* of Charlie's spinal cord. His friend Ed probably saved his life that night—or his capacity to walk—by giving the policeman in charge second thoughts about moving him. Charlie is completely fine now.

When I was a kid and Virginia was mad at me, she sometimes told me I had "another think coming." I always thought, oh goodie, I get another think!

At first, Scott was angry with me for leaving town to do an acting job only two weeks after Charlie's operation. But I didn't feel guilty. Charlie was out of danger—especially with Scott looking after him (and Connie, who was living with Scott now, near UCLA).

Chapter Thirteen

The first instinct isn't *always* best. Sometimes it's vital to make good use of those second thinks. I'm trying to rethink the spirit of some of Linda's books. According to one of them, I'm trapped in Babylon with all my guilts and fears, when what I ought to do is refuse to believe the door to the cell I've shut myself into is locked. The books are telling me to rethink that. They're suggesting that the door is *not* locked, that there is no guard, nobody but my own ghosts preventing me from opening it and walking out.

But your guilt is entirely warranted, you self-aggrandizing phony!

These are muscular ghosts. They've been in training for a long time.

CHAPTER FOURTEEN

Abigail sends me her one-month chip from AA, which makes me well up, which then makes my wife remind me that I cry at card tricks (in my defense, it has to be an unusually moving trick). I call Scott in Minneapolis, where he teaches math (his wonderfully charming wife Connie is a law professor at the University of Minnesota. Their son Aaron, my first grandchild … goes to school).

Scott answers the phone. This week, he's putting in a new bathroom—doing the whole thing himself. He can do that: carpentry, wiring, plumbing, plastering, anything. He learned some of his handyman skills from me—like changing light bulbs, replacing fuses, putting new washers into the handle thingies in the kitchen and bathroom sinks (that one took quite a long time for me to master). I don't know where he picked up the more complicated skills. He has a mind-boggling list of resources and talents. I tell him about Abigail's chip and he's delighted.

Later we talk politics. He's the only one I do that with. We agree with each other. I only talk politics with people who agree with me, partly because I am consistently baffled by politics. Did the founding fathers mean for it to be *this* adversarial? I know *they* were adversarial.

But they couldn't have thought it was a good idea for it to get so *mean*. Scott and I talk about that. We agree. At least he *says* he agrees. Tender as my feelings are for him, I can't say I know his soul. Well, a little. I do know his heart.

I go on, telling him that when I was young you had no choice but to listen to both sides of the news, that there were zero websites and blogs, and only four or five dependable television channels, and not so many mulish corners of the culture where people could go hide with their my-team-is-always-right intolerance, cut off from everybody who isn't looking at the world from exactly *their slant*.

I call Charlie. He's an actuary. He lives in Pacific Palisades with his wife Kim, a fascinating, multitalented woman, a music producer, and masterful rockabilly singer. (She and her band, the Jaguars, have a worldwide fan base.) They have one child, Riley, my second grandson. Like Aaron, he's a great, smart kid. Charlie and some of his actuary partners have recently invested time, money, and a significant amount of physical labor in a winery. It's called Pali Winery. I've found this idea very appealing and have recommended that they concentrate on Chardonnays. I'm not sure Charlie was paying attention. He likes Pinots.

He's not home, which disappoints me. I'd like to talk to one or both of my sons about some dreams I've been having lately. I forgot to bring them up with Scott. Maybe I was too embarrassed. Anyway, my sons are usually willing to discuss anything with me. They're good listeners. I'd like to understand what my dreams are telling me—which now that I think about it might be harder to do than I thought, because I don't exactly remember them. And even if I did, I don't know what question I'd ask or why I would expect anybody who lives outside my brain to be able to answer it. I think of my boys, the mathematicians, as being able to solve anything.

Chapter Fourteen

These things are on my mind now because I have the sense lately that some little nothing of a personal uneasiness is escalating into a crisis. It may have to do with Debby. I'm not sure.

The only recurring dream I remember is one I've had intermittently for most of my lifetime. It stars a large number of snakes. When I was in kindergarten, a boy who was three or four years older than I was had been enlisted by my parents to walk me to school across a big field near Lincoln, Nebraska, where my father was stationed in the Army Air Force. The boy made me jump over what he told me were snake pits. I reported this to my mother, but she said she didn't believe me; I sensed she was afraid of approaching the boy's mom. I still have the occasional nightmare about those snake pits.

Linda says I should turn the nightmares into good dreams. I'm puzzled, and seeing that I am, she says it no doubt didn't happen the way I remember it, that I've just interpreted it that way.

"Snakes are snakes," I tell her.

"What did the snakes look like?"

"I don't know. I didn't *see* them. They were in the pit. I just knew they were there."

"But you *didn't* know they were there. They were a rumor."

"Okay, maybe. But what's the difference? I've still got that idea in my head."

"Change your idea."

"How do I do that?" I'd really like to know. Maybe she's onto something. "I'd have to talk myself out of believing something I've always believed," I tell her.

"Then do that. You are what you believe."

Where does she get this stuff? "I believe what I believe."

"You don't *have* to."

"But I watch myself—too much, I know—and I *see* what I do, what I *am*. And it doesn't fall under the heading of any of that 'affirmation' crap—pardon me—in all your damned books—at least not enough for me to have a clue what to do with it."

Her look indicates she understands this about me. She sighs and says, "Believe in health and prosperity and most of all that you're a good man, then watch what you do. People do what they believe. You may be surprised. Maybe those nightmares will go away."

She's probably making sense, but I'm still not able to read between the lines, where I assume the important stuff lies. It seems to me that to try to change my mind about something I've always believed is like telling Abigail, when she was taking drugs, to "just say no."

I see Greg Aamond, whom I jerked off with one night as we leaned against a cement retaining wall. The wall was next to the grade school we'd gone to up until a couple of years before. We talked that night about girls we'd known in that school, then decided it might be fun to see who could come the fastest.

Greg is in LA for a convention and calls me. He has some time on his hands and has gotten my number from a mutual friend. We meet at the bar at the Sportsmen's Lodge on Ventura Boulevard and Coldwater Canyon and sip Heinekens. We talk about old times, which we remember not as history or cautionary lessons to review and re-digest, but as personal myth and legend with the artificial wheel of colors that attaches to it.

He asks me what it's been like to be in show business. I say nothing that satisfies him *or* me. I can't do that any more than I could tell him the meaning of life. It's like everything else and nothing else—

Chapter Fourteen

as mundane and exhilarating as life. He tells me the bones of what he's doing now, renting trucks and hauling equipment. Maybe I'd care if it were about anything that I could *feel* in even the smallest way. But my God, his children come out sounding like they're truck frames or canned goods or a brand of cigarettes he gave up ten years ago. What we're doing is sitting in a saloon, talking about trivia that seemed to matter as we were living through it. But it doesn't anymore. Not to either of us. We are total strangers.

On top of that, he looks seventy years old! He has a right to age, but he doesn't have a right to look *this* old. He's decrepit. Worse, he's old—or atrophied—in spirit. He has no connection with the Greg Aamond whose father was one of the first Americans killed in North Korea, who was passionate about girls and sports, and with whom I spent a few casual minutes one evening at the age of thirteen, jerking off.

I think of Dixie Thorpe who broke his neck when he was nine and probably never got to jerk off once, let alone fall in love or hold his children or feel for a single second the grown-up joy of giving everything you possess to someone.

I am deeply ashamed of hurting the people I've hurt, and sorry for every second I've wasted crying over irrelevant losses and wishing I have things I don't need.

I wish I could lose my gift of hindsight.

The last time I see Goldie Hawn, it's three years after *Cactus Flower*. This is around the time she's stopped returning my calls. One day she answers the phone herself, instead of her prickly secretary.

When I suggest we get together, she tells me her friend Julie Christie is in town (it's shortly after they've done *Shampoo* together) and is going to be staying with her and she doesn't have any spare time.

I pout and she half-heartedly relents: "We'll probably play some tennis Thursday. I guess you could join us."

It's a brush-off. Anybody playing with a full deck would recognize it.

When I inevitably call her Thursday morning, her secretary says, "She's not here, Mr. Lenz." When I press her: "She may not be back for some time. She's got a houseguest. They're playing tennis this morning. I'm sorry, I can't tell you where."

But I *know* where—a well-kept clay court in the hills above Brentwood, hidden behind a grove of eucalyptus and Italian cypress trees. According to Goldie, it was once owned by Boris Karloff. Now, a small group of movie people, including Goldie, own and share use of it.

I experience rejection, humiliation, and rage, all of it curiously focused, like whatever's going on in the brains of the pod people in *Invasion of the Body Snatchers*. I shower, shave, put on fresh tennis whites, and lumber myself into a situation that, if it were food, I'd be able to smell it had gone bad and would have the common sense not to take a bite of it.

I don't care. It feels like everything I've ever worked for is at stake and I *cannot* let that go any further. It doesn't matter that this is the most suicidal act of my professional life. I'm angry with Goldie—and everyone who has *ever* aggrieved me. I understand such feelings have probably been snowballing into this "transference" or "displacement" (or whatever a shrink might decide to call my condition) since I was a child. But knowing that doesn't deter me. It's not a scene I'm proud of, but the truth is that although I wouldn't do it *today*, I no longer blame myself for doing it *then*.

I walk out onto the court, get a cold look from Goldie and an equally icy message from Julie. I don't have whatever it takes (such as balls) to turn around and walk away from this awful moment. Also, under severe pressure my small talk becomes desperately feeble. When I feel that happen, I try even harder which only makes me come off weaselly.

Chapter Fourteen

I play brisk tennis with two rich and famous movie stars who hit nothing but apathetic shots back at me.

For a few minutes, I feel avenged. I'm a better tennis player too.

Julie gives me about the same look she gave Rod Steiger in *Doctor Zhivago* as he was about to rape her.

The weasel mortification *really* sets in.

I go over to a gym I'm a member of, in Panorama City. If there were an unobstructed panorama in Panorama City, you couldn't see it without being in a tall building and there are no tall buildings in Panorama City, only miles of strip malls and "beach shack" houses poignantly far from the Pacific.

As I semi-jog around and around the carpeted indoor track, looking down at the weightlifters, treadmill-walkers, stairway-climbers, and a panorama of various other bodybuilders on their high-tech machinery, I think about a friend of mine. She knows me quite well and after she's heard something of my story, says, "You want to make sure you don't come off bitter."

Bitter? For some reason I didn't ask her *how* she thinks I'm coming off bitter, but I'm *shocked* that she thinks that.

Well, maybe not *entirely* shocked.

Still, considering all the ignorant things I've done, I've come out with so much good fortune it's crazy. Sure, there have been certain ... *moments*. But my friend has no conception how *not* bitter I am.

I feel a little fearful, the way I've always felt on airplanes, or like a memory I have of being on the IND subway, riding under the East River, and dark angels of amazing indifference are tinkering with the barrier that separates me from the crushing waters. I remember as a kid I stepped on a tack. My babysitter told me I should wash the wound *very* well or I might get lockjaw from the bacteria and never be able to eat again, and then I'd starve to death. I went into my room, crying, and mourned my passing for the rest of the evening. That's what I have to watch out for: that old devil bacteria.

I had a colleague and friend, Robert Moore, who died of an AIDS-related illness many years ago. He was a first-rate actor and later on he had great success as a director. His first directorial hit, the one that got the attention of Neil Simon and started Bob's deserved good run of stage and film jobs, was the stage version of *The Boys in the Band* by Mart Crowley. It was the first successful breakout play openly about homosexual men. It's a funny and heartbreaking—perhaps by now a little dated—but still moving story about eight gay men and one straight one who have all come together for a party. I ran into Bob in New York about six months after the play became a hit. He told me the actors in it had gotten a bit puffed up by their success. He said, "Now that bunch of old gypsies think they're the Moscow Art Theatre."

I thought of that line years later when I was auditioning for *The X-Files*. Especially as you get older, auditions gone awry are not always the actor's fault. A lot of times, the creators of a hit television show come to believe they're geniuses, when the truth is that they're surfers who *happen* to have caught the big wave. And then gradually, their distorted impressions of themselves begin to cause whatever artistic judgment they do have to turn south.

You didn't get the job, did you?

Sometimes, when I was a young auditioner, the adrenalin and youth of my attack masked my potluck of self-sabotages. Much later,

Chapter Fourteen

given the quality of most of the writing I was now asked—at my level—to try to breathe life into, I found it harder and harder to cover my anger, my displaced (or whatever) disdain for *them*. One time, I did a reading for a television show. I was standing at the end of a long conference table with five or six extremely Beverly Hills-ish execs sitting around it in blue jean overalls, designer T-shirts, that sort of thing. When I'd finished reading, I tossed the script down on the table. It made a sharp *thwap.*

I glanced briefly up at the executives and got a fleeting picture of the not-so-mixed message I'd just sent them. None of those Beverly Hills farmers had ever done anything to me. Who did I think I was punishing?

Them?

I guess it's just ... *possible* that it's not only my friend's sadness projected onto me when she says, "You want to make sure you don't come off bitter." I suppose it is *conceivable* that there's a *little* corner in me in which some bitterness that's not a reflection of hers—that's mine only—*has* survived, like a piece of food that doesn't get chopped up in the Cuisinart, a lump of anger I've always carried with me and never until now noticed, and that, if I'm not terrifically careful, I might end up choking on it.

CHAPTER FIFTEEN

I often wonder what celebrities are thinking. When I was a kid and Dwight D. Eisenhower was running for president, he came through Jackson. I remember seeing him from my child's perspective, far across Michigan Avenue on a dais in a little town park, speaking over a tinny loudspeaker system. I don't recall what he said. I certainly couldn't have made sense of it. I wonder if they took him to see the rocks that mark the birthplace of the Republican Party. Probably. They would have had to. He *was* a Republican. I wonder what he thought? Maybe: "Here I am, the Supreme Commander of the Allied Expeditionary Force, the guy who orchestrated D-Day, standing under a diseased elm tree on Washington Street in one of over three dozen towns and cities named after a general and president I never thought much of, saying hello to a bunch of rocks and pretending I think any of this means anything. Ain't life a funny old duck?"

Years later, I'm doing *A History of the American Film* by Christopher Durang at the Mark Taper Forum. We're doing the show in repertory with two other plays. One of them is *Angel City* by Sam Shepard. I'm in the back of the theatre one day, mouthing words, going over my lines, and I see Shepard off in a corner talking to a skinny guy with limp curly hair. I think my eyes have probably bugged out. The other guy is Bob Dylan.

I wonder what these famously standoffish artists are talking about. It could have to do with how much they hate celebrity. I know they both think it's silly. Maybe they secretly wish they worked in an air conditioner factory, all hunched over, operating screw guns, assembling the units I tried to sell in the Detroit ghetto. But that seems unlikely. I do know these artists love the common man—at least they don't hate him. I believe they save most of their hostility for guys in suits. And celebrities. They hate the whole idea of celebrity. But *they're* celebrities—especially Dylan. I'm sure they *think* they didn't ask for it—but *kind* of, they did. Are these guys close? I don't know. What *do* creative geniuses talk about with each other?

"I like that song you wrote about society being bullshit."

"Thanks, man. I loved your play about the pointless banality of life."

"Thanks. Want to come over to my place and have some peanut butter cups and ginger ale? We could watch a little *Green Acres*."

"Nah, I think I'd better go write a song."

"What are you going to write?"

"I'm calling it 'Fuck You'."

"What a coincidence, man. I'm writing a play about that."

Maybe Dylan is simply telling Shepard he can't hear the dialogue in *Angel City*. Or it could be Shepard is asking Dylan to write a new musical score for his play.

At one point, I hear something Dylan says. It sounds profound, like it has what Woody Allen calls "heaviosity." I'm still trying to remember the exact words.

One night when I'm first in Hollywood, I meet George Cukor, the brilliant "woman's director." He's widely known to be gay. Does

Chapter Fifteen

he think when he meets me, "Wouldn't it be fun to go all upside down with this attractive young man?"

Once, as a newbie in New York, a famous director, whose brilliantined hair capped his bird of prey face like a slick black helmet, had me come to his hotel. It was the final audition for a part in a play that was scheduled for a pre-Broadway tour. It was a pretty good role. But it turned out it wasn't my acting he was auditioning that evening. After the interview in the bar downstairs, he asked me if I'd mind coming up to his room to kiss him goodnight. I told him I had a pretty tight schedule and didn't think that would be possible. I may have added that I had a crushing headache and that perhaps it was the beginnings of the flu. Or cholera. I do remember I didn't want to burn any bridges by going "Eek" and running out of the bar.

One time I saw Johnny Carson in a restaurant in Malibu. He smiled at me as if he recognized me. I guessed that everybody smiled at *him* as if they recognized him, and after thirty-plus years of that, he'd just come to think that's how human beings relate.

I picture Bob Dylan on Jay Leno's show, or Oprah's: "You bet, Jay. I just adore fielding your oblivious questions." "Sure, Oprah, I do think my work is defined by my feminine side. Gosh, I'm in seventh heaven just thinking about it!"

He hops up on her sofa and jumps up and down ecstatically. "I just love this deconstructionism!"

The audience goes wild and demands a fleet of new Cadillacs.

I'm doing a major Disney film called *Scandalous John*. After I've signed for it, I have a meeting with Peter Bogdanovich. He's considering me for the role of Timothy Bottoms' mentally challenged brother in

The Last Picture Show, a part Timothy's real-life brother Sam will end up playing.

Peter tells me categorically not to do *Scandalous John*. He says it will wreck my career. That seems excessive. I don't ask him *how* it will wreck my career. Anyway, it's the romantic lead, I'm already contracted to do it and furthermore, he doesn't give me the role in *The Last Picture Show*.

Scandalous John flops—although it really isn't bad. We shoot it in South Dakota, New Mexico, Arizona, and at Fox Ranch in Malibu Canyon (California). The sets and cinematography are beautiful. Rod McKuen's score is better than the one he did for *The Prime of Miss Jean Brodie*. It's a lively modern retelling of *Don Quixote*, but it doesn't capture any imaginations in the sense of hoards of moviegoers deciding they ought to rush out to see it. It is a little too "Disney" around the edges, but the big problem is that the lead, capably played by Brian Keith, is supposed to be an eighty-year-old: a feisty codger who won't let land grabbers have his ranch, even though he can't keep up the payments. Brian is only fifty, and seeing it years later, I realize he looks like a burly stud wearing old man make-up in a bad community theatre production. The Disney people originally offered the part to Jimmy Stewart, but for reasons unknowable to me, they wouldn't pay him his price—which at the time was $750,000, peanuts by today's standards. I don't think it's unkind to call that decision poorly thought out.

Making *Scandalous John* is my favorite film experience. Alfonso Arau, the Mexican actor/director (he acted in *The Wild Bunch* and directed *Like Water for Chocolate*), has a lot of Zorba the Greek in him. He plays the Sancho Panza character. His wicked grin and sense of fun could easily lead some innocent young Alan Bates type down the road to ruin like the nefarious Fox and Cat do with Pinocchio. Hanging out with him, I learn to drink like a *borracho*. I was already coming along pretty well in that area of my well-roundedness.

Chapter Fifteen

One night—we've been drinking tequila for a little while, *quite* a little while—I say, "Alfonso, look at me."

He does, grinning, holding my gaze for a long time. Finally, he says, "Yes, Rick? Why are we doing this?"

"Sorry, I just wanted to see if there was something behind me you needed to *get* to. You know, the way some actors ... some ... some people do?" My tongue is too thick for my mouth. "The way they seem to look for some nameless ... *something*, right over your shoulder, that might save their lives ... if they could just ... *get* to it somehow?"

Alfonso thinks about this. His eyes light up. "I *know* the look!" he says. "It's the confusion and sadness you feel when you're on a high-speed train and all that scenery, everything you might want to look at, or touch or taste, vanishes before you have the chance to ... separate what you've *really* seen from all the other shouting in your brain. And you know *this* is your life and that you're on the track you always *wanted* to be on—except now it hits you like a ... *pedrusco* ... a giant rock—it's not taking you where you want to go."

One day before we begin filming, I'm rehearsing at the house of my leading lady, an insanely sexy young ingénue named Michele Carey. She gets a telephone call and whispers to me, "It's Frank."

She means Sinatra, whom she met and got involved with when she worked on a movie titled *Dirty Dingus McGee*.

They chat for a few seconds, then I hear her say *very* casually, "Oh, I'm with a friend. We're rehearsing." Pause. "Rick Lenz. He's playing my boyfriend. ... Sure, okay." She smiles mischievously at me and says, "Frank says hi."

My guess is Frank is not just communicating "hi" to me.

On our sixteenth wedding anniversary (May 15th, 1998) Linda is just leaving Valley College, where she's taking an Italian class. Passing the Grant High School football field, surrounded by a quarter-mile track and bleachers, she notices people jogging. Over the loudspeakers, Sinatra is singing "I've Got the World on a String." Linda tells me about it when she gets home. That is so cool—to do your workout in the open air, accompanied by the silky harmonies of Nelson Riddle and Old Blue Eyes.

Later, we hear Frank Sinatra had died earlier that day. It was still cool.

Brian Keith is an interesting man and a good natural film actor. He's kind to me and generous in the work, but there's something deeply sad about him. He will take his own life in 2004, which gives me a jolt, but isn't truly a surprise.

I see him starring in *Da* on Broadway several years after *Scandalous John*. In his dressing room afterward, he's happy I came back to say hello. But as we talk, I feel between the lines—even more than when we worked together—the black Irish sorrow in him. Later, Ann Stuart will prompt memories of Brian. They were not alike in any way but one: Neither of them could find a breathing way out of their grief.

Maybe reliving the past isn't entirely bad. Maybe the second time through, if you're not focusing so much on yourself, you may see things more clearly. Then at some later critical moment, you might be able to help somebody else, somebody who seems destined to get hurt, or to die too early, or simply to be lonelier than they ought to be.

I know what it was about Ann Stuart! She reminded me of Hollywood extras—waiting most of the time, off to the side, in a field, or

Chapter Fifteen

at the end of some idle back lot street where nothing is being accomplished; living their lives for scale, always in the unimportant place at the important time, superfluous, suggesting hopes and plans gone awry, dreams that never come true.

That's unkind to extras. The difference is that Ann couldn't go home at the end of the day's shooting. She couldn't escape. She was trapped on the sidelines forever with nothing to comfort her but a guaranteed spot in the checkout line at Rite Aid, waiting to pay for cigarettes and whatever brand of vodka was marked down that week.

Perhaps it's having seen Greg Aamond, I'm not sure, but I find myself thinking I'm the worst company Linda could possibly have right now and that I *must* change that, so I tell her I'm going to get out of the house for a couple of days. It looks like tears are about to form. I head them off by telling her everything's fine, that I'm just working on something that's going to take all my concentration and that I'll call her.

"Have you gone *insane*?" She's raised her voice.

"Listen," I say as soothingly as I know how, "I realize it may sound a little nuts, but I've got this idea that I can work some things out if I can just be by myself for a day or two. It doesn't have anything to do with *us*, I promise. It's something I need to do on my own." She stares at me as if she's thinking about something that has nothing at all to do with me. "Honey, this feels *really* important. Maybe it's Debby, I don't know—but it feels like I've *got* to do it. You'll be glad I did. I *know* you will."

She turns and starts to walk away. As I move around to intercept her, she stops and looks up at me.

She closes her eyes and I feel lost, shut out. I want to know what she's thinking, but I don't ask.

Finally, she whispers, "Go."

Trying not to notice how softly she's said it, I tell her, "It won't be long. I promise. I'll call you. We'll talk in a little while. I promise." I head for the door.

"If I'm still here."

You know you're being an asshole.

Well, duh!

I turn them and my cell phone off.

CHAPTER SIXTEEN

I've noticed this hotel once before. It's downtown. No one will ever try to gentrify this one. I've picked it because it reminds me of my first place in New York. The room they give me on the fourth floor exhales ammonia and room fresheners futilely employed to mute the lingering vapor trail left by a few thousand former residents. Its gray walls need painting—after they're re-plastered. The old single metal-frame bed wants a new mattress and box springs so badly it moans in pain when I sit on it. The sink needs a new faucet *and* a new sink. The whole bathroom, about five-by-seven with a tiny bathtub, needs to be re-plumbed.

Another fine selling point is the view: urban desolation—exactly what I want right now. I'll think better here.

I turn on my cell phone. Two messages. Both from Linda. I'll call her soon.

I think about my therapist, Susan, whom I have nothing—*almost nothing*—but the kindest thoughts about. Shortly after she quit her practice, she moved to Santa Fe, where she's become an artist (oil paintings—I Googled her. She's amazingly good). I never actually knew much about her—one of the precepts of therapy is that you're supposed to know as little as possible about the personal life of the therapist. I've spent a lot of time wondering anyway. I still think of her as my *good* mother, even though I haven't seen her in ten years—since I decided I was *cured*.

Oh, you're a model of mental stability now, living in what might as well be a set from Blade Runner.

Ever since Susan moved away from LA, I've kept her number in my wallet, in case of emergency. She told me I could call her if I ever felt the need. Even though I have no specific purpose in mind, it can't hurt to check in.

I dial the number and she answers on the fourth ring. I tell her who I am and she seems pleased. There's something like warmth in her voice.

"I'm fine," I respond to her first question.

There's silence as the burden of being the one who has to initiate this hits me. "I called because I'm … I mean even though I'm doing okay, I've got some things that …" This is *exactly* the conversation we had when I began therapy with her. "Well, maybe not *quite* okay."

I give her a summary of what I'm doing, what my family's doing—including the fact that Debby is terribly sick and Abigail's in rehab and maybe on the right track for the moment. I tell her I'm reviewing my life, that I haven't suddenly gone schizoid, and that I'm not taking drugs or drinking.

"Where are you?"

"Downtown LA. I don't know the name of the place. I'm not sure it has one. There's just a sign that says 'Hotel.'"

"This sounds like old behavior."

I remember why I quit! It's the *jargon*. Words become mysteriously infected. "That's the point," I say. "I've got the feeling if I can live

Chapter Sixteen

through this—and please don't tell me I'm acting out—if I can live through this one more time, sort of almost ritually if you know what I mean, and do it as a grown-up ..." She sighs (not a good sign). "If I can do *that*, I can finally get rid of this ghost that never really went away."

"Which ghost would that be?"

I try a different tack. "Mostly, I'm trying to understand my reason to *be*. I've read a few spiritual books in the last couple of years. And I believe I'm a positive contributor to the world." I sound like a bad talk show. I've unscrewed the cap of the fifth of Gordon's gin I brought with me. I take a swallow directly from the bottle. "I mean I do my best ... I've done what I can for Abigail. I can't change the course of what Debby's going through."

"I still don't know what this is about."

"Neither do I ... exactly." I know from the time I spent with her in person that I'm dipping into some madness here, and that it's time to finesse my way into what I need to say. I start more measuredly: "Listen, I was watching television a couple of nights ago. I saw a program on the homeless poor in New Orleans—Jonathan Demme directed it. Then, after that show there was a young woman, not a line in her face—this was on PBS, I think, both these shows were. This woman had just written a book about China and India—not just China or not just India, but both goddam places. I learned from her that they graduate several more million people from college every year than we do in this country and probably every one of them knows more about the world I live in than *I* do ... Are you there?"

"Yes, I am."

"And what do *I actually know*? I know a little about *Law and Order* and for God's sake, *The Love Boat*. And I'm talking about most of my life!" More hushed breathing from her end. "I'm sorta wandering here. See, the thing is, I'm trying to decide what I ought to do with the rest of my, *you* know … existence. I mean it's still my *life*. It ought to be worth *something*!"

"Of *course* it is."

Oh, good! Thanks for that. I'm a well man now.

"What about Linda? What does she think about this?"

"She's tired of my jokes and my funny faces. I'm not so sure she wouldn't be better off without me—once she got used to it."

A pause, more breathing, louder now, and she says, "What do you expect me to say to all this?"

"I don't know. Whatever occurs to you. I'd especially like it to be something that answers all the questions I need answered, like why should I go on … the way I've been going. Do you remember my snake dreams?" Her silence tells me she's heard lots of snake dreams in her time and can't place mine at the moment. "Well, anyway …"

"I can give you the names of some good people there in LA."

"I don't WANT to go into a new therapy! I just want you to give me some simple answers and then I'll be okay. Yes! Linda loves me. I *know* that. But Linda loves most people. She's like that. She has simple answers. Wouldn't it be better if she had someone to love who was capable of loving her back in a nice honest way that *meant* something—the way she deserves? I mean, if I *really* love her, isn't that what I would wish for her?" Silence. "Listen, I just want to vanquish some demons." *That* feels right, as if maybe I'm finally starting to get a bead on what I need to tell myself. "Or maybe all of this is because *this* moment, right now, *today*, is the last time I'll ever get to do this! *I mean I cannot come back here again! I* KNOW *that!*"

There's another silence on her end before I realize my phone has gone dead. I forgot to charge the battery before I came downtown. I plug it in and watch it for a while, wondering if Susan has Star 69 on her phone.

Chapter Sixteen

My phone doesn't ring.

I ponder this for an indefinite length of time, then I *don't* call her back. I don't want any more help today. Also, I think I've only made a limited jackass out of myself so far; I'd like to leave it at that. I think about "egocentric predicaments," one of which Susan used to tell me I'd managed to trap myself in for most of my life. "It's not being able to view reality outside of your own perception," she'd said. I also remember her telling me about the other side of that, the optimistic side: *The universe I live in is of my own making.* So why not make a nicer one?

For a few moments, I actually feel better. When I leave here, my feet will carry me away—not because they decide to, but because I give them that direction. So it is with everything I do, the direction I give the rest of me will make it happen—if I let it. All I have to do is award myself better guidance. Simple. I'm dealing with two parts of myself: the part that's used to getting what it thinks it wants (the habit part), and the part that knows better. The first part is like an old worn-out skin that I've been tripping over for longer than I can remember, the second part is simply developing some new behavior and choosing ... *freedom*. Which one do I pick? Duh.

I look around me at my current universe, at this awful place, and rephrase to myself the last thing I said to Susan—the only words from this session that stand out:

I Cannot Come Back Here Again. This is the last time.

Who says?

However, for now, I direct myself to do what I've always done, because ... it's there. I have a few more shots of gin. Relief mutes anxiety and I've *sort* of escaped.

Of course, in the end, where I've escaped *to* is the center of a city most famous for its lunacy, as a place you escape *from*—e.g. *Them, Night of the Comet, Earthquake, Miracle Mile, Escape From L.A.* The most common line in movies is, according to the first edition of Trivial Pursuit, "Let's get out of here." It must be the most common line said in LA. But when you're young and dumb and living in Jackson, Michigan, you don't have any way of knowing that—neatly camouflaged as LA is, under 451 square miles of glowing, glimmering, gleaming glamour, Gladys.

My mother's house features a white living room we can't go into. It's the biggest room we have, but it's for company. You can eat off the floor of my mother's big white living room. I once fumble with a girlfriend's bra and panties and make serious contact while on the big white couch next to the big white fireplace in the big white living room, and I think it leaves scars on me. It's the first time a girl has ever given me permission to go that far, but I suddenly break off my slick seduction and say, "No, I respect you too much," or something equally silly. The truth is the thought of making a mess in the big white room gives me an adrenalin attack and my pulse races. That room connects with my light comedy mandate—not too serious, not too risky. Sometimes it pretends to get near the edge of the rabbit hole, to become messy, but it doesn't *really*. It never takes the chance of killing the neat, obligatory happy ending where Bing Crosby is home from the war for Christmas, just as he promised.

But Christmas *and everything else* had *better be white*. I hear a voice that sounds like Maximilian Schell's in *Judgment at Nuremberg*: "You *vill* be home for Christmas! You *vill* put your poops in ze potty, or zer vill be *conzequenses*! Undt *ezpecially*, you vill *not* get bodily fluids on ze vite couch."

Chapter Sixteen

It goes without saying, light comedy has to be funny. In the words of Abe Burrows, the brilliant playwright and wit of the nineteen forties through sixties, "Everything does not have to end with a joke. But a joke has to end with a joke. It's a rule."

He did not, however, include anything about whiteness in his rule. In fact, logic is more and more telling me, the less whiteness a joke has, the better its chances of ending funny.

That doesn't mean a good joke can't be light or … *puffy* maybe. I think puffy would be all right. Maybe even dark. But white—not so good.

Little nap.

When I do *The Shootist*, I'm on the set one day when Jimmy Stewart is working. He talks to me for a few minutes and I tell him that a lot of my reviews have mentioned his name. He frowns. "That's no good," he says. I tell him, "I know that. I can't help it that I look … *somewhat* like you." I quickly add, "It could be a lot worse … *You* know … I mean, someone less committed to excellence." I guess I want to please him. He *is* Jimmy Stewart and I'd like him to like me.

He gives me a sad smile. I remember hearing that he suffers from depression and I panic for a second, thinking maybe I'm bringing him down. Or maybe he's going to tell me to just go away, that I'm sounding like a fan and I've already taken up too much of his valuable time.

He says, "Just keep doing what you're doing"—he shrugs—"always your best, and you'll be fine."

He smiles again, moves off in the direction of his trailer, and it occurs to me there's not a lot I can actually *do* with advice like that. I remember he was a bomber pilot during World War II. He flew twenty missions over Germany. Imagine that—getting your neighborhood blown to smithereens by Jimmy Stewart.

Mr. Smithereens goes to Germany.

I smell lilacs.

Not everything can be comic. I think of a moment in *Joanna's Husband and David's Wife* that always brought tears to my eyes. This was on stage at the Pasadena Playhouse. Betsy (Elizabeth Forsythe) Hailey was the playwright. Joanna has left David and he's remembering a place they'd lived in together—specifically he sees an upswelling of morning glories in the ivy outside the house. The story is actually about Betsy and her playwright husband Oliver—both dear friends—and the writing of Betsy's first novel, *A Woman of Independent Means*. I played Oliver and their daughter, Kendall, played Betsy.

I've had a lot to do with the Hailey family. I do staged readings of two other Hailey plays, *The World and His Wife,* by Oliver, opposite Kres Mersky, and *Home on the Range,* by daughter Brooke, opposite Lily Tomlin. This one affects me, as I work on it, almost as much as *Joanna and David*—it was written not long after Oliver's death.

I smell lilacs again, a scent I associate with Linda (she carried a bouquet of them the day we were married) and now I turn to look for her. But in the gin-soaked time it takes to feel the pinch of a frown I realize I've stuffed one of her scarves into my jacket pocket and that *that's* the agitator of this un-nameable longing I'm feeling.

I study myself in the mirror. I remember applying age makeup to this face when it was younger. Now, I don't need it. Now, I barely recognize this face.

Chapter Sixteen

There *is* intelligence in these rheumy eyes. The wisest of all Shakespeare's characters is Prospero in *The Tempest*—an old man. Authorities agree that Shakespeare himself is the character of Prospero. (Actor tries to firm up wobbly neck skin, can't figure out how to engineer it and gives up.) A player has to look ahead—*not too far!* When time takes away the beauty of youth, he has to recognize that and be prepared. He has to concentrate on character-actor skills. The number of juveniles and ingénues who had their fifteen minutes and were then tossed into the garbage is staggering. Think of Howdy Doody, Charlie McCarthy, Mortimer Snerd, Lamb Chop—all cut down in their prime because they couldn't do character work.

Aside from needing something to eat, I realize I'm out of gin, so I go down to the nearest liquor store, buy another fifth of Gordon's, a loaf of rye bread, a jar of Skippy peanut butter, and some Cokes. No one gives me even a curious glance. I come directly back to my monk's garret. Being alone promotes spiritual growth; it's clear that's what I need. Of course, who's going to know about my spiritual growth if there's nobody here to see it?

I splash cold water on my face from the filthy sink in the filthy bathroom and drench my shirt and pants, too. Water drips into my shoes.

Slathering peanut butter onto rye bread with the handle of my toothbrush, I remember that I've already learned what I came here to learn. I just can't *quite recall* what it is. I don't think it was anything ... exactly ... *spiritual*.

Sometime later—after dark—there's a knocking at the door. It's some drunk, hollering for Maury. I say, "There's no Maury here."

"What are you doing in Maury's room?"

"It's not Maury's room. It's *my* room."

There's a long pause and he says, "What's your name?" I don't want to answer him, but he insists. He raises his voice: "Hey, buddy! What's your name?"

"I don't know." And now, under the pressure of his third degree, I'm not kidding. "I honestly can't think of it." It occurs to me that being alone, but not knowing who you are—because you're stupefied—can't possibly enhance your soul. I am thrilled at this insight; it even sobers me up a little, but I still can't remember my name and I say through the door to Maury's pal: "I knew it when I got up this morning."

His tone suddenly becomes friendly: "That's okay, buddy. It'll come back to you. Happens to me all the time. Just get yourself some sleep and you'll remember. Hey, buddy! 'We are such stuff as dreams are made on,' okay, buddy?"

Wondering briefly if he may be right, that I actually *am* Maury, I hear his footsteps recede down the hall.

Off in the secret distance, I hear a door being unlocked.

CHAPTER SEVENTEEN

I wake up with the old post-binge guilt, the kind that makes you want to crawl under something and hope you'll evaporate or be sucked up out of the universe. But neither of these things happens. Everything continues to function according to the laws of science, and unlike my father and my sons, I was never very good at that. Someone—I can't remember who—said, "Life should be mystical and glorious, but living is a science."

I drink a Coke. It has caffeine in it—which infuses my blood with adrenaline, giving me a temporary boost. Science.

I turn on the television. They're talking about celebrity. High-minded journalists denounce the whole notion—even as it's providing them a lavish living. Someone is talking about all those red-blooded American men nearly breaking their necks to get their names on the birth certificate of Anna Nicole Smith's daughter, of whose money and fame they were—"there's no other word for it," says one of the talking heads—"jealous." "They fantasize having Swiss bank accounts and being on TV," says the pundit. "John Hinkley shot President

Reagan so he could be famous and impress Jody Foster. The fact is, they're all stuck in their own egocentric predicaments; all of them solipsists, stuck in their conviction that only they and the gods of their idolatry exist."

So what does that prove? This show is no different than the phenomenon it's discussing. Pretty soon—if they aren't already—these talking heads will feel like stars too. We're hardwired to recognize celebrities as our family or friends, or both. Our cerebral mechanism knows better. That piece of our brain tells us, "*C'mahnnn*, don't be stupid! That man is no more than another random television personality with a hairstyle as hard as stucco." But the most inward part of our thinking apparatus—the bit that lies at the base of our skull: the cerebellum, right behind our ears—the chunk of our brain that helps us out with the *real* stuff, like not falling down—that "lizard" part—responds, "Unh-unnhh!! That's m' buddy ... or else, maybe m' daddy or m' brother—I don't care. All I *know*—all I gotta know—is that dude has deep meaning for me!"

Celebrity (the concept)—the down side (for the celebrity):

When our friend Dian Parkinson was on *The Price Is Right*, she got an enormous volume of mail, for a while even more than Bob Barker. It's a good thing to get mail (though maybe not more than the star). It means you're valuable to the show. The bad news for Dian was that, as a former beauty queen—and never mind that, a beauty—she was the one her bosses most often dressed in scanty costumes and because of that and her open, friendly personality, she drew the attention of the most crazies. She received a bewildering number of death threats.

I ask her why being gracious and exceptionally pretty should inspire people to want to kill someone.

Chapter Seventeen

"Sometimes it was because I wouldn't have their baby."

"Huh?"

"A lot of these men are literally crazy—institutional crazy. They have lots of time to watch daytime television. They fixate on the performers. Sometimes two guys in the same place will fixate on the same woman—especially if she's wearing swimming suits all the time. They get competitive. They both want her, but they realize they can't both have her." Dian scowls as if she's bitten into chocolate and found out it's bitter. "Then these guys realize that a *lot* of people want the 'pretty girl.' They've gone through their whole lives being shut out. They're outsiders. Not being able to have the pretty girl makes them angry. Then after a while, they get *really* angry. And the anger takes all kinds of forms."

Her gaze wanders away and she shudders.

"Like what?" I ask.

She looks at me with a rueful smile. "I got two dozen roses two or three times a day for a year and a half."

"That doesn't sound so bad."

"I didn't mind the roses. I gave them away. It's just that the notes that came with them got nuttier and nuttier. I told the *Price* people it was making me nervous, but they didn't know what to do. The notes weren't crazy enough to call the police." Her mind jumps to a parallel track: "I had a lot to do with the police and the FBI in those years. Once they had a twenty-four-hour watch on my house for four months in a row." Dian often talks about all the subheadings of a subject at the same time. "One time a guy smashed through the heavy glass doors at CBS with a sledgehammer, announced 'It's time to kill Dian' and came marching right toward our studio."

"What happened?"

"They caught him. Stopped him. Beat him up, probably. I don't know." She shudders again. "I think he went to jail for six months.

When he got out, he came after me again." She spreads her arms in a big shrug. "They put him in jail again. I saw all kinds of notes and placards during those years: 'You're going to have my baby, nobody else's. If you don't have my baby, I'll kill you.' Or sometimes it was just a simple announcement from some other part of the country in the mail: 'I'm on my way to kill you.'"

"What happened to the guy with the roses?" I say, but her mind goes where it goes.

"After Rebecca Schaeffer, the girl who was on *My Sister Sam* with Pam Dawber—after she got murdered right in her own doorway, I realized the same thing could have happened to me."

"Jesus!"

"The guy who did that—who killed her—got her address by going to the DMV and giving them some story about a traffic accident that involved her car and they gave him that poor girl's address." She shakes her head. "They've changed the law since then, but it was too late for her."

"And you were saying—about yourself?"

"Well, a few months before that, some guy had come to *my* door and said, 'Do you have a yellow Mercedes 450 SL?' I told him yes I did, and he said, 'You hit my car.' I told him 'I haven't been in any accidents.' He said, 'Can I see your car?' I said, 'Sure' and opened my door to him—idiot—and went to get my keys.

"The very *second* I got back into the room, I immediately knew this was all wrong. He had that … *look*." Her gaze skips away from mine as she recalls it. "He was staring at my … at my chest. And the look in his eyes was all lost and wrong, but sort of purposeful in a nasty way."

"What happened?"

"Both of us suddenly felt Sunshine on the stair landing."

Chapter Seventeen

Sunshine was Dian's Doberman and according to Dian, a particularly good-natured dog, who genuinely liked people—but not this time.

"I'd never seen that look in Sunshine's eyes before," she says. "She was standing tall and very ... I don't know, *ready*. Her ears were straight up and she was ... bigger somehow and very, very still, and focused on this man. And the man said, 'Is it friendly?' And I said, 'No, *it's* not. It's attack-trained.'" She sees the glued-to-her-story look on my face and takes a deep breath. "Well, the guy backed out very slowly, never taking his eyes off Sunshine. And Sunshine kept her eyes on him." Dian's whole upper body drops, the reawakened moment over. "And then I went and locked the door. And I ran up to Sunshine. I was half-hysterical and crying and I hugged her and I told her she was the best girl in the whole world. And she *was*."

And that's saying something. Nobody loves her dogs better than Dian, and she's had *a lot* of dogs and more than one has helped her out in moments of crisis.

"I found out later he'd gotten my address from the DMV. Just like Rebecca Schaeffer. The name and address he'd left them—for himself, so he could get the information on me—was fictional." She stares at me. "He was simply *after* me."

Finally, I say, "What about the man with the roses?"

She frowns. "Yeah. Well, one day this guy showed up at the studio and I was right there and he had a lot of roses. And I asked him, 'Are these for me—from the guy with the roses?' And he said, '*I'm the guy.*' And then I saw he had the same *look* in his eyes." She seems to stare right through me.

"Well, what *happened*?" She's still lost in the memory. "*Dian?*"

Now, she drags her gaze back into focus as if she's being forced and shrugs minutely. "Oh, they ran in and got him. Somebody realized this guy had gotten through. They put him away and I never heard from that one again ... I guess he found somebody else to ... think about." She hiccups, then smiles. "Excuse me. Imagine—you remember people wanting to kill you and it gives you the hiccups. Isn't that silly?"

"But you're not in that world anymore."

"Right. They used to write things like, 'You belong to me. You're mine. If I can't have you, I'll kill you.'"

"That's all behind you now."

"Sure."

One of the remarkable things about Dian is that she's still open and friendly, even with strangers.

I read some articles on celebrity. One quoted a Hollywood publicist as saying, "There are worse things."

Dian would probably find that debatable.

Down on the street, people are moving without much seeming enthusiasm toward their destinations, in most cases home, I imagine. I see a fat lady on the corner, sorting through some papers. A child stands nearby, gazing up—it looks like—at me. It's a warm day. Hardly anyone is wearing a coat.

Afternoon sunshine floods the street, the rosy smog-sifted light playing off the pavement and the parked and passing cars. There's life down there, unquestionable life—warm, sunshiny, coatless. The people may look subdued, even indifferent, but the whole scene has one tremendous virtue for most of them: It is life. The sun will shift in a moment and the picture will too. But the life will remain. And where there's life—for most people—enthusiasm can strike at any second.

I think about my mother—which I don't do much anymore. I know she didn't know how to stop herself from punishing ... *someone*.

Chapter Seventeen

I know that peace is the best policy; that you don't want to spend your last years in a fog of resentment. And honestly, I *can't* think of any vicious thing Virginia did that I haven't obsessed about and forgiven her for over and over. The only things about her that still haunt me have to do with Debby.

I even have good memories of her. I can still see the look of worry in her eyes as my father sutured my forehead after the Nelson twins chased me into the basement door.

Maybe I should have just forgiven her once. And *believed* it.

Once, when I was a teenager, she and I were driving somewhere on the south side of Jackson. It was an area that was being redeveloped—new roads and new construction. Everyone was confused, drivers most of all. We saw a car on the other side of the divider lose control. It could have been that the driver became disoriented by the changes in the landscape. Maybe he'd been drinking or had had a seizure—anything. The car had been going too fast and it ran off the road, skidded, flipped around twice and then stopped, the front end up on a pile of sewer pipes, wheels spinning lazily.

Virginia looked as if she'd had a heart attack. She pulled over, breathless. It was clear she was terrified. The terror came from some part of her I was not familiar with.

Finally, two people climbed out of the front of the runaway car. They walked around slowly, obviously dazed, but they seemed okay. A police car pulled up. In the distance we heard an ambulance siren.

I stared at my mother. After awhile, looking straight ahead, she whispered, "I thought we were going to die."

"You mean *them*."

"No," she said, "I mean *we*."

My God! She'd included *me*! She leaned over and hugged me as hard as she could. Her cheek was wet with tears that were for *me* as well as her. Here was a soft, compassionate part of her I'd never seen in my life. It was momentous!

Shortly after I started working on stage in and around New York, I decided to audition for the Actors Studio. At about the same time, I was invited to join the playwrights' unit of the Studio, and was allowed to work in either the East or West coast branches in any capacity—including acting—which I did, so I didn't see the point, I told myself, of going through the arduous actor's auditioning process (Harvey Keitel did it eleven times before he got in). I probably should have; I might have found a solution in advance to my years of auditioning yips.

"The Method" always baffled me. If I break "the work" down into handy capsules or Stella Adler's "common language of the theatre," I get all stiff and left-brained. Besides, when I was working at the Studio, there was too much screaming testosterone for the whole process to be of value in nurturing creativity, at least in me. The teaching was impenetrable and curiously pedantic. It's nearly impossible to teach acting anyway.

That doesn't mean there aren't brilliant teachers out there—Milton Katselas is gone, but Joan Darling (my favorite "acting" teacher) still works at it. There are lots more who are excellent: Jon Korkes, Robert F. Lyons, and my old teacher Michael Howard, who said, "It's not about being natural, it's about truth."

But most of the time, it's like the guy in the fourth grade who ran faster than all the other kids. He was simply born *fast*. He had a gift. You can develop the gift for acting by learning specific craft things like, for example, how to sit down as if you've had some experience

Chapter Seventeen

with chairs, and by hard work. An angel of a teacher/director at the University of Michigan, Claribel Baird, once told me, "Instinct isn't enough, Ricky."

There *are* principles—like discovering how to really concentrate, learning not to "act the result," actually listening to the other actors instead of collapsing into the thousand forms of not listening, understanding and accepting that the reservoirs of human feeling run so mysterious and deep that very often there is no applying words to them—and a few dozen other basics. But after you learn these things, the main thing still is: Can you run fast?

You can't run at ALL—not anymore.

So what am I doing here?

You overheard what the singer said to the playwright.

Did I? And what was that, please?

"It frightens me, the awful truth of how sweet life can be." —Bob Dylan

And now I hear the poet *sing* it in that way that only he can, and *this time* it feels as if it gains the tiniest foothold in the back of my brain.

CHAPTER EIGHTEEN

I'm doing a movie called *The Little Dragons*. I'm the father of an eight-year-old girl who's going to a karate camp. My wife is played by Sharon (Weber) Clark (*The Billion Dollar Hobo* and *Lifeguard*; she was also a Playmate of the Year quite a few years ago). Witty, mordant, frighteningly overweight Ann Sothern is also in the film, although I don't have any scenes with her.

For me, the best things about this job are Charles Lane, and Curtis Hanson, who will later "helm" (as they say in *The Hollywood Reporter*) *L.A. Confidential*. He's one of the brightest and nicest directors I've ever worked with. Charlie, who's been a character man in Hollywood forever, will eventually be honored at *age one hundred* for his significant contributions as an actor. One of his many memorable roles was the bank examiner in *It's a Wonderful Life*.

One day he tells me about his first job. It was 1936 and he was working for Frank Capra in *Mr. Deeds Goes to Town*. Charlie was a stage actor just in from New York. His first scene was with Gary Cooper. The following day, Capra asked him if he'd like to see the dailies. Charlie said sure and Capra ran them for him.

"The first shot was on Cooper," says Charlie. "He was … well, Gary Cooper. Just doing what he always did. You'd hardly know he was acting at all."

The next angle was the matching shot on Charlie. Looking disgusted and amused, he tells me, "And there I was, a spastic monkey, acting my little heart out."

"It couldn't have been that bad."

"Yes, it was," he says in his signature barky tones.

"What'd Capra say?"

"He patted me on the shoulder and said, 'Don't worry, Charlie, I'll re-shoot it tomorrow.'"

"I've got a few things I wish I could re-shoot," I say.

He shows a dry, smirky smile. "You get very few second chances. Unless you're some kind of a lucky sonofabitch, take one is all you get."

But Charlie Lane *was* that lucky. He lived vigorously and fully compos mentis to more than a hundred—and at least that one time along the way, he got a second chance.

I must have left my cell phone on when I plugged it in because I'm hearing a tinny version of Bach's Concerto in D Minor for harpsichord. Scott programmed it in for me.

I open the phone, say hello, and hear Linda: "Didn't you get my messages?"

"No, no, I've been … busy."

"Where are you? You said you'd call."

She sounds as if she's been crying, and I can almost see the look in her eyes when she talks about Grace or one of the kids when they're in trouble. "I was just about to."

"Where *are* you?"

Chapter Eighteen

"Downtown."

"Why are you doing this?"

I have no sensible answer. "Is Abi okay?"

"What? *What?*"

"Sorry. She just flitted through my mind."

I remember Abigail telling me about being by herself when she was doing crack—the paranoid delusions, the hallucinations. "A whole different world is produced," she told me. "Then, I *know* people are outside—talking about me: cops, enemies, drug enforcers, monsters I haven't seen since my kid nightmares. My friends are out there … my family. But now *they're* monsters, too. And they can see through my windows. They're gathered together, whispering about their plans to … 'save me.'"

"I'm okay," I say to Linda.

"Ask me how *I* am."

Abi told me she loves being high. "I love the … *ceremony,*" she said. "Getting the gear together. I love that. I love the people. They're *alive*! Jesus, maybe they're stupid sometimes but they're *interesting*! It's a fascinating, exciting world."

"I know," I say to Linda. "I'm sorry."

"Abigail's in rehab," she says. "She's safe. *I* don't feel so safe right now."

"I understand. I am sorry."

"And even though I know I have to get sober to survive," said Abigail—it's burned into my memory—"what I *really* want is that crazy life that kills me!"

To Linda: "I've had a little—" I start to say "slip," but stop myself and tell her: "I'm sorry I didn't call you. I really am. Honey? Are you there?"

"I'm going to drive up and see my mother. She's not feeling well."

"I'm coming home," I tell her, as if this bit of magnanimity answers anything.

"Don't forget to feed Dash," she says.

"Okay. How long will you be?"

"I don't know."

"Can't you wait till I get there before you go?"

"I don't think so," she says. "I'll call you tonight—at home. You *will* be there?"

"Yes." I tell her. "Yes, I will be there."

I haven't given enough space to Dash the Wonder Dog, and he must be documented. He's our eight-year-old standard poodle and he's not a dog; he's a black, curly-haired mind reader who knows what you're about to do, and also what you want, before you know you want it. He has a bagful of tricks: plays the piano, fetches the toilet paper, and more. He's patient with kids and other dogs, but he's not a wuss either. If a big dog attacks him, he's a warrior. But mostly, he's a lover. If either of us is sick in bed, he periodically checks on us, burrowing his head into our nearest parts, offering solemn affection. He's the lovechild we never had.

Checking out of my hotel, nobody says come back real soon. Outside, the winds are swirling. Catalina Eddy is running head-on into Offshore Flo and an edgy vitality grips the LA Basin.

Transferring from the Glendale Freeway to the Golden State, on my way back to North Hollywood, I notice my gas tank is nearly empty, so I get off at Los Feliz and head east toward the nearest station. As I'm filling up with unleaded that costs per gallon what I can remember paying for a week's groceries, I notice a Fifties-style coffee shop called Eatz next to the Los Feliz public golf course. I've been here before and

Chapter Eighteen

I could use a wake-up cup, so I stop in and order it, along with eggs, bacon, and a side of pancakes.

The waitress serving me from behind the polished Formica-and-chrome counter regards me with mild curiosity. As I'm finishing up my breakfast, she says in a husky voice, "Like another cup, honey?" I'd guess she's in her early fifties, her once-blonde hair gone steely gray and pulled back into a droopy ponytail, her face deeply creased, especially around the eyes and lips, from a lifetime of cigarettes.

I smile and nod. She pours it and says, "Used to be on TV, huh?"

I feel as if I've been given a loving pat by somebody whose face I recognize as an old friend.

"Still do it?'

"Not lately." I feel like I'm letting her down. "I've got something coming up, though."

Her eyebrows go up as she makes a crinkly smile. "Oh, yeah? What?"

It just pops out of my mouth: "I'm doing *Man of La Mancha*—on stage."

"Really? Where?"

My brain is still a little fuzzy. I can't think of the name of a single grungy, obscure theatre. "Downtown," I say. "At the Music Center."

"What are you playing?"

"Don Quixote," I tell her. She frowns. "You know—to dream the impossible dream?"

"No offense," she says. "But aren't you just a *little* old?"

"Don Quixote *is* old. And wise."

She smiles again and nods. She seems pleased I stopped in today. Even if I am a big fat liar.

When I get home, Linda's Mazda Protege is in the driveway. She hasn't left yet. She's in the kitchen, cleaning the stove.

"Sorry," I say for a greeting.

She looks at some point a foot away from my eyes, taking me into peripheral consideration, not smiling, then returns to her work. "Your sister called."

"What did she say?"

"You'd better call them. Frank will tell you. Debby sounded weak and put Frank on."

"She's fine. I *know* she is! Debby has a life force I don't think even she's aware of!"

She stares at me. "Will power doesn't cure cancer."

"It's not a matter of will power. It's something deeper and I don't know if it's learned or if you're born with it. It's an infinite, unshakeable faith in the value of life. I'm *sure* Debby has that."

She gazes at me several seconds longer, her look softening, then goes back to her work.

I phone Arizona and Debby's husband Frank tells me they've determined Debby has stage III ovarian cancer and that they couldn't get all of it during the exploratory surgery. It feels as if all of the blood has drained out of my head. When I ask him if it's metastasized, he tells me they don't know, but they've already set her up for six chemotherapy treatments, three weeks apart, in Phoenix, starting in a couple of weeks.

I remember a time Sarah and I were in my folks' house. We had the boys, who were still toddlers, with us. My mother and father and I were all on the winterized porch, drinking. Sarah was sober and not a part of the family psychosis, except as reluctant witness.

Chapter Eighteen

Hoping, in the bonhomie of the moment, to unearth some kind of long-lasting solace, a bit of truth and understanding, I *humorously*—and I have no idea what I really had in mind—brought up the time my mother had beaten me with a cane for putting scuff marks on her new recreation room floor, steadily whacking me on the back and shoulders as I cleaned up the shoe smudges from something my friends and I called knee football. I was about twelve. My mother claimed to have no memory of the incident and her retaliatory fever blew through the top. She told me I was a spiteful liar and I yelled something equally useful back at her.

Debby was fourteen. Awhile earlier, I'd been aware of her hovering in the kitchen, within hearing range. Now, I looked out the porch window and saw into her bedroom, across a corner of the backyard. She was watching us, looking like someone staring at a highway accident, but from behind the white gauze curtains in the nearest window of her bedroom. I could make out that she was sobbing and I knew she was crying for me, for herself, for all of us. I have always felt exactly the same about her and now the thought of her suffering feels like a frozen sword stabbed up my spinal column.

As Frank's and my phone conversation runs down, I tell him she's going to get through this and be radiantly healthy before we know it.

But I don't think it helps. He puts Debby on. She sounds frail and scared and tells me she doesn't want to die.

I say with every bit of passion I can summon that she's not going to, that she's going to get well.

Linda and I get into an argument over my recent conduct. I'm at a disadvantage: She's right and I'm wrong.

What makes me crazy, though, is that she acts as if she doesn't have her own piece in this puzzle. I mean, we're both a part of each other's picture. If the pair is emotionally blocked, it can't be only one person's fault, can it? It's not just one half of a human equation that causes the congestion. If it *were*, the un-diseased half would get up and leave, wouldn't it—out of a simple need to survive?

Linda appears in the doorway and tells me she's on her way up to the Central Coast to see her mother.

CHAPTER NINETEEN

Arthur Hill was an actor who remains alive to me. He always greets me with, "Hi, lad. How's it going?"

I first meet him when I play his son in the pilot for a series that lasts for three years: *Owen Marshall: Counselor at Law*. Arthur plays the title role. During the second season, I play his nephew; in the third, I'm a psychotic killer. They used to do that kind of thing in the old days if they liked you—let you play different roles in the same series.

Arthur was fairly well-known in film for a while: *The Andromeda Strain*, *The Ugly American*, *A Little Romance*, *Harper*, *Futureworld*, *A Bridge Too Far*, to name a few. But his finest work was on Broadway: *The Matchmaker*, *Who's Afraid of Virginia Woolf*, *All the Way Home*, and *Look Homeward, Angel*. To watch him on the stage was to see masterful acting, direct and truthful.

When I'm working with him on the *Owen Marshall* pilot, we have lunch together one day. Afterward, we go back to the soundstage and do a scene. It is now later in his career, after his Broadway triumphs and much of his film work. During one of his close-ups, he loses his way almost at the beginning of a long speech. We shoot it again and the same thing happens.

It happens twenty times before he gets it right. I'm relatively a kid, new in the film business. I know very little and he's a great actor. I wish I could help him but I don't know how. I have an overwhelming urge to either run away from the set or hug him.

He dies last year from complications of Alzheimer's disease.

He had back trouble when he was young. After I've had my first spinal surgery, the first telephone call I get is from Arthur. "Hi, lad. How's it going?"

I'm fine, Arthur, better for having known you. I wish I could talk to you today.

I give my old therapist in New Mexico a call and apologize for being insane.

"That's okay. What in the world was going on with you?"

"I sort of crashed." I don't elaborate because I don't know what else to say. She doesn't pursue it.

I thank her and tell her to bill me for her time—which she does not do. She keeps to her principles, which reminds me of the compassion I remember in her eyes when I was seeing her and I'd told her something especially revealing about myself. She could be tough-minded, but she was invariably kind. And that reminds me of a quote from Dame Edith Evans that has no particular reason to be here, except that it appeals to me: "When a woman behaves like a man, why can't she behave like a nice man?"

I get a call from Abigail's counselor in Mississippi.

She's missing.

Chapter Nineteen

Shit! Everybody is conspiring to destroy my happy ending. What is the *matter* with her? Her mother and Linda and I have gone through hell trying to persuade her to go on living and now she's trying to kill herself again. She'd just sent me her three-month-sober chip. She was on her way. She was on her goddam way. God damn it!

I drive out to Venice. Heading west on Pico, I open the window, a luxury I don't allow myself in The Valley because of all the pollens and particulates in the air. I feel a chill, but I don't mind. Smelling the sea air, feeling the soothing, satiny texture of it, has helped me stop dwelling on Abigail for a few seconds at a time. It feels good to be out in the city, but away from the choked-up heart of it.

On the corner of Ocean and Rose, I spot the famous rock singer who turned Abigail onto crack—I'll call him Nicky to protect the guilty. I'm startled to see him here, but not really surprised; Venice is a small town in Los Angeles, even smaller for the many artistic types that frequent it.

I think of the pistol Linda has. When she was working in her dad's jewelry shop they were held up five times. One time, the masked robbers told Linda, her coworker Gunnar, and her dad that they were going to kill them. They tied them up and left them on the floor while they gathered watches, rings, and necklaces.

Then they left.

Gunnar and Linda and her dad worked themselves free, went next door, bought lots of miniature bottles of liquor, and got properly pissed. They had being alive to celebrate.

Now, Linda keeps a Browning automatic in a safe place in our house.

Seeing Nicky, my skin goes all prickly like I've swallowed a bottle of niacin tablets. I imagine that I've got the pistol in the car; that it's on the seat next to me.

Nicky walks out onto the beach from the Rose Avenue public parking lot.

I park, and I *imagine* that I get out and follow him, the Browning hidden in a towel.

He settles down in the sand, fires up a joint, and gazes out toward the sea. Still stoned from the night before, there's a dull cast to his eyes. I walk up and sit next to him, the towel in my lap. He looks over at me, pissed off that I've entered his territory. He says, "You're a little close, dickhead."

I turn toward him, shading my eyes from the sun. "Am I?" I squint, but I'm smiling. "Have I invaded your space?"

"Look, old dude, get your ass up offa the sand and move away from me or I'll break all your teeth for you."

"That would be cruel. I've got a brand new bridge." I point to the upper right side of my mouth.

"Listen, fuck. Go away or I'll stomp your fuckin' bridge to dust."

I take the pistol out of the towel. No sudden movement, nothing dramatic. I ease it out and point it at him. "You got any crack, young dude?"

His eyes go wide. He whispers, "You're a crazy old man."

I nod, agreeing. "You still want me to get up and leave?"

"No no no, I'll go." He's raises his hands slightly, like somebody reluctantly giving in on some minor dispute.

"I'd prefer you stay."

"What do you want, dude?" Fear has crept into his voice.

"*Dude*? You're actually calling me *dude*, like I'm one of your drug buddies?"

Chapter Nineteen

"Whatever, man. I'll call you whatever you like."

"That sounds good. Okay, call me the father of a girl you introduced to crack. He's thought about it quite a bit and realizes he's really pissed off about it and wants to shoot you fucking dead—*dude*."

I smile again but he doesn't return it. His hands move from surrender into cowering and covering himself. His body curls up. His eyes are even wider and I can see they're bloodshot from whatever poisons he's been ingesting lately.

And now—GODDAMMIT—I'm feeling *sorry* for him. Some damned vigilante I am. I resolve to throw away my books about the Dalai Lama. But it's too late. I'm not going to be able to kill this little shit. The Dalai Lama told me the nasty prick just wants what I want, to be happy and not to suffer.

"Get the hell out of here," I say in my mind, as I start down Ocean Avenue, making my way toward Abigail's mother's house so we can share with each other the helplessness we're feeling about our wayward daughter.

Nicky scrambles up and scurries down the beach. I imagine he goes home, shoots up some new designer drug, and writes a song about unprincipled old men.

Jessica is not home. I head back to North Hollywood. The 405 Freeway is a parking lot, so I get off at Sunset, inadvertently bypassing Beverly Glen because I'm thinking God-knows-what at the split second I should be ready to make the quick slide into the left-turn lane. I continue five miles east on Sunset until I reach Beverly Hills, where I turn north on Whittier. I take a right on Lexington and drift east between towering sugar pines and Mexican fan palms to Beverly Drive. Even ordinary cars seem to glide like Rose Bowl floats through certain neighborhoods of Beverly Hills. I hang a left on Beverly and head over Coldwater Canyon toward the San Fernando Valley.

A mile or two up, I notice the street Jessica and I used to take to Laurence Harvey's house. He was away in London then, and after that, doing a film on location. We were visiting David Janssen, who had leased the house from Harvey. David lived with his girlfriend at the time, Rosemary Forsyth. Rosemary played my wife in *How Do I Love Thee?* We used to sit in the bar that overlooked a circle of boy statues that, atop marble coping, peed graceful arcs of water into the swimming pool. The first time I noticed this, David, who had a quick, wry sense of humor, said, "You must forgive the boys, they just woke up."

He and I played pool—the kind with balls, which the eleven lads a-leaking lacked. Sometimes we stayed up all night. Next to him I was a social drinker, but one day I went to work with a morning face that looked as damaged as Richard Boone's. Boone even managed a grin at me through his own hangover pain. I spent an hour having ice applied before I again resembled the young man I still was.

I think of Jessica in those days—how much pleasure she took in her social life, in adventure. She loved—*loves*—sharing with people, having and giving a good time. She draws people to her, always has. She's a great storyteller; has an exuberance and joy in life that's irresistible. Abigail is exactly like her in those ways. Jessica has always been generous and faithful to those she's cared about. She's always loved Abi unconditionally, sometimes I've thought overly so, but I'm not so sure anymore. The last day of the eleventh grade, Abi went to her and said, "I hate school, Mom. I want to enroll in The Music Institute." There were tears in Jessica's eyes. She nodded and said, "First, we have to take a look at it." In recent years, Jess's qualities of compassion and kindness have only increased.

Chapter Nineteen

I know another thing about her. After our separation, she never once said a single bad word about me to Abigail.

I'm thirsty by the time I get home from not murdering Nicky. I have a couple of gin and tonics as I dwell on Abigail, remembering that Laurence Harvey's daughter died of an overdose in her mid-thirties. They made a movie about the last sad months of her life, called *Domino*, starring Keira Knightley.

I think of somebody's line—I forget whose—about dealing with personal grievances: "Sometimes it isn't worth whining, it's just a fact."

But that's not *true*. I whine about facts all the time.

Abigail calls. She *wasn't* missing. There was a miscommunication. She was exactly where she was supposed to be, and everything is fine with her.

When I'd heard she was missing, I said, "Please, please, please let her be okay." Did that count as a prayer? Is it *that* easy? Jesus.

As I'm microwaving a turkey potpie for dinner, I think of my father and wonder if he didn't enable my mother's drug addiction out of what he took to be his best wisdom at the time. I remember him waking me up in the morning, saying, "Good morning, sir," and fixing me breakfast before his long workday. There were times, when I was feeling sick, he'd sit on the bed next to me, tap my chest, feel my forehead, then tell me it was "nothing but a nothing." And it always eased my anxiety—even if something *was* wrong with me. His touch and ceremonial ministrations alone always made the ache disappear.

He must have had a *calling* to be a doctor. Maybe he was in fact a *healer*.

If so, where was the healer when it counted—when Virginia overmedicated that night? He gave her a shot of Demerol, then went to bed in my old bedroom. He knew the pills were on her bedside table. In addition to being a healer, was he an accomplice?

Awake in the middle of the night, I remember another time I'm clenching my eyes shut, trying to sleep—I've taken one sleeping pill, then another. It's five in the morning. I look in Linda's Day Runner calendar to see when we had the bedroom air conditioner put in. Maybe the filter needs to be changed and that's contributing to my recent nighttime asthma flare-ups and to my lying awake right now.

Looking for the date, I see notes she's made a lot of days in a row about her back hurting. The notes were written just before she had a cyst aspirated that was pressing on her sciatic nerve. I had no idea it was causing her so much pain; she hardly said a word about it. I think of the diary entries by Ann Stuart—being "disgusted" and "discouraged" and all alone and sad with her vodka, her turtle, and her birds.

The next day, I call Linda as many times as I can get away with. She needs to spend time with her mom—since she's there, after all—but I want to hear her voice. I talk with her for just a few minutes each time. She asks me how I'm doing—she's thinking about Debby. Each time I say I'm fine.

Everything seems okay with her; she's forgiven me. But I know when I'm losing her attention, so I tell her I love her and she says it back to me. After we hang up, I think about how she almost never feels sorry for herself. I just love that in a human being.

Chapter Nineteen

I go out to the pussycat feeding station and give Willy some tuna, his favorite. Later on, I give him catnip and stay outside for a while, playing with him. He's more interested in the catnip than he is in me, but I don't care. It crosses my mind to see how he feels about coming in and spending the night with me.

"What do you say, darlin'? Just this once? You could curl up next to me. For old time's sake?"

He shakes his head emphatically, sidle-hops off into the ivy, batting at a moth, then tumbles out of sight. He has other plans.

CHAPTER TWENTY

When Linda was young she wanted to be a torch singer, then either a bomber pilot or an artist. She finally picked artist. (She occasionally torch-sings in the bedroom. She also keeps her bomber piloting hush-hush.) She went through an early Ayn Rand period when she wanted to run a railroad or some huge company. That was the most unlikely because she's organizationally challenged—a dreamer, a wafter. It might appear that she drifts through her daily tasks by chance, but she's aware of what she has to do; it's just that she does those things only as they float into the meadow of her consciousness.

On the other hand, she can be shortsighted and preoccupied when it comes to my concerns. And her phone skills: The best word I can think of to describe those, after lousy and unsatisfying, is absent. *Presence* is the thing with her. I understand all her words; they're okay, but it needs her living, intimate self to make an encounter with her fulfilling the way I've come to need her.

One time, I'd opened in a play by S.N. Behrman, *No Time for Comedy*. Linda had to leave town right after the show. Later that night, we talked on the phone. I said, "Did you like it?"

"Yes, very much."

I waited for her to amplify. "In what way? In what *way* did you like it?"

"I enjoyed it. It was good."

"Yeah, but tell me how."

"It was funny."

"In what *way*? Like—what about *my* part did you find funny?"

"You were amusing ... very entertaining. I laughed."

"Was it my *character*? My physical language? What *made* you laugh?"

"I don't know. It was good. I *liked* your character."

"Yeah, but he's not exactly likeable. Did you like me better than the others."

"You were *all* good." Then, quickly, "Especially *you,* though."

I imagined her reaching through the phone line and popping my eyes like bubble wrap, so I gave up.

Now that I think about it, I should never be surprised by her telephone manner. She can be pretty taciturn *in person*. In fact, her best communicating is between the lines. Sometimes, that can be quite effective.

Her only brother Tim was killed in a car accident when he was twenty-two. I never knew him, but I feel as if I did, even though she's never talked about him much. Tim comes through certain of Linda's quiet moments, and I can almost see his reflection in her eyes now. It's like completing a familiar shape in your mind when you can't quite make out the whole thing. I actually miss Tim—as if he'd departed from *me* as well.

But Linda's phone skills: fuh-geddaboudit.

Chapter Twenty

Shortly after I do my episode of *The Greatest American Hero*, the producer of a theatre in San Diego asks me if I'd like to come down and play Elwood P. Dowd in *Harvey*. I'm a little reluctant because the character is so eternally associated with Jimmy Stewart, but it would be a joy to play.

I do the job and have one of the best times I've ever had on a stage. My only problem is that Elwood is really, *really nice*. After playing him for a few weeks, living every day in the skin of an almost saintly, lovable man (well, he boozes a bit, which, after every show, I do too—I put it under the heading of actor's research), I begin to feel, percolating up inside me, a Mr. Hyde, who's looking to go out—when I've concluded my after-show drinking bouts—and commit the odd murder in the gloom of night.

Then I would get a good day's sleep and return to the theatre in time for my next performance as sweet, pixilated Elwood—sanguine again, no longer sanguinary.

After the show closes, I begin therapy with Susan, whom I spend a couple of new cars' worth of our savings on to learn that I have a dark side. Maybe I should have listened to what Linda's mom said when she heard I was going to start that therapy: "Just have him call *me*." I wonder how Grace is at prayer. I've been thinking more and more about such things lately, but I'm ignorant and mistrustful in this area and the Yellow Pages has no listing for "prayer coaches." Most of my questions couldn't be answered by another mere human anyway. Like: Why does He have me learning a ... *lot*, and in the same breath, knowing *nothing*?

I don't have any prejudice against people who pray. But I don't think I have the gift. When I was ten, my mother told me to pray for Dixie Thorpe. It didn't work. That was depressing, because if a boy can't pray for his friend not to be dead anymore, and it *is* a sincere prayer because it was all the boy's fault in the first place, then why should that same petitioner have any more luck now that he's not so innocent any longer and is aging like an out-of-control brush fire?

Anyway, may Debby and Abigail bloom. And you, Grace.

Positive thoughts, keeping counsel with yourself, but not taking it so far as to withdraw to a lamasery—because you've learned you're not the type, or are too much the type—that's the only way to go. But a sensible goal like that seems no better than an outside chance for someone the advertising kids dismiss as being "over fifty and hopelessly set in his 'old-to-dead' ways."

But what do *they* know? They have so little experience. If they had experience they wouldn't dismiss the value of experience.

One evening a few years ago, Linda and I were lying on the floor watching a movie on television. I got up and sprinted into the kitchen to get something to eat. The lights weren't on. Linda had left the sliding breadboard sticking out. Racing gazelle-like because it was a good movie and I didn't want to miss any of it, I ran into the corner of that breadboard, giving myself a wound that reminded me viscerally of a football injury I got when I was in the tenth grade. I'd broken a tangle of blood vessels in my thigh and my dad had to take me to the hospital where, in a painful procedure, they drained my leg of all kinds of alien fluids I was instructed not to look at, and then they gave me a transfusion.

When I smashed into the breadboard, I let out a yelp they probably heard on the campus of Valley College a half mile away. Linda hugged me and was sweet about it.

Understandably whiny, I told her I was worried that this might be the broken blood vessel thing all over again.

The next day my leg and my anxiety were worse. Finally, Linda said, "My dad was wounded in World War II and he didn't complain

Chapter Twenty

this much." Her father fought in the Battle of the Bulge and received a Purple Heart, a Bronze Star, and a battlefield commission.

Come on! No fair! This is nothing compared to what my father the war hero went through? So now, I was in hideous agony *plus* I wanted to strangle my wife.

However, I took a positive lesson out of this, and changed some of my "set-in-my-ways" behavior. *Experience.* It's taught me that sometimes you have to lick your wounds all by yourself, like a dog with his curative saliva. No one is going to understand the depth of your pain and worry—even if they caused the goddam problem in the first place by leaving the goddam breadboard out. I learned some self-reliance and found some inner resources. You need to have those. Even if your mate is normally everything you ever dreamed of, sometimes you have to seek advice from your own inner advisor—the God within you, I believe is the term.

When I reminded Linda of this recently, she agreed with me—about the joys of keeping this sort of thing to myself. She added that I shouldn't dissipate the force of my epiphany, even now, by telling her about it.

I know she's right. That way my prayer won't dry up and die before it gets to where it needs to go. Also, since that advice came from her, I'm not even bothered by the sarcasm.

I return to my previous topic: experience, versus the accrued wisdom of the extremely young. There's nothing more old-to-dead-spirited than *knowing* all the answers when you're so young it's next to impossible to know *any* of them.

There are so many blessings that come with experience.

Being able to hang on to a train of thought for example.

Another thing I could pray about: It's now Monday night and Linda is not home yet. She said she'd be back about noon. Her mother says she left there around eleven this morning. It's a three to four hour trip. I can't reach her on the cell phone and it's starting to give me the whim-whams. I picture a GPS navigation map, an especially sophisticated, teleological one. My imaginary electronic map shows the whereabouts of *people*.

But it doesn't help; I can't distinguish Linda's blip from the rest. Maybe I didn't hear what she said to me.

I remember the Coen brothers' *Barton Fink*. John Goodman (as amiable insurance salesman Charlie Meadows) says a line to John Turturro (as the title character, a self-important playwright) that's etched in my mind forever. The most satisfying moment in the film comes when Fink, after undergoing a series of mishaps, laments "Why me?" and Meadows thunders, *"Because YOU DON'T LISTEN!"*

I think of the time I was first in Hollywood and hanging out with a lot of young actors. Many of them listened to you only as a preoccupied pause in their monologues while they planned what they were going to tell you next about themselves. They rarely knew what you'd just said, let alone given it serious thought. If you don't listen, you've stopped learning. More than that, your generosity skills will waste away, just dry up like a tadpole in the hot sun.

Linda arrives home a little before midnight. Her cell phone had lost its charge. I ask her why she wasn't home before dinner.

"I told you I wouldn't be home until now. I told you I was going to stop off in Shell Beach and see Harriet."

"Who's Harriet?"

"Weren't you *listening*?"

Chapter Twenty

Abigail sends me her five-month chip. She has a job working with Alzheimer's patients and she's dating some guy on a regular basis. I'm happy about the chip and the job—she seems in a great mood—but I'm not so pleased about this guy. His name is Josh. I don't want to hear about new men in her life. He's a foreman in a resin factory and she tells me he's a good writer, trying to get me on this one's side, but it doesn't work. New boyfriends always seem to portend the beginning of some new slide into hell.

Debby got her first CT-125 blood test reading since she started tri-weekly chemotherapy and apparently the score is extraordinarily low: a "9." She's thrilled and relieved, dragged out from the chemo, but still managing, after a couple of days, to go in to her job as a nurse and do a full day's work.

In the late '80s I do a Fox series that has a one-season run. It's called *The New Adventures of Beans Baxter*. We shoot in Vancouver, British Columbia, and Linda has joined me for a few days. I am the title character's father, Benjamin Baxter Sr., super-spy—in a spoof, not bad casting. (I always wanted to be the heroic type, but I had to look in the mirror and narrow my eyes just right to make that work.) One time, my contact is jammed into a street corner mailbox. Richard Mulligan, the same actor I understudied in *Mating Dance*, plays that role. He doesn't remember telling me the rat should get the girl. Another time, I'm held prisoner by Soviet agents: Mr. Sue, played by Kurtwood Smith, whose credits include *RoboCop* and hysterical dad on *That '70s Show*; Conju, played by punk singer Wendy O. Williams; and a brute called Vlodia, given a brave go by Bruce Wagner, now the brilliant Hollywood-skewering novelist. Bruce is open, guarded, kind, caustic, and funny; good company, although occasionally he gets a wild look in his eye and bolts away to scribble furiously until the next set-up is ready.

One night, Bruce, Kurtwood, Linda, and I are having dinner. At a nearby table is some of the cast of one of those awkward nostalgia movies, *The Return of the Six Million Dollar Man and the Bionic Woman*. I speak to Richard Anderson, with whom I'd been friendly when I worked on both original series. It makes me feel a little jealous, seeing them, injured that they haven't asked *me* to be in their nostalgia movie. Or maybe what I'm feeling is just more of my old crush on Lindsay Wagner.

I speak to her. She's very warm; she had substance problems of her own for a while, but came out the other side glowing. It feels like encountering an old flame—after all, she *was* my girlfriend, and before that, my wife—even though it was just on film. Cognitive dissonance never entirely goes away.

I see Lindsay recently at a *Bionic* Tribute Dinner—which ought to be a story in itself, but the fans there are not actually much different from stamp collectors; the only real distinction is that these very pleasant hobbyists collect everything to do with the first versions of *The Bionic Woman* and *The Six Million Dollar Man*. It's not surprising that Lindsay is more charming than ever. I am amiable but inarticulate with her. I try to be "cool," with the usual result. A little later, I realize it doesn't matter. Those days have passed.

I'm sentimental about pretty girls I used to have a crush on. I don't want them carnally (well, maybe a little), but I was a child of World War II and mostly just want to come home safely for Christmas and have a nice Hollywood ending: live happily ever after with Rita

Chapter Twenty

Hayworth and Grace Kelly—not at the same time, of course—and Ava Gardner and Cyd Charisse; Mitzi Gaynor, Audrey Hepburn, Vera Miles, Romy Schneider, Anouk Aimee, Barbara Hershey, Nancy Wilson, Marilyn Monroe, Giulietta Masina, Eva Marie Saint, Rita Moreno, Marcia Gay Harden, Natalie Portman, Simone Signoret, Janice Rule, Diana Lynn, Carmen Lodise, Lee Remick, Jan Sterling, Catherine Deneuve, Lindsay Wagner, and Kim Novak—especially Kim Novak.

When I first meet Linda, her eyes remind me of Kim Novak's—looking hypnotically into Jimmy Stewart's eyes.

I'm at a party a long time ago. Loretta Young is there too. I have an awkward, gin-inspired exchange with her. I've seen several of her movies and behave as if we're neighbors, even though she's never laid eyes on me before. It's another weaselly moment (Hick From Sticks Fawns Over Slick Chick's Pics), but she is gracious anyway.

A few minutes later, an actress, who is my age and has fangs as I remember her, tells me in front of several people how unappealingly I've behaved. It's one of those social sequences you wish you could rewind and run some other scene instead, but you can't, so you go on feeling embarrassed and I think of Annette Mirza, the sexiest girl in class. I'm walking home from school one day with her and Dave Daugherty, the coolest guy in my school. I trip on a crack in the sidewalk and Annette says, "Walk much?"

Shortly after the Loretta Young incident, I go into therapy so I can learn not to be so silly so often, and that when I inevitably *am* silly, it shouldn't bother me so much.

Years afterward, I'm at a party with the actress who called attention to my awkward behavior with Ms. Young. She's with a much older Rod Steiger, who doesn't date her very long because maybe she nips at him a few too many times with her stinging wit, and soon he'll be escorting Elizabeth Taylor to various Hollywood affairs. I don't remind this actress about my embarrassment with Loretta Young and her part in it.

Sometime after that, I'm in a television movie with Elizabeth Taylor: *Malice in Wonderland*. I don't have any scenes with her; mine are with Jane Alexander, a Matisse among actors.

Peter Lawford is also working on that film—a job Ms. Taylor got him. I'm in one half of a tiny trailer. Peter is in the other half. It strikes me as a hell of a comedown for the former MGM golden boy, but looking at it now, maybe it wasn't. Maybe it was necessary for his soul. As we wrap for the week on a Friday evening, Peter says, "Goodnight, Rick. Have a pleasant weekend." He seems oddly earnest about it; I didn't think he knew my name. When I go to work the following Monday, there's a new actor in the other half of that trailer.

Peter has died over the weekend.

Another time I'm offered a role in a mini-series based on a James Michener book. I can't do it because I have another commitment that fall. The actor who does play it is sleeping in his trailer on location in Colorado one day. There is a carbon monoxide leak in the heating system of the trailer. When the assistant director knocks on his door to call him for his next scene, the actor is dead.

It couldn't be that the Deity thought that was good for his and his family's souls. I place the blame on the studio people. Their advertising revenues can pay for scandalous executive salaries, but they can't pay for basic safety precautions for the workers. It reminds me of a B. Kliban cartoon: The rear end of a large draft horse is pooping out little men in buttoned-up suits, smoking cigars. The caption is: *The Birth of Advertising*.

Chapter Twenty

Linda does a terrific impression of Ethel Merman singing "There's No Business Like Show Business." She wrinkles up her nose in mock-disdain and belts out: "You're *reg*-ular and you're *orrr*-dinary—and *weeeee're* show people ..."

I tell her show people *are* regular.

"You don't have to convince *me*."

My friend and agent, Stanley, calls me today and tells me he doesn't think he's giving me the representation I deserve and that I should probably look for a new agent.

Shit! Some pal! Forty-plus years in the business and he tells me to take a hike and find new representation. Agents don't drop *me*. I drop *them*.

I can't think about it!

Maybe it's not such a terrible thing that Abi has a boyfriend. We've been having talks, and she seems happy. She took her GED test and passed it with no trouble. She's looking after herself and being independent. I recall a picture she drew when Linda and I were first together. Abi got up before us on weekends. This particular drawing was of a crafty-looking little dark-haired girl. She had big, almond-shaped eyes and a sneaky, mirthful smile. Beneath it she'd written: "Abigail's Spy Agency. Spy anyone on block."

When I tell her Debby's cancer is in remission and that it looks like it may stay that way, she's as elated as I am (she's always a joy to share joy with). Debby lived with Jessica and me for a year when her first husband, Chuck, was in the Army, stationed in Korea. Debby and Abigail, who was a toddler at the time, became very close.

Because I sometimes think of my daughter and my sister in the same thought balloon, I recall another one of Abigail's drawings from those first months Linda and I were together. It was a little girl under a big, multicolored semicircle.

The caption beneath it said, "Saved by a rainbow."

The image of a little girl protected by a rainbow suddenly grips me with anxiety—not because of Abigail, because of *me*. Whenever I realize my mind has jumped to something that feels sentimental, or "over-earnest," it sets off my *un-cool* alarm and I expect the blow. If I linger in that frame of mind long enough, it'll come. I expect it *now*—in its recent form, the *voices*. Not knowing why, I goad them by entertaining other—I admit—schmaltzy images of Abigail as a little girl. I think of Debby when she was a baby, this miraculous gift given explicitly to *me*. The first Christmas she was alive, I used to sit next to her crib and sing Christmas carols to her. I don't think anybody else heard. I did it quietly. I did it for myself as much as her. It made me feel good. It *was* corny. I know that.

And now, I sense the *voices* nearby, as usual, those heartless deniers of joy, those reminders of all unkindness.

And again Abigail and Debby appear clearly to me, both of them safely sheltered beneath rainbows.

Now, the voices crescendo and echo back at me, declaring with a twist of sadistic sparkle: *"Any cool you ever had is dead."*

I concentrate on coming up with a coherent lesson out of recent events.

Today, I succeed. Driving on the 405 Freeway on my way to see my allergist on Slauson Boulevard in Culver City, I'm doing my best to focus the laser of my brain on all the *positive* things that have been

Chapter Twenty

happening lately. I pass one of those signs on the freeway that gives the traffic and weather conditions, or AMBER Alerts. In bold letters, it says: Go With The Flow.

For the next five miles, I'm *euphoric*. I've been handed a sign, so to speak, a cosmic answer to the big question. And my mind races over all the ramifications of that.

Then I see the next sign still off in the distance.

My hands go all clammy on the steering wheel. I feel this pious kind of anticipation. I'm being given important information here—in plain, useful language.

And now, I'm able to read the second sign.

It says: Avoid Slauson Exit.

I don't have a lot of accumulated wisdom from what I've been dwelling on during this journey. But I now have five rules with which to guide myself:

1. Men always take the biggest half.
2. Nobody likes to hire damp people.
3. If you don't want to be noticed, get out of the spotlight.
4. If you stay by yourself in a hotel room too long, you may end up forgetting your name.
5. Avoid the Slauson Exit.

I'm awakened by a phone call from Abigail. She's in high spirits. For a few minutes she makes me forget I've been dropped by my agent and that for now I'm as cold in the Business as that male penguin sitting on the egg, waiting for his wife to come back and reward him with a gulletful of regurgitated fish.

Abigail has only positive things to say about her life in Mississippi, about her rehabilitation and the people she's working with. She says they've asked her if she'd be interested in working as a counselor once she's got a year of sobriety under her belt. She's still going with Josh and I'm feeling less alarmed about it. He's also in recovery; has two years. If I can believe Abigail—and I can usually feel when she's solid in her sobriety—he's really not a bad guy.

I don't ask her any hard questions, like how do you qualify to be a drug counselor? That's not my job. I could be an advice-giver again, but I hear Charlie's words from when he lived with Linda and me—as I often do lately when I've said something especially weighty: "Can I go to bed now, Dad?" So, demonstrating the better part of wisdom for a split second, I tell Abi I'm proud of her and happy for her and then, biting my tongue so as not to pass on some invaluable nugget of cutting-edge advice from the potty-trained-too-early, I shut up.

I nuke the coffee Linda left me, which my daughter-in-law Kim says will likely kill me because microwaving turns the atoms upside down or something. She's probably right. I've read Masaru Emoto's *The Hidden Messages in Water.* It says, "The distilled water heated in the microwave resulted in a crystal similar to that created by the word *Satan.*" You don't have to hit *me* on the head.

But my coffee has gotten god-awful tepid and I don't want to reheat it in the pot. I sit down to flip through the *Calendar* section of the *Los Angeles Times.* I'm off hard news lately. It harshes my mellow.

Calendar seems unusually trivial so I pick up the *Travel* section. On the front page is a big photograph of a Rocky Mountain landscape. I remember riding over mountainous terrain like it when I was little. My father was in the Army, stationed in Colorado Springs. I was in the back seat, looking down at the sheer drop-offs at the side of the road—there were very few guardrails in those days—and my father,

Chapter Twenty

glancing at me in the rearview mirror, said, "Don't worry, son, the captain is at the helm." This translated to: "God is at his post." It was like feeling sick and the captain—when he *was* still the captain; the doctor, my dad, God—told me it was "nothing but a nothing."

Maybe the only thing I have to fear *is* fear itself. That's what I always told my kids whenever I saw that look in their eyes—that the real danger was inside their heads, not lurking out in the darkness somewhere.

I've been convinced for a long time that if everyone's survival depended on me or my father or any one of us—or even the brainiest group of us—the human race would be in serious danger. But also, it does feel like a shadowy gate has swung open and my life is not skipping around quite as crazily as it used to. I'm building roads in the mountains. Most of the work is uphill, but there are plateaus with brilliant views here and there—once the work is modestly underway. And there is a small voice inside me now that's beginning to whisper, "Epiphany, epiphany!"

But why should I believe it? I have no history of being able to trust *any* of my inner voices. Is it possible this faint, recent one actually has my best interests at heart?

Maybe I'll just try my hardest and keep on building my little roads—believe that God *is* at his station, and that there's no more point in telling Him what to do than there is in running up to the front of the Boeing 767 I'm on and telling the pilot to be careful.

CHAPTER TWENTY-ONE

Abigail is pregnant and is going to marry Josh, who, the more she describes him, sounds not so bad. There's confidence in her voice. I once went to fifty AA meetings in fifty days (after my last meeting, I went out and drank myself into a stupor—to celebrate my sobriety). Alcoholics Anonymous veterans, the ones who've filibustered the portals of Hell, have an aura about them that is touching in its humility and hard-earned insight. I'm hearing that in my daughter's voice. All at once she feels like somebody I might ask serious advice of, which may say more about me than her. I *do not* mean to put overconfidence into the air about Abigail. She and Josh plan to live in Mississippi for about two years, then move back this way, but probably not to LA, center of many of Abi's good times and most of her bad.

They're going to be out here in August for the wedding, which will take place on the twelfth at her mother's home on one of the canals in Venice. It will be their second wedding; they'll have a first ceremony in Mississippi for Josh's family and friends. Debby says she'll come, so she's obviously feeling better. Our friend Dian, who is Abigail's adopted godmother, will be there; and my old friend Michael Norell;

and Scott (Connie is working and Aaron is in school); and Charlie, Kim, and Riley.

I've been writing all day. Out of complete silence, I hear the most devastating shriek I've ever heard. Linda is screaming, "RICK!" so that it could carry beyond Valley College.

I leap up from my desk and tear out into the dining room, where the front door is.

She's crying it out again as I round the corner, "RICK!" Now, she adds with all the pain of Medea, "*I think Willy is dead*!"

She's standing in the doorway, tears streaming down her face, Willy's limp orange body in her arms.

He's been hit by a car. The driver didn't stop.

Neither of us gets over this for a while, and then only slowly. I think for Linda, it's also grief for her brother Tim and for her father and for all the losses she's ever suffered or ever will.

Gordon Gray is an actor I meet in New York when we're doing shows in adjacent theatres. He's the friend from those times I miss most.

Debby stays with Jessica and me for a while when we're in New York, and again when we move to Beverly Hills. She grumbles about being overweight, which she's not. Gordon is often at our place cooking, cheerfully telling stories, laughing, and smoking his habitual menthol cigarettes. He tells Debby she's the only woman he's ever met who is "dead solid perfect." Debby is very fond of Gordon.

One night in New York, before Abigail is born, Gordon and I ride home together on the subway and go to a small party given by another friend, named Nerissa, and her fiancé. Nerissa is a bright girl with an

Chapter Twenty-One

acerbic wit. She doesn't like Gordon's type, even though I don't think he says a single thing to her that is anything but friendly. She just flat-out doesn't like him. All evening, in front of a lot of people, she uses him for target practice, calls him Mr. Broadway. She and a handful of others delight in her contempt. He's a good-looking actor; they're budding intellectuals—maybe, maybe not.

The more Nerissa attacks, the more it runs off Gordon like water off a duck's back. He's just a person who doesn't react to insults. The more he deflects her assaults with his best good will, the angrier she becomes. Her friends are getting embarrassed for her. Personally, I would like to smash her with a brick.

Finally, her fiancé yells at her, "Nerissa, knock it the fuck off!"

Gordon, gorgeously *immune*, doesn't appear to notice.

Gordon and I are close for many years. Later he quits show business and goes into construction, eventually becoming a building contractor. He gets married, and although I don't see him as often during that period as I wish, I still think of him frequently.

Nerissa crosses my mind again, not in anger because it's so long ago and what's the point anyway?

For a while, I used to think about dropping a note to her: "Dear Nerissa, the show is over. The curtain came down early and Mr. Broadway died tonight." He was most of a lifetime too young.

It was the menthols.

I told Jessica, then Debby. We all felt like pure malevolence had ripped away a large piece of our lives, lives we thought we'd been guaranteed.

Tonight I doze for two hours, then, as often happens, I wake up and can't get back to sleep. I go out to the kitchen, have some cereal, then lie down on the couch in the living room and find myself thinking about Mr. Broadway. I miss him, more than twenty-five years later.

I slip past the look I remember on Linda's face when she was holding the shell of Willy in her arms, and into thoughts about Debby, and Abigail, about whom I remain uneasy despite all the good news from Mississippi.

Still on the couch, I drift, but remain sleepless; my insomnia won't be reasoned with. Then, unaccountably, something from that damned Sunday school of my childhood pops into my head: "Ask and ye shall receive." Normally, I hate that kind of debris loitering in the back of my brain, but tonight I think okay, why not?

For the fun of it and to kill some time, and maybe partly because I've been browsing again through some of Linda's books, I come up with two things I would like to ask for. The first is Debby's complete restoration to health. Then, because I've only slept for two hours and feel crummy, I assemble a trio of sensations I'd like to experience right now, all related: peace, well-being, and joy. (I know it's jargony, but I can't think of anything better.) I start saying these three words over and over: "peace, well-being, and joy."

It feels as if I'm turning God into a waiter. "I'd like an order of peace and well-being, please. Oh, and let me have a side of joy."

"And how would you like that joy prepared, sir?"

"Oh, I don't know. Sunny side up."

I go back into the bedroom where Linda's sleeping like a baby, lie down next to her and silently carry on with my new mantra. It doesn't work.

I whisper to Linda; ask her if I can have a hug. She's always available for that. Sometimes in the past, it's helped me get to sleep. As she holds me from behind, I keep thinking: peace, well-being, and joy. It still doesn't work.

Chapter Twenty-One

But after a few minutes, she does something she's never done before. As she continues spooning me, she rests an elbow lightly on my side and lays her palm across my forehead. It feels warm, and I remember it's supposed to be a cool hand on the forehead that eases distress. But hers feels almost—I begin to imagine—as if it's imparting some kind of healing energy.

Slowly my anxieties melt.

That's the last thing I remember until morning.

My computer is being fixed so I go with Linda to downtown Los Angeles.

She's inside an eleven-story building doing some business. After awhile I decide to go down and sit in Pershing Square until she's done. It's a mild day. The sky is clear. I can see the tops of the San Bernadino Mountains to the north, the two highest peaks capped with startlingly white snow.

I sit on an empty bench and lean my head back, enjoying the rare sensation lately of sunshine on my face, but also feeling a pang of the blues, remembering that Willy is gone and I've been ditched by my swine of an agent.

I feel the bench jolt sharply and look up to see a large black street guy, wearing shabby clothes. He's sat down on the opposite end of the bench.

Seeing me glance at him, then away, he says, "Don't worry. I'm harmless."

I smile perfunctorily because the truth is that adrenalin *has* surged through me—that reptilian reaction before your brain's contextual apparatus has had time to kick in. But my fear ebbs quickly and is replaced by a surprising visitation of tranquility.

"So am I," I say. "I'm harmless too."

He looks over at me with a slow, crooked grin. "Yeah, I figured."

"How? *How* did you figure?"

He chortles deep in his throat. His eyes are bright, the irises a rich amber. They're shining despite the whites being bloodshot. "You look pretty harmless," he says.

"I could be a mad killer."

"Yeah, I guess you could." He smiles again. "But you're not."

"I wish I knew how you *know* that. Because that's what I've been striving for lately—to be just as harmless as I can be."

He narrows his eyes at me appraisingly, then looks up at the top of the Bank of America Plaza, I assume thinking over what I've just said. "Yeah, there's worse things to be." He points at a rail-thin man with ramrod posture over on the corner of Sixth and Hill streets, facing two other men, gesticulating angrily. "He's harmless too."

"Could be," I say. "And if he is, I think of it as a good thing."

"Maybe."

"If you're harmless, it probably means you're not trying too hard to defend something."

He gives that some thought. "Of course there's people," he says. "Sometimes you gotta defend people."

"I can see that."

"Course people gonna do what they gonna do. You can't watch 'em all the time." He's staring at me.

"Yeah."

"So maybe we both oughta just go off and be harmless today." He sighs and looks up at the top of the B of A Plaza again. "Can you spare five bucks?"

"Yes, I can."

Chapter Twenty-One

Out of nowhere, I get a call from an old friend named Harry Marx, whom I was in a play with many years ago. He tells me he's heard I've left my agent. I tell him it was the other way around, but he ignores that and asks me if I'd like to come with him.

"Where?"

"Where?" He sounds hurt. "You don't know?"

"What?"

"I've had my own agency for fifteen years."

"I'm sorry," I say. "I don't follow the business very closely lately. Congratulations. I had no idea. You're saying you want *me* as a client?"

The hurt leaves his voice. "If you're interested."

I don't think it over. "Sure, Harry. I am. I'm interested. Are you any good?"

"Fuck you. Give me a ring later in the week, bring in all your stuff and meet the other agents. I'm on Sunset in the building Wally Hiller used to be in. Fuck you, Rick. Glad to have you."

"Fuck you too, Harry. Thanks."

Linda and I are in the kitchen. I'm doing a bit of what, if I were really pressed, I'd have to call blowing my own horn. Linda listens quietly, or maybe she's turned me off, I don't know. She *has* such a button for me, and again if I'm honest I need to admit that in her place, I'd have one too, for moments like this. I am capable of being a one-subject man. On this night, I'm doing sous chef duty, using paper towels to pat the lettuce dry for a salad.

I say: "Do you think I'm as self-involved as I used to be?"

She chuckles in the back of her throat, then frowns. "Don't *squeeze* the lettuce, *spin* it—in the spinner. You always get it all wilty."

"The spinner's underneath the stove."

She opens the cupboard, gets out the OXO salad spinner, and sets it decisively on the counter.

I put the lettuce in it and do it her way. "Okay, it's *in* the spinner. See? I'm spinning it. Answer my question."

She gazes at me, suppressing an evil grin. "Self-involved. No, you're not as self-involved as you *used* to be." She goes silent as I pump the salad spinner as fast as it will go. "You're still the most introspective man I've ever met, but no, I wouldn't describe it *exactly* as self-involved." I stop pumping. "Spin it till it's dry."

"It's *bone* dry *now*!" She opens the spinner to look for herself. "It's just that I'm looking back on all the acting and realizing that I didn't get what I aimed for."

"Who does? Spin it some more, it's still moist."

I pump the thing vengefully. "I mean I'm not really sure what I was aiming for in the first place, but the point is, I wasn't the best."

"Who says you have to be the best?"

"Why get into something if you can't be the best?" I say. I know I can't win this argument.

"I'm sorry, but that's just stupid. Why would you *expect* to be? That's like being angry you didn't win the lottery. You're good. You're a wonderful actor!"

She *says* I'm wonderful but her face is getting flushed. I'm so wonderful she's pissed off at me.

"And what are you complaining about? You just got a new agent. I just said you're wonderful." She looks at me, sighing. "If acting were some other kind of art like, say, playing a musical instrument, you'd be outstanding. You might even be first chair"—her features slide into a well-executed deadpan—"playing whatever acting instrument you'd play in … oh, a medium-ish-sized city."

"Thanks a lot."

Chapter Twenty-One

"I'm serious."

Linda's sense of humor is quite useful sometimes if I can take it in the right spirit. It's not so much witty as a pretty well tuned sense of proportion.

"Besides, you might *still* be the best," she says. "You're not dead yet."

"Maybe I've limited my experience of life by my own unique pattern of perceptions," I say. "By my ... egocentric predicament, my ... *solipsism*."

She stares at me. "Your *what*?"

"It means someone who—in effect—doesn't believe anyone exists outside of himself. I've had, maybe, a *few* moments like that, here and there—from time to time ..."

She blinks twice, then her lips go up very slightly at the corners. I gaze into her eyes and realize they're smiling too.

"I'm going out to pick some basil." She turns and walks out of the kitchen, out the back door and into her herb garden.

CHAPTER TWENTY-TWO

I call Michael Norell in Pennsylvania. He moved there after his wife Cynthia and he separated. He was tired of Los Angeles. He's had a good career, won a Writers Guild of America Award for *The Incident*, starring Walter Matthau, co-written with his brother, Jim. He's also "penned"—as they love to say in the cubicles of *Variety*—about fifty television movies on his own, all of them inventive, none of them standard TV fare. Michael and my friend Don Eitner, the dramaturge and director, are the only geniuses I've ever called close friends.

Michael now lives back in South Central Pennsylvania across a country road from his brother. I call him just to talk and he tells me he can't come to Abigail's wedding, explaining he has to honor a previous commitment to direct a play. The schedule got moved up, which makes a trip to California impossible for him right now. I whine at him for a while, which he tells me he needs this day like a third nostril.

So I drop that and move on to complaining about my life having gotten—"small," I say.

"What's the point of a big life?" I can see his aggravated frown, all furrowing black eyebrows. "You have to keep too many balls in the air to live a big life. It wears you out, makes a liar out of you."

"I don't lie anymore." He doesn't respond to that. "I'm more direct than I used to be."

"More than *that*. You've gotten painfully straight. You seem to be turning into an elderly Candide."

"What do you mean 'painfully'?" We've known each other for almost forty years.

"I mean you used to want that penthouse on Central Park, remember?"

"Yeah?"

"Well, now you live real modestly in that North Hollywood 'your-asthma' of hanging particulates. At least in New York you had some culture down the hall, down the block, around the corner."

"You're saying totally different things."

"I know," he says. "It's crazy. A guy leaves a questionable burg like Jackson, Michigan, and ends up in a place even more dubious."

"You just hate LA."

"That's not the point."

"What *is* the point?"

He thinks about that for a couple of seconds. "I don't know. LA made me moderately rich. Why would I hate it? But shit, man, you've got plenty of reason to in recent years. But there you are, still living in the exhaust pipe of the nation."

"Don't you remember the end-to-end beautiful days out here? The smell of the ocean, the bougainvillea, the LA light?"

He sighs. "Yeah, I remember. I miss it—twice a year. But there's no traffic here. I can't *see* the air ... I guess I'm saying you left home trying to get away from life's biggest question and you end up right in the middle of the same question."

"Yeah, but at least I'm more peaceful about it. What question?"

Chapter Twenty-Two

"You started out wanting to be this callous sophisticate. And how do you end up? Simpler than ever. And the funny thing is, basically you seem more contented than I can ever recall." He laughs. "But that doesn't stop you from banging around like the Energizer Bunny, demanding to know 'Why?'"

"Why what?"

"How the hell would *I* know? You're the one asking the question."

Last night we have a party. I'm worried I've lost my ability to relate to people. Recently I stay home and write or paint every day and except for Dian, with whom we often watch movies at night, I don't see much of anyone other than Charlie, Kim, and Riley every few weeks.

It's early, I haven't had my coffee, and I just glanced up and realized I've typed, "We *heave* a party," which is sort of the right word. Anyway, we gather our courage and *heave* a party for thirty people. Our house is quite small, so it's a little like all those sophomores in the Fifties cramming themselves into telephone booths, or the New York bash in Holly Golightly's *Breakfast at Tiffany's* apartment.

We have the food sent over from Papa Cristo's, a Greek restaurant in Hollywood. Linda's bought roses from Costco and has about fifty votive candles set out all over the place. Dian lends us enough dishes and flatware to serve fifty people. The house looks great. I'm in charge of the music, but you can't hear it because of the lovely babble of old and new friends.

God, I sound like I'm writing for "Life In These United States."

Later on we all get naked and go over to Hollywood. But nobody notices.

I'm back at Century City Hospital for the second day. Yesterday, Linda had the cyst on her spine removed, finally—the aspiration wasn't enough. Dian and I waited through the surgery, then through a long afternoon of worry because Linda's heart rate had dropped dangerously low—down into the low thirties—from the anesthesia. At seven-thirty in the evening, the cardiologist showed up in the ICU and told her he wanted to do an echocardiogram and a CAT scan today. My mind jumped to her father's heart disease, then to Debby's illness and, as I tried to go to sleep, it continued to race over everything in the world that could possibly go wrong.

This morning during rush hour, without Dian today, I inch along the 405 from The Valley over the Santa Monicas into Sawtelle and east to the botched solid-geometry assignment called Century City. Watching a series of pathologically incoherent and repetitious talking heads on TV in the waiting room, I'm approached by a friendly black nurse's aide with a bandage around her knee. She is going to have a knee replacement soon and has just walked down a football-field-long hall to get me. She tells me Linda is back up from her CAT scan and I can go sit in the ICU with her.

For most of the afternoon, Linda sleeps and I wedge my head up against the back of a visitor's recliner, propping one foot carefully on her bed. I stare up at a strip of sky between two elongated and characterless structures that look like lazy illustrations for an H.G. Wells novel.

After awhile I notice a long, extremely thin triangle of sunlight creeping down the edge of one of the buildings. I can actually see it lengthening and realize that from my ant's-eye perspective, I'm watching the earth turn. I'm seeing something spectacular; it's quiet, like the 99.9 percent of the world's wonders I don't notice except during those rare synaptic flashes when I see a whopping trillionth of a percent more and imagine I've become exponentially wiser.

Chapter Twenty-Two

Then, just as abruptly, my new feeling of insight vanishes.

Later, they give Linda a clean bill of health and release her. We've cheated the devil.

Today, the day after Linda's surgery, I'm trying to be useful around the house as she recuperates. Abigail's wedding is Sunday. Scott gets into town on Saturday. Charlie will pick him up at the airport and they will all come here, bringing dinner with them—I hope—or else they'll have to eat my cooking and they'll be sorry.

Debby can't come to the wedding after all. I knew Michael's schedule might get complicated, but I'm upset about Debby. She has to have a minor surgical thing—nothing to do with the cancer—and I'm confident about her health, but I really wanted to see her.

It's okay. She'll be out soon.

When Debby lives with Jessica and me, during the time her first husband is in Korea, she works for a department store in Beverly Hills. One day she's arrested in the Valley for shoplifting. She didn't do it, but she's arrested for it. That night, she's upset and I don't know how to talk her out of it. She can't sleep or even begin to relax. It's been an ordeal for her, so I give her a couple of tranquilizers and some sleeping pills.

I have plenty of those. I get all I want from our father, who's from a still-widespread school of physicians who think distress is best coped with by knockdown sedation. It's a handy belief if your family has a sizeable habit of its own. Except for Debby. Her one indulgence is a little pot. Anyway, this night I give her some pills.

Her lawyer asks her if she wants a jury trial, in which case she could collect considerable damages; or she could have a hearing in front of a judge. If that happens and the judge rules in her favor, she will get a modest, pre-determined settlement. I don't understand why at the time but Debby doesn't want the jury. She'll take the judge and the smaller satisfaction.

Several months later, at the hearing, I have to testify. Debby's attorney asks me about her state of mind the night she was arrested. I say that she was very upset and add, on the lawyer's prompting, that I gave her tranquilizers to help her deal with it.

Then, the department store's attorney examines me and asks if I have a license to prescribe medicine. I say, "No." Only I don't just say no. I tremble with guilt like I'm playing a lying weasel on *Perry Mason*.

Every word Debby says feels timorous and self-conscious, and I realize why she hasn't chosen a jury trial. She knew she was going to come across guilty.

She wins her settlement because she didn't do anything wrong, unless you count being embarrassed and shamefaced.

But hell, we've both done that forever. We always had to work the angles every second and behave like lying weasels just to survive our mother's erratic dictatorship. When we'd complain to Dad, he'd sigh and say, "Well, you know your mom." Usually he'd already had a drink or two when he said it, which, as I know I've mentioned, was *his* way of dealing with the domestic madness.

I didn't set out to be whiny and bad-tempered and to go on like this, but I believe that having to live that way when she was a child caused Debby's merciless anxieties and that *that* caused her first cancer, and now it's caused this one. And even though I say I've forgiven my parents, *I HAVE NOT*.

Chapter Twenty-Two

Frank calls last night and tells me her cancer has metastasized—to her liver. They've found three spots.

Debby won't talk to me at this moment, but I call her back later and ask her how she feels and she tells me, "Not good." She has pain throughout her body. She's going in for a bone scan in a few days, but it looks bad. She sounds in pain, frail, scared—and curiously brave. When I get off the phone and Linda and I have recovered from the first wave of grief, I'm flooded with a rage I can barely control. Debby seems so much cooler than I am.

I don't care how much my mother suffered her own devils or how evolved I'd convinced myself I was becoming. I can't stop myself from hating Debby's killer.

Linda tells me, "Somehow she's going to be all right."

I just stare at her.

"I have a feeling."

For some reason this enrages me all over again.

"Miracles happen."

I don't know what to say to her.

"Pray for her. And get on a plane."

Movies I like: *To Kill a Mockingbird, Wings of Desire, Enchanted April, Closer, Fargo, Working Girl, Howard's End, Room with a View, Proof, Mostly Martha, Red, Blue* (the second and third films in Kieslowski's *Three Colors* trilogy), *Laura, Lost in Translation, Tootsie, Broadcast News, Groundhog Day, Casablanca, Trucker, North by Northwest, The Big Chill, Shopgirl, Sleepless in Seattle, Breakfast at Tiffany's,* anything by Kirosawa or Mike Leigh, *The Reivers,* and *Now, Voyager.*

Also *Umbrellas of Cherbourg, Black Narcissus, The Third Man, A Man and a Woman, Born Yesterday, Love Actually, The Apartment, The*

Wizard of Oz, Roman Holiday, Double Indemnity, Brief Encounter, The Searchers, Melvin and Howard, Under the Tuscan Sun, The Accidental Tourist, Dark Victory, anything by Fellini (especially *Nights of Cabiria), Sundays and Cybele, Il Postino, Shakespeare in Love, The Snapper, The Man Who Would Be King, Emma,* anything with the Marx Brothers, *The Spiral Staircase, Picnic, The Bridge on the River Kwai, It's a Wonderful Life, The Adventures of Priscilla, Queen Of The Desert, Raging Bull, Lawrence of Arabia, Strictly Ballroom, Blow Up, Flight of the Red Balloon, Leave Her to Heaven,* anything with Catherine Keener, *Life Is Sweet, Four Weddings and a Funeral, Hannah and Her Sisters, Radio Days;* two thirds of the films by Woody Allen and Merchant/Ivory, *Twelve Angry Men, I've Loved You So Long,* Leonard Cohen and various, mostly Canadian singers in *I'm Your Man,* Roy Orbison in *A Black and White Night,* and *Attack of the Crab People.*

And *Intolerance* and *Who's Afraid of Virginia Woolf* and *It Happened One Night* and *Steamboat Bill, King Rat, Postcards from the Edge, The Bicycle Thief, Run Lola Run,* and *City Lights* and *The Maltese Falcon.* Oh, and *The African Queen, Bringing Up Baby, Network, The Crying Game, Rear Window, Little Manhattan, The Graduate, Angels in America* (the TV mini-series) and *Once.* Plus at least a couple hundred more.

Directors who miss their big chance and don't hire me: Tyrone Guthrie (for *Dinner At Eight* on Broadway), Billy Wilder (for *Avanti!*; he casts a much older Jack Lemmon, who couldn't save it), Otto Preminger (for *Such Good Friends*; he's the only one I ever meet, who I know if he doesn't kill me, I'll kill him), William Wyler (for *A Walk in the Spring Rain,* with Ingrid Bergman, who suggested me for it, and Anthony Quinn), Steven Spielberg (for *The Sugarland Express*), and Gene Kelly for *Hello, Dolly!* (He is charming to me. I'd sell my soul

Chapter Twenty-Two

for this one—but Michael Crawford is a better dancer, not to mention singer: *The Phantom of the Opera*.) I audition for the original Broadway production of *The Lion in Winter*. Arthur Hiller sees me for *Love Story*, but although I always wanted to be, I'm not really a jock type.

One time I do a pilot for the American version of a popular BBC program, *No, Honestly*. It's a Burns and Allen relationship (the Gracie Allen prototype is the lovely Shelley Fabares). The other two characters, Shelley's father and a butler, are to be played by Burgess Meredith and Joshua Logan. It's a marvelous show, written by Madelyn Davis and Bob Carroll Jr. who wrote *I Love Lucy*. Sitcom veteran and friend Bill Persky directs. Shelley's character is wacky, but smart—not a dumb blonde as NBC is worried she will be perceived. She simply operates on another wavelength. In the end, NBC goes with Instinct B: It's a dangerous time to take a risk on a dumb blonde stereotype and the show doesn't go to series.

Lots of actors have similar stories. My friend Marcia Rodd (a sublime stage and film actress) was offered the role of Maude's daughter in the television series of the same name. Marcia said no thanks. I'm not sure if she regrets that, but, knowing her, I doubt it. I'm pretty sure she's happy with the choices she made. Nevertheless, you can't help *sometimes* thinking about the what-ifs in any life.

For example, I sometimes wonder *what if* my mother had gotten some help with her fucking emotional problems and had not dumped *so many* of them on my sister?

Talking about directors I never worked for, I forgot to mention whoever directed Lanford Wilson's *Lemon Sky* Off-Broadway.

It's winter when I audition for him at the Eugene O'Neill Theatre, where I did *Mating Dance* for one night a couple of years earlier. It's icy cold outside. I've just worked the nightshift at my desk-clerk job at the Americana Hotel.

I go down to the coffee shop, have three cups, and read the audition scene over and over till I can't look at it any more. I'm not bad casting for this role. I'm feeling, if not confident, genuinely hopeful. I leave in plenty of time to walk the few blocks to the theatre. It's freezing cold as I hurry toward the O'Neill.

As soon I sign in, they're ready for me. I walk onto the stage a bit breathless and unsteady, but I've been here before; I know what to do. I call out a jovial hello to the invisible director and the rest of them in the darkened theatre. They're not exactly cordial, but I know the schedule they're keeping to and I understand.

The stage manager gives me my first cue.

The words come out of me like I'm a seal begging for fish. My mouth is frozen. I make a jumble of sorrowful noises. As I near the climax of the scene, I get louder, trying to *force* myself anywhere close to the deeper meanings and the emotional pitch Mr. Wilson intends.

But it amounts to no more than a garbled scream.

I keep hoping it's a dream and I'll wake up, but it's not and I don't.

They cast Christopher Walken instead of me and I can't argue with that.

CHAPTER TWENTY-THREE

Debby's dog Tally died last year. Debby and Frank returned to Wyoming just before the most recent bad news, and she called me from the park where Linda and I had gone with her years ago for a picnic. She told me she'd just given Tally's ashes to the wind. She said it was a beautiful day and she'd known for a long time she was going to do this, but she felt sad; Tally was really gone now.

Does Debby imagine *her* ashes blowing in the wind? I can't imagine she won't go on forever.

I won't say goodbye to her, and I don't mean her *spirit*, I mean the *fact* of her: Debby as Debby, as she's always been—at heart—full of life and enthusiasm, and each day less and less vulnerable to primordial fears.

But what does she dream of now that there's so little time left for dreams? What comforts her when she's facing the dark? And how did she get to be so courageous in the face of this?

Ann Stuart didn't want a funeral service. She is buried at Forest Lawn in the plot she'd bought many years before—not near any family because there *is* no family except her mother and for reasons unknown to me she didn't want to be buried near mom. So she is alone out there somewhere in that big field of stones across from Disney Studios along the northern edge of Griffith Park.

At the appointed hour, Linda and I are standing at her gravesite. The crowd consists of us, two men from the mortuary, and a Forest Lawn representative. No clergy. It feels to Linda and me as if the whole thing is being done for us. There's a big pile of red dirt. Next to it is a rectangular hole in the ground that looks like a backhoe dug it. Above the hole is a coffin with two slats of wood beneath it. We assume that Ann is in there. This hole is not in a line with any others. I guess this is the start of a new row. It looks for the moment as if Ann is going to be off to the side again, by herself.

It's a sunny California day, not much wind, but enough to pick up some pollen, arouse my asthma, and remind me that I will be among the un-present myself in a finite number of years.

Neither Linda nor I experience what you could call grief; maybe bleakness is the word. I think of Ann's opaque eyes, reflecting only her paralyzing fear. I'm glad she's not (*really*) here. She'd hate this.

The coffin is a simple wooden box. She'd paid in advance for the no-frills deal.

One of the men from the funeral home asks us if we'd like to say anything. Neither of us has considered this possibility. I step up to the coffin and say, "Heaven rest you now, Ann." The notion of adding, "Or Anitra or Alice Ann or whoever else you may have been inside your unknowable self," flashes through my mind, but I don't do it.

Linda slips out the two slats of wood. The other three men and I, by means of canvas straps, lower the coffin down into a cement vault

Chapter Twenty-Three

already in place at the bottom of the hole. Linda and I each throw in a shovelful of dirt.

We wait. The men leave.

We stand there alone, wondering when they'll be filling up the hole.

Now, two young guys riding on a machine the size of a large pickup appear from over a hill. The machine whirrs toward us, turns around, then backs over several graves and finally comes to a halt by Ann's. Then, with a big paddle, it puts dirt alongside the cement vault in the grave. One of the guys jumps down into the hole to pack the dirt in along the sides of the cement, then effortlessly climbs back out.

The guy still on this nifty entomb-o-matic contraption now scoops red earth into the hole with the finesse of a surgeon. The machine looks like an agile giant with a tablespoon and a tiny whiskbroom, something perhaps SpongeBob SquarePants would use. When this is done, the driver switches on a tamping mechanism. It makes a terrible pounding noise that makes me imagine for a moment that I'm alive and in that coffin, eyes and ears open, hearing the suffocating finale thundering down on me. I hate cognitive dissonance.

Finally, the men take out four rolls of sod, spread them over the tamped-down grave and tamp them down too. And then *they* leave. The whole process has taken about fifteen minutes.

Linda has been holding flowers, daisies. I see her frown. The wind is picking up. I'm ready to go, but I understand she wants to do something with the daisies.

Because it's the newer part of this vast, rolling graveyard, Linda and I both realize we don't know for sure which end of the grave is the "head" where they'll put the stone when it's engraved and ready. The cemetery people must have some system, but for now, no one who doesn't work for Forest Lawn or who isn't in the burying business could possibly tell there was even a body here, let alone which end used to do the thinking and which end used to propel her from here to there.

After a moment, Linda arbitrarily picks an end and lays the daisies on it. Then, she turns, still kneeling, and looks up at me.

She's crying. She looks back down at the daisy end of the grave and whispers to it, "I know that's not you, Ann. You're not in there."

Dabbing at her eyes, she stands up and joins me again. We both stare for a while at the shoved-together pieces of fresh sod and the daisies and the abstract bits and pieces that lie on top of Ann's former life.

Then we walk back down toward Disney Studios and our car.

Linda answers the telephone and says, "Hi, Debby." Listening, she begins to smile, then silent tears form in her eyes and my spirits rise like a geyser. I put my ear to the receiver too.

The three masses, the tumors they found on her liver, were hemangiomas—like the arrangement of dilated blood vessels she'd had in her lower lip when she was a little girl; technically tumors, but actually no more than three patches of benign nothings that mimic cancer nearly exactly.

Except they're *not cancer.*

Debby's oncologist called and told her that with her CA-125 score continuing to be low, what she's experiencing does not add up to anything calamitous. It's not in any way related to the ovarian cancer. The pain has apparently resulted from not being able to exercise because of the chemotherapy, which has in turn caused her normally controlled backache to become critical—so much so that Debby *and* the doctors confused it with cancer pain.

Chapter Twenty-Three

And now, she'll begin to exercise, using all the industry and good judgment she's got, and she'll do it with patience and without fail. And she will get well.

And all of us will keep praying.

I wait for the *voices* to say something cynical, but they appear to be gone, or just keeping quiet, or *maybe* I can't hear them anymore. I *like* that idea. I remember, from Genesis, Jacob wrestling the angel. In that parable, Jacob thinks at first—our problems never appearing to be anything but earthly—that the angel is a man. It's only in retrospect that he realizes it *is* an angel and that the angel has helped him transform his life and that the very struggle has given him new life.

Jesus! In the Bible, man means woman too. Is it possible my angel was my own *mother*? I thumb through one of Linda's spiritual books, something Eastern about reincarnation, but it doesn't tell me a thing about angels showing up as your mom.

I wonder if the picture of Michael Curtiz's mother that he autographed was a compassionate gift to Ann because of the rotten mother *she'd* been dealt? Is it possible that *he* was a ... Nah.

Mariette Hartley calls me. She's a great actress who made her film debut in *Ride the High Country*, directed by Sam Peckinpah. Since then, she has worked more consistently than any actress I know of. A lot of people remember her from a series of Polaroid camera commercials she did with James Garner in which she was as utterly charming as she is in real life. I've known her for a long time. We were in Raymond Burr's next-to-last *Perry Mason*, both of us red herrings. (I can't remember who committed the murders, but I do recall the first victim was Regis Philbin. He's a nice man, but as an actor, it's probably a good idea to kill him as early on as possible.)

Mariette has heard about Debby's illness and Abigail's recovery. I tell her the most recent good news and she says, "Some people get all the breaks." She's joking, but it comes gently, from her heart. She wrote a book called *Breaking the Silence*. Her grandfather was behavioral psychologist John B. Watson, who believed children should never be held or cuddled. Mariette was raised that way and getting over it was a long road. Early on in her career, recently arrived in Hollywood from her years as a New York stage actress, her father committed suicide. Her uncle and a cousin died the same way. How do you keep from taking that a little personally?

Mariette has spent her life as an advocate for people in trouble, trying to be useful before unspeakable things can happen.

Linda and I like to read each other to sleep. Well, I read to *her*. The "nice droning" of my voice puts her almost immediately out. We read the aforementioned *The Hidden Messages in Water*. Emoto says that because a cloud is made up of water, and *we're* mostly water, that if we focus on a cloud long enough with relaxed concentration and tell it we would like it to dissipate, that before long it will.

I realize the following may sound indescribably silly to some people. But.

This morning Linda was already up when I came out. She told me she had caused a cloud to disappear that way. I made a cynical face, then, feeling sorry or at least guilty about that, gazed through the kitchen window out at a fair-sized cloud to the south of us. At first I couldn't relax but finally, I silently said to it, feeling very goofy: "I am focusing the laser of my mind on you (what-*ever*) and I'd like

Chapter Twenty-Three

you to please dissolve." *I really did try to be sincere about it.* I made myself hold the thought.

Within a minute, the cloud was gone. I blinked. It had to be an optical illusion. But when I looked back, it still wasn't there. I said to Linda, "Does it *stay* gone?"

She nodded. "Now, say thank you." In the book, Emoto says it's important to do that.

So I did.

Finding out you can dissolve a cloud, even if you can't think of anything practical you'll be able to do with a skill like that, calls for a bit of ... *something*—humility, maybe. The funny thing is, I've told this story to several people and almost all of them use the same tone of voice with me you use when you're trying to carefully deal with a lunatic, or just being delicate in a way that won't hurt the poor crazy person's feelings.

But it *works*! I called Abigail in Mississippi and told her about it. She was getting out of her car at a park. She said "Just a minute," took a few steps into the park, chose a small cloud and dissolved it.

When I woke up this morning, Linda was still asleep next to me. I watched her for a long time. Her face looked older, more settled on the pillow. It touched me with unimaginable tenderness, like there's a new kind of beauty in it I was too ignorant to see before.

CHAPTER TWENTY-FOUR

Josh was at our house last night with Abigail; so were Scott, Charlie, Kim, and Riley, who's six-and-a-half now. It was the night before the wedding. At one point, Abi and Scott and I were sitting on the bed with Riley pummeling me and being a little boy. Abigail said to Scott, "This is good." And Scott smiled and nodded, and Abigail—full of outgoing and indwelling life—looked at me and beamed, and I was contented to be there. Linda picked tomatoes and made pesto from the basil in our garden, and even though she was only five days out of surgery, she didn't want anybody else to cook the steaks Charlie'd brought. She wasn't on painkillers any more and said she felt fine. I offered to do all this, but she wouldn't allow it.

I thought about the last time I did *Same Time, Next Year*. Vera Miles and I had closed in our original production more than half a year earlier. Now we were doing it one last week at the huge Neal Blaisdell Concert Theatre in Honolulu. Since the show had been staged a year earlier by Harvey Medlinsky, the producer didn't want to pay for a director, so he asked me if I would brush up Harvey's work. There was nothing I could think of to brush up, but I knew if my name didn't go on it in that capacity, then the producer's probably would, and he might go all artsy on us and screw something up—so I said okay.

One afternoon during the short run of our little play in this barn of a theatre, the next show was rehearsing. Abigail, Scott, and Charlie had come to Hawaii with me, so we all went to a stop-and-go run-through of *A Chorus Line*.

In that brilliant show, there's a director (a character in the show) out in the audience, directing the performers on stage. As the surrogate director of the current show, accompanied by his kids, I watched the *real* director of this production of *A Chorus Line* direct the actor who was *playing* the director, as he pretended to direct the performers on stage (who were also being directed by the *real* director), and I imagined that I *had* directed *Same Time, Next Year* and felt a rush of something like self-worth.

Last night, as the patriarch of the family gathering, I felt a similar sensation, except it was a little less delusional.

Yesterday evening was the wedding. Jessica gave the party at her house and as always was a superb hostess, one of her best things.

It was a benchmark in Abigail's life, not only because she was marrying—technically, she'd already done that in Mississippi a month earlier—but because it made a lovely punctuation mark to her first year of sobriety and the million changes that have happened in the twelve months since I picked her up at the convenience store in Hollywood the night she talked to God.

Whatever He said to her, it worked.

She was radiant.

Chapter Twenty-Four

Scott was there, and Charlie, Kim, and Riley. Dian drove out with Linda and me. They were both radiant. The whole family was radiant.

I was radiant.

Charlie is in some ways the more centered of my sons—I'm not sure why I say that, because Scott is also my hero. My guess is that as the second son, and with Scott doing most of the raging at Sarah's husband during the bad times, Charlie took a philosophical tack and was able to cope with more flexibility.

After the wedding, Charlie and I are standing on the bridge over Sherman Canal, just west of Jessica's house, having a glass of wine. Actually, it's *his* wine, an excellent Pinot, from his own winery. They don't make Chardonnay yet, but he tells me he thinks they will soon. I hope he's not doing it just for me.

After we talk for a while and he lets me know what's going on with his work and his home life and all the latest about Riley, I tell him some of the things I've been thinking and some of what's happened. I tell him about the books Linda's brought into the house that I've been perusing, and that I've sent some off to Debby during her illness. Charlie has read a couple of these books and is much more naturally inclined to understand that you *are* what you *think* you are and all that.

"I don't remember your being involved with any of that mystical stuff," he says. "You didn't used to, did you?"

"I've changed."

He squints at me. "Have you?"

"Yeah, I think so."

"How?"

"Well, I'm not exactly sure."

"Then how do you know you've changed?"

"I *don't* really. I feel different—*better*. I haven't quite got a handle on it yet, at least not enough to explain it."

"Wow."

"What do you mean 'wow'?"

"You *love* to explain."

"Whether I've got a handle on it or not, huh?"

He smiles. "Yeah, I remember you explaining a few things to me."

"Was it ever useful?"

"Sometimes."

"That's good."

"Sometimes not."

I nod. "Well, it was still early in my learning curve."

He smiles.

"Anyway, with what Debby's had to deal with and all the problems Abigail's gone through, I started to order some of these things from Amazon myself."

"Did you read them?"

"Parts. I skimmed through other parts."

"They don't seem like skimming books."

I watch a gull land on a stanchion where a short dock used to be, a couple of houses away. "Well, I don't have the patience to just sit there and read. Linda's the reader. I write or paint all day. Then at night, I usually watch movies on TV."

"Did Linda read these books?" I guess I frown because he says, "What's the matter?"

"I think she's read all of them—maybe more than once." I'm not sure why I'm surprised to realize this. "When I'm gone, she doesn't watch television. Whenever I go away, I don't think she turns the thing on. The television's mine."

"Pardon?"

Chapter Twenty-Four

"You know how certain areas get to be one person's, and the other things are the other one's domain? Linda's never really learned to use all the TV remotes. I keep teaching her, but she won't retain any of it. I don't think she really cares."

"Yeah? What don't you do that she *does*?"

"Quite a few things ... She puts the cartridges into the printer and takes care of the sprinkler system, and God knows I have no clue how to work the washer and dryer." I'm feeling embarrassed. "Well, I'm in charge of the *audio* equipment."

"When does she have time to read?" I just look at him. "I mean with taking care of the garden and the shopping—so you don't have to spend too much time out in the LA air—and running her business and taking care of your printer."

"She finds time."

He's watching me with his damned inscrutable smile. "So, you're in charge of the television and the music, but she washes your clothes, does all your errands, and feeds you, body and soul?"

"Yeah, that's about it."

He's still smiling at me. And suddenly I'm aware of where we are, and the air that's pretty much perfect on my skin, and a tremendous ease that seems to be washing over me.

In the afterglow of Abigail's wedding day and the beautiful evening on the canal, Charlie says, "You're my hero, Pop. You're the Leonardo of philosopher/artists. You know how to delegate and still turn out beautiful work."

I take a sip of his fine Pinot. "Thanks," I say. Even if his words are a little tongue-in-cheek, even if life is swimming around me very fast, for the moment I'm in the peaceful eye of the storm with Charlie, and it feels good.

When Scott and Charlie were eleven and ten, Jim and Sarah took them aboard a thirty-foot sailboat, a sloop, Jim had chartered in Jupiter Inlet in Southeast Florida. Even though there was a small craft warning in effect, they set sail toward Grand Bahama Island. Jim was anxious not to waste any of his vacation time. The National Weather Service doesn't give a definition of a small craft, so Jim undoubtedly thought they were safe. Once at sea, he relaxed, cruising under mainsail only, for a long time—too long.

They were leisurely drifting southeast when the storm hit.

The Gulf Stream moves north. The winds were gusty from the east. The four of them were suddenly, as Charlie remembers it, surrounded by thirty-foot waves that didn't know which way to break. "They were as tall as trees," he recalls. Scott says, "We were in the Bermuda Triangle. I knew that. That didn't help our frame of mind. It was all adrenalin and trying to hold a course in the rolling waves and doing our best to cope with the notion that we might not live through this."

After twenty-four hours of fighting it, Jim could no longer handle the tiller.

Sarah, who had never sailed in her life, took over. Controlling the tiller of a thirty-foot sloop in seas surging as high as the deck of the *Titanic* takes enormous strength and determination. Sarah's not small, but she's not big either. She was at the tiller for eight hours. Jim woke up once in awhile and checked their bearings, then left it to Sarah.

When either Scott or Charlie talk about their mother, it's not just with love, but also admiration and respect—not only for bringing them safely in sight of Grand Bahama Island on that occasion, but for having the same guts and strength all through their childhoods. While raising a family that not only included Scott and Charlie, but

Chapter Twenty-Four

also Jim's three kids from an earlier marriage, Sarah earned a bachelor's degree in Psychology at SUNY, Stony Brook; then a master's degree in Social Work. She co-designed and still runs a children's bereavement summer retreat, called Camp Good Grief, "for children who have experienced a loss." The rest of the year she works at East End Hospice as head of the social workers there. She has written on the subject of grief and grief counseling and continues to be the best mother the boys could possibly have.

When I reflect on the awkwardness that existed between my father and me, especially after I'd grown up, I think—as I often do anyway—about my boys, grown men, and how it was a form of lunacy to be off pretending to be other people when I had a critical role in my sons' lives that I only rarely played. I know that the curtain will never rise again on those lost opportunities. I regret that I was not there when it really counted and I'm constantly amazed and also proud—though I have no right to be—at what good people they are and what good fathers they have been and continue to be to their own boys.

All of this in no small part due to Sarah.

The day following the wedding: I'm home painting and Linda calls me after seeing Dr. Goldstein, who'd operated on her a week ago today. When she was through with her appointment, she says, she was making her next one and saw, ten feet away, Al Pacino. He was waiting to see Dr. Goldstein and was talking on a cell phone. She smiled at him and says he gave her a warm smile back. Actually, she says, "*killer* smile."

Thinking of Al, I feel that kind of nameless ache for a thing I had for awhile a long time ago. Then the ache goes away as I remember that everything is okay because the thing I thought it was, was only in my imagination, and that Al's killer smile is no more than what it is, a good man's warm smile at a pretty woman.

And this makes me think of being in Hawaii a few years after I'd done *Same Time, Next Year* there. I was doing a *Magnum, P.I.* The first day, Linda came onto the soundstage and I introduced her to Tom Selleck.

It was the only time I ever saw my wife go gaga over a big star. I guess Tom *was* at the peak of his good looks. When I said, "Linda, this is Tom," she reminded me of Jackie Gleason as "The Chef of the Future" in the episode of *The Honeymooners* where he was on live television selling a kitchen gadget called the Handy Housewife Helper, and had such stage fright he turned into gibbering Jell-O, or maybe it was Woody Allen she reminded me of, in *Sleeper*, when he's just come out of the "Orgasmatron." She might as well have been made of Silly Putty. God knows Tom *was* charming to her, but you'd think she'd just met Adonis or something. It was embarrassing.

Scott fixed the broken garbage disposal and the shower yesterday, mended two broken chairs, and put a new lock on the back door. This morning he's out in the living room doing yoga. He moved all the furniture off the area rug in front of the fireplace and now he's out there doing whatever he does while I'm in here doing whatever it is I do. Later on he's going to level the ground for a potting shed we're putting in the back. Or maybe he'll build a suspension bridge.

Last night, I was playing the piano. Scott and I each had a beer going. Linda was cooking. Scott sat down on the piano bench, facing the other way, put a hand on my shoulder and said, "This has been sweet."

Chapter Twenty-Four

Very late one summer night when I was older than I care to reveal, I was sitting on our back porch, drinking something heavy-duty: turpentine—if that's what there was. Linda had gone to bed. I was reading a local stage trade paper. It dealt mostly with Equity Waiver theatre. Someone had received a lifetime achievement award. I began to wonder if it was possible that I could be honored that way. I read the story again and realized that although I was younger than the honoree, my accomplishments, added up, were *somewhat* comparable.

As I sipped my turpentine, I began to plot how I could get one of those awards. I would convince someone to submit my name. I would write some higher-up. I didn't have the details worked out of exactly who that might be—Mike Nichols springs to mind, although I don't know Mike Nichols, nor he me. I would subtly suggest that I too be considered for a lifetime achievement award. I had won some individual acting awards in the past (transparently insignificant ones). I had been honored a little, but I wanted to be honored a *lot*. I didn't know where it would take me. Nowhere. It would be meaningless in the larger world of show business. Even within the Equity Waiver stage world, as very little time passed, it would be forgotten. But it didn't matter. I wanted the Wizard of Oz to give me my *Testimonial*.

I'd like to say this was a breakthrough; that the next day I began to restructure my magic show values, and make an effort to look at the lives of people with problems that mattered. But it didn't work that way. I continued to concentrate most of my energy on making sure I had enough *importance* to get me through—like Fagin in *Oliver Twist* hoarding away enough plunder, enough sparklies to bedazzle and overcome mortality. I hadn't yet realized that occupations other than acting and drinking were open to me. I hadn't learned to be grateful for the gift of what J.K. Rowling calls "the fringe benefits of failure, and [for the] the importance of imagination."

I'd lived in that restricted frame of mind my whole life. Victims of the fire can't be expected to carry buckets of water to it. Anyway, *they* didn't *start* it.

Yesterday, the Saturday after Abi's wedding, Abi, Linda, Dian, and I drove over the mountains to Venice. Linda and I said we'd get tattoos when Abigail hit her one-year sober mark—which happened a few days before the wedding.

Abi had made an appointment with Kevin, a ferret-like ex-punker with the ink-gun hand of an angel and a likewise appealing way about him. He's got maybe four-dozen tattoos himself. The walls of his space—a small room in the back of a good-sized barbershop in The Venice Circle, where the boardwalk begins—are plastered with thousands of beautiful designs he's capable of embedding in your hide. He has an iBook, and can go to the Internet, locate thousands of other shapes and patterns, print the ones you're interested in, blow them up or shrink them to any size you choose, and use them as templates for illustrating any mark, character, icon, or pictogram you choose. If it pleases you, he can turn you into an epic poem.

I thought I might get a circle of five letters: L, A, C, S, and D, the first initials of Linda, Abigail, Charlie, Scott, and Debby. But in the end, that seemed to lack any poetry, plus it left out my grandchildren, and my kids' spouses—and then there were Dian and others who are dear to me, so I decided on the Chinese symbol for "love." I was told it would hurt to get it on the tender skin of my inner wrist, which is where I'd decided to wear it. It did. Kevin etched the fine lines of love on me in bluegrass green, and Linda and Dian watched me keenly since they were to follow. I had to fake bravery. They said my cheek twitched some, but otherwise they thought I was quite stoic.

Chapter Twenty-Four

Next, Linda got the Chinese symbol for peace on the inside of her left ankle.

She said it didn't hurt. She never lies, so I guess it didn't, which I find irritating.

Dian went last. She got a paw print—also on an ankle—in honor of her many dogs. She'd been unsure about doing this. We'd all told her she didn't have to, but in the end she said she wanted to. Next to the dog paw print she got a small heart. She said none of it really hurt, which would have irritated me too, but I had some kind of tattoo buzz happening by then and felt too good for anything to bother me. Dian got a second one, a larger heart on the back of her shoulder and the name of her late Doberman, "Sunshine." I think if we hadn't told her "absolutely not" she would have gotten a couple or ten more. Abi said perhaps she has "an addictive personality, just like us."

Maybe. I wouldn't know.

A few years ago, Uncle Stu, who was so kind to me during my first days in New York, called me. Childless, he was all by himself in a retirement home in Atlanta. He'd gotten it into his brain that he needed to talk to Robert Urich. He didn't know Robert Urich; he'd just decided he had to talk to him—Uncle Stu was obviously not in his right mind. Bob and I had worked together a couple of times and had been friendly.

I felt bad for Stu, but I wouldn't have liked Bob to sic a crazy uncle on me.

I said, "Hold on, Uncle Stu. I think he just walked in." Then I came back on the phone in a different voice and said, "Stu? Bob Urich. What can I do for you?"

And they straightened out what they had to and Uncle Stu cried, happy. If it had been now, I'd have gotten on a plane and gone to see him before he died.

Halloween:

This evening, a little after dark, Abigail delivered a baby girl—without anesthetic, screaming obscenities the whole way. The baby's name is Frances (after Jessica's mother) Palmer (Virginia's maiden name, my middle one) Broome. Josh's last name works well for a Halloween baby. I e-mailed Scott and Charlie that they were uncles. On the subject line I wrote "New Person." Charlie e-mailed back, "It's funny, I think that this person is exactly the person the world has been missing."

Christmas Eve:

Abigail and Josh show up with Frannie, who at two months is a dead ringer for Abigail at that age. There's no point in trying to describe a beautiful baby, except to say it's hard to imagine a better feeling than holding my daughter's daughter, or to watch Abi napping with Frannie nestled in her arms, sleeping too, their faces no more than three inches apart, breathing each other's air.

Recently, I was talking to Linda about the night I picked Abigail up, the night she talked to God. Linda asked me what He'd said. I said I didn't know, Abigail didn't tell me the words.

Linda said, "I think He said, 'You'd better straighten up. You have to have Frances.'"

Maybe praying for help does work. Cervantes said, "Maddest of all—to see life as it is and not as it *should* be."

Chapter Twenty-Four

In the old days, you'd have puked before you'd evoke Cervantes at a moment like this.

Maybe if you "meditate" for others first—ask for the best, *expect* the best for them, and if you mean it, something like that comes to *you* as a nice little side reward.

Gag me with a spoon!

I thought you were gone. Go away.

Let's get out of here!

And they fade to black (at least for now).

Late Christmas Eve:

With Frannie asleep between Linda and me, I read—as I have for twenty-five years, to Abigail and Linda, and tonight, Josh—*A Child's Christmas in Wales*.

> … I turned the gas down, I got into bed. I said some words to the close and holy darkness, and then I slept.

CHAPTER TWENTY-FIVE

Linda and I will visit Abigail, Frannie, and Josh soon. At one time I thought I'd be going to Arizona to help Debby, but she called today with further good news: She's had a PET scan to see if she has any cancer in her body and she's clean as a whistle.

She said her oncologist came in, grinning from ear to ear. *Those* people are the ones—doctors, nurses, drug counselors, caregivers of every description, men and women who work directly for the good of others, the peacemakers, the kindhearted: the VIPs.

The only crabgrass left on the park-like grounds of my existence turns out to be back operations. Shortly before I began working on this story, I had an operation to remove the hardware from my spinal fusion of several years earlier. My orthopedist had decided the metal in me might be causing the pain I was still having. He was wrong. After that operation, it still hurt. So, after several injections of this steroid and that numbing medication, which didn't help either, my *new* orthopedist (Dr. Goldstein) thought it might be best to go in one more time and re-fuse me.

I told my friend Michael I didn't think this made very interesting subject matter for my Hollywood story. But he pointed out that lots of people haven't had *one* back operation, let alone four, and that maybe I should tell people what Munchausen's syndrome is really like.

Then there's the *pump*. They place a little morphine pump in a handy quick-draw position. All you have to do the first couple of days is reach out the smallest distance, give the button a little click and *whoppo*, no more pain—just that druggy, blissful, glad-you-opted-for-surgery feeling; it vaguely occurs to you this might be the solution to world turmoil: Give everybody a pump—*a peace pump*.

Eventually they don't let you use the pump anymore, no matter how sincerely you promise them you won't get hooked. And that's when the post-op fun really begins. The good news is the only thing you remember about pain is that you had it, and the truth is you can barely recall what it feels like.

When I get home from the hospital, Linda nurses me. It's like I'm up there with one of her cats. Or Dash. She fixes me pancakes every morning. (Twelve days after the operation, when I have to go back for my first post-op appointment, I will not be able to button the top button on any of my pants.) It's as if I've gotten wounded in battle and she's one of those angel nurses in the old World War II movies. She bathes me, then I lie down on some towels on the bed, with my head at the edge. First she washes my hair, massaging my scalp with warm water from a basin in her lap. Then she gets my arms, chest, and shoulders. Finally, she rinses my hair and massages my head and neck some more.

I drift off and remember our trip to Mississippi a couple of weeks earlier. We've traveled to visit Abigail, Josh, and Frannie. It's April and I want to get this in before my surgery. We make a connection in Memphis on our way to Hattiesburg. There is a storm cell over Memphis International Airport, so we have to wait awhile before we

Chapter Twenty-Five

can land. I recite the 91st Psalm, a medium-long piece I've learned—just to keep my memory exercised—seven or eight times as we circle. We are above what the lady next to us, whose husband is a pilot, tells us are vertically developed clouds, which means there's a storm down there.

The 91st Psalm says, "Angels shall bear thee up in their hands lest thou dash thy foot against a stone." And: "There shall no evil befall thee." I am still doubtful about God. She doesn't feel what I would call reliable—my litmus test for God's relevance to me. I do more and more think of Her as feminine, because I'm quite sure any particle of wisdom I've managed to absorb is thanks to the women in my life.

As we finally start our descent and the airplane begins to quiver and bounce like a tin can on the street in a hurricane, the speed of my inward recitation increases. I'm advised by almost anyone who claims to know about those things that God is not best communicated with by mechanical repetition, but it's all I have to offer. I know I've already said I'm not creative when I'm terrified, and my cognitive dissonance is now clearly announcing to me that we're doomed.

At least Linda is with me. Then, as I think about it, I realize that doesn't really help; the thing I can stand least in the world is seeing her unhappy or in pain. So I find myself wishing she *wasn't* here. If I have to die while setting a world record in speed-recitation of the 91st Psalm, I don't want her to lose everything she loves about this life at the same time. And she seems to love all of it. There's no place she doesn't want to visit or live; no food she doesn't want to try; no pain she doesn't want to relieve. I couldn't stand to see her lose that.

As I tear through the greater part of my spiritual learning, I'm gazing at Linda. I concentrate on her, the words to the psalm feeling more and more mechanical. I wish she were safe in our house in North Hollywood.

Then, all at once, I feel peaceful.

I think it's *possible* that all those ministers, those dubious "holy men" who represent God as looking down at us—decreeing from His Olympian perch that we are all born miserable offenders with nothing to save us except maybe a lifetime of groveling—are cruelly missing the point of, for example, the Sermon on the Mount; and that the *essence* of what's really going on is that God is inside all of us, approachable by each of us, loving each of us, exactly as most of the great prophets have patiently explained.

The plane is still lurching, but it no longer bothers me. We land and everything is fine.

Mississippi is fine. The area around Hattiesburg feels like the Jackson, Michigan, of my youth, only with mega-gluts of shopping malls. The people are nice. It's very kickback. The Southern hospitality and kindness are genuine.

There does appear a crack in my rose-colored glasses one day, through which I see a church with a sign outside that reads: "The good don't go to heaven. Only the redeemed go to heaven." I stop to take a picture of that sign. Then I realize my instinct to do that is unkind.

Abi called me recently and told me they had a new sign in front of that church: "God loves you. But only if you obey." I know this is another wicked instinct, but I don't even want to shake hands with a God who puts "Buts" on loving me. I know it's not Godlike of me, that it probably falls under the heading of not obeying, but I think that's one of the things a loving God *will* forgive me for. I even expect Her to forgive my impudence in thinking that some of the time I can distinguish truth from bullshit.

Linda tells me to change the picture I have in my head of the boy who made me jump over snake pits and of the vipers I imagined I saw in those pits.

Chapter Twenty-Five

"I can't just eject those snakes out of me like a stereo spits out a CD."

"Stick in another CD, a nicer one," she says. "One that features things you enjoy thinking about, something noble and worthwhile—you know, fairness and justice. You like digging around in those thoughts."

"I'm not sure I'd know where to begin."

"Think of that little girl at Halloween."

It was years earlier. Jessica had taken Abigail out trick-or-treating. I had to receive the kids who came to our house even though I was uncomfortable with it each time I went to the door. I greeted each set of children with an uneasy smile and appropriate reactions to the costumes, wishing all the time I was in my room, too self-conscious in my solipsism even to appreciate the neighborhood kids in their vampire and ghoul get-ups.

Toward the end, I went to the open, screenless front door and saw two big black boys at the exact moment they saw me. It felt like my adrenaline might shoot me through the roof. Then I noticed they were with a small black girl, no older than five. One of the boys who'd grasped and probably anticipated this, said, "She's our sister." As I looked down at the little girl in her princess costume, then back at the boys, I saw that they all had the same beautiful eyes.

"Simple as that?" I say to Linda. "I just think noble thoughts and I'm all better?"

"It's a beginning. But you've got to make sure to keep your eye focused on this new picture and not let your mind wander back to your snakes."

I wish all the changes I've gone through had begun a long time ago. I wish they'd begun before Dixie Thorpe and I went swimming that day. I wish I hadn't been so stupid and unkind during my first two marriages—unable to give comfort, unable to do anything but seek it. I wish I'd been smarter and nicer to women I now admire and respect. But that's another one of those things you don't get retakes on.

I'm a better husband and father now. But the changes I've made don't seem to be as much the result of courage as of good luck or The Universal Creator within me. Maybe they happened because I ended up married to the only blind date I ever had. I never would have guessed the night I met her that this woman, this feminine Holy Spirit, would raise me out of chaos and restore my soul.

When Goldie Hawn and I were first working and hanging out together, I felt a kinship with her that developed out of us being *the kids* in an experience that was crazy and wonderful and seemed HUGE at the time. She and I alone shared this thing.

I was recently looking through a box of old pictures, clippings, and letters. I came across one of the last notes I've gotten from her. At the end of it she wrote, "I have always held you close to my heart."

Me too, Goldie.

EPILOGUE

I wake up the night after I've finished this with my habitual insomnia and an awareness that I've been looking for my usual reward and that I haven't gotten it. I always play for the audience's approval, but I don't hear any *applause*. There's no smell of greasepaint, no roar of crowd, only silence.

CLOSE-UP: Actor tells in a manic rant what he thinks happened as he wandered here and there, preening, strutting, and playing the fool on other people's stages. If he's gotten it right, that's okay, but he's due no applause for it, it's just his life, at the time—what he felt compelled to do in the frenzy of his youth.

If I'm lucky and somebody enjoys the story, I get no credit for that either. It's absolutely accidental and came only from my eternal need to please.

Or, if I'm wrong about that—and I do find this thought comforting—then, whatever good has come, came from some point of origin that uses me only as a means of expression, a mouthpiece: an actor.

If that's the case, I'm grateful.

When Linda and I first met, she wouldn't call me Rick. She admits it was from a kind of snobbishness. She preferred Richard. Now, she likes Rick. Sometimes I imagine us at the airport, doing the final scene from *Casablanca*, which was shot at the Van Nuys Airport, six miles from where we live.

It's foggy. You can barely see the plane behind us. But in this version—and it could have happened this way; they seriously considered alternate endings—it's the leading man (me, not Bogey), who's going off with Ilsa Lund; only it's not Bergman, it's Linda. Unlike Bogey, I don't have any heartfelt and idealistic insights to pass on because what the hell, I'm getting the girl.

Paul Henreid looks at Linda, broken-hearted, but captivated as always by her registered lethal weapons. He glances briefly at me, then looks at Linda again. He says, "If you ever get tired of this guy, let me know."

Linda says, "Why? Do *you* want him?" She smiles up at me. She wouldn't give up the North of Hollywood guy for anything.

And now the two of us make our way out into the fog. It's impossible to see where we're going, but we don't mind. We feel confident we're headed toward the night plane to Lisbon and freedom.

www.ricklenzauthor.com